The English Renaissance in Popular Culture

Reproducing Shakespeare: New Studies in Adaptation and Appropriation

Reproducing Shakespeare marks the turn in adaptation studies toward recontextualization, reformatting, and media convergence. It builds on two decades of growing interest in the "afterlife" of Shakespeare, showcasing some of the best new work of this kind currently being produced. The series addresses the repurposing of Shakespeare in different technical, cultural, and performance formats, emphasizing the uses and effects of Shakespearean texts in both national and global networks of reference and communication. Studies in this series pursue a deeper understanding of how and why cultures recycle their classic works, and of the media involved in negotiating these transactions.

Series Editors

Thomas Cartelli, Muhlenberg College
Katherine Rowe, Bryn Mawr College

Titles

The English Renaissance in Popular Culture: An Age for All Time
Edited by Greg Colón Semenza

Forthcoming Titles

Extramural Shakespeare
Denise Albanese

The English Renaissance in Popular Culture

An Age for All Time

Edited by

Greg Colón Semenza

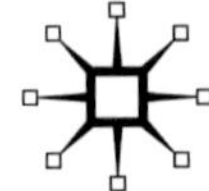

THE ENGLISH RENAISSANCE IN POPULAR CULTURE
Copyright © Greg Colón Semenza, 2010.

First published in 2010 by
PALGRAVE MACMILLAN®
in the United States—a division of St. Martin's Press LLC,
175 Fifth Avenue, New York, NY 10010.

Where this book is distributed in the UK, Europe and the rest of the
world, this is by Palgrave Macmillan, a division of Macmillan Publishers
Limited, registered in England, company number 785998, of Houndmills,
Basingstoke, Hampshire RG21 6XS.

Palgrave Macmillan is the global academic imprint of the above companies and has companies and representatives throughout the world.

Palgrave® and Macmillan® are registered trademarks in the United States,
the United Kingdom, Europe and other countries.

ISBN: 978–0–230–10028–2

Library of Congress Cataloging-in-Publication Data

The English Renaissance in popular culture : an age for
all time / edited by Greg Colón Semenza.
    p. cm. — (Reproducing Shakespeare)
Includes bibliographical references and index.
ISBN 978–0–230–10028–2 (alk. paper)
    1. Shakespeare, William, 1564–1616—Adaptations. 2. Shakespeare,
William, 1564–1616—Film and video adaptations. 3. Renaissance—
England—Historiography. 4. England—In popular culture. 5. History in
popular culture. 6. Popular culture—History—20th century. I. Semenza,
Gregory M. Colón, 1972–

PR2880.A1E64 2010
822.3′3—dc22   2009032107

A catalogue record of the book is available from the British Library.

Design by Newgen Imaging Systems (P) Ltd., Chennai, India.

First edition: April 2010

10 9 8 7 6 5 4 3 2 1

Printed in the United States of America.

Contents

Illustrations

Acknowledgments

I wish to thank board members of the Shakespeare Association of America for supporting a 2007 Workshop called "Representing the Renaissance in Modern Popular Culture," which was the first step toward completing this project. Katherine Eggert was kind enough to serve as a respondent to our wonderful group of participants; her enthusiasm for this project has been much appreciated. Also at that conference, Kathy Rowe mentioned her new co-edited Palgrave series and, since then, she and Tom Cartelli have been extremely helpful series editors. Brigitte Shull, the acquisitions editor at Palgrave Macmillan, has been a most generous supporter. The thorough and incisive readings of the anonymous readers for the press helped me and the other contributors to put forward stronger work than we otherwise could have done. Finally, I am grateful to my contributors, who often were willing to revise their drafts over and over again, and with whom it has been a pleasure to work. Richard Burt has been particularly generous in offering feedback and suggestions.

Mark Thornton Burnett has been leading a well-funded two-year symposia series on "Early Modern Film and Performance" at Queens University, Belfast; he was kind enough to invite me to speak about the Sex Pistols in a forum whose ideas proved crucial to the development of this project (and he and Ramona Wray were kind enough to feed me at their lovely home). My fellow participants over three stimulating days in Northern Ireland were Robert Shaughnessy, Sue Doran, Adrian Streete, Christie Carson, Stephen O'Neill, Ton Hoenselaars, Jerome de Groot, Susanne Greenhalgh, Ruth Abraham, Majella Devlin, Adele Lee, Ros Barber, Jesús Tronch-Pérez, and Tatiana C. String.

Other friends and colleagues who have contributed ideas and support for this project include Thomas Anderson, Jean Howard, Bob Hasenfratz, Barbara Hodgdon, Douglas Lanier, Bambi Mroz, Ryan Netzley, Scott

Newstock, my entire "Shakespeare and Popular Culture" Graduate Seminar, Karen Renner, Cathleen Schultz, James Siemon, Garrett Sullivan, Catherine Thomas, and Robin Worley (for ordering me literally hundreds of CDs and DVDs).

For watching dozens of mediocre movies, I appreciate the work that my wife Cristina put into this project. And since my last collection proudly mentioned Alexander turning one, this one is for Benjamin, about to turn three.

Introduction: An Age for All Time

Greg Colón Semenza

Although English Renaissance literary scholars have written extensively on popular historical and political appropriations of Shakespeare—theorizing the cultural capital accrued through contact with the central canonical English author—such work has downplayed the fact that Shakespearean appropriations are merely part of a wider popular culture interest and investment in the Renaissance as an imagined historical period. Renaissance literary scholars will be quite familiar, for example, with the political functions of Laurence Olivier's film of *Henry V* (1944), whose depiction of the seemingly miraculous English victory against the French at Agincourt was intended to boost the morale of British troops in Europe during World War II. A relative lack of attention to William K. Howard's 1937 film *Fire Over England* and Michael Curtiz's 1940 *The Sea Hawk*—both of which emphasize parallels between the Spanish Armada and the Blitz—has more to do with how the scholarly industry governs inquiry than the relative political complexity, economic success, or artistic quality of the films. In the nine years between 1935 and 1944, in a moment of international crisis, at least four major films (add Arthur B. Wood's 1935 *Drake of England*) turned to the Renaissance as a historical source of national pride, inspiration, and even moral authority, and the Renaissance was celebrated in several less overtly political films of the period such as Curtiz's *The Private Lives of Elizabeth and Essex* (1939), John Ford's *Mary of Scotland* (1936), and John Stevenson's *Tudor Rose* (1936). Nor can it be said that this period's interest in the Renaissance is historically anomalous in any way since, if anything, popular interest in the Renaissance beyond Shakespeare has proliferated at the same rate as the popular culture industry itself. For instance, 2008 alone saw a Hollywood adaptation of Philippa Gregory's 2003 novel *The Other Boleyn Girl*, commencement of the second season of the Showtime hit series *The Tudors*, the release of *Elizabeth: The Golden Age* on DVD, and the beginning of production on a major film version of Milton's *Paradise Lost* (production on a separate indie film version of the poem began in 2009), just to mention a few examples.[1] Nor are contemporary engagements of the Renaissance any less politically involved than those half a century ago as, say, the post-9/11 debate in the mainstream media regarding Milton's advocacy of, or opposition to, religious terrorism would demonstrate.[2]

An Age for All Time encourages readers to think about popular culture's rich engagements of the history, thought, and figures of the English sixteenth and seventeenth centuries. While a major contention of this volume is that scholarship has been too Shakespeare-centric, its chapters in no way seek to exclude Shakespeare, since many of the richest modern engagements of the English Renaissance have, of course, been inspired by his writings.[3] Ranging from "period films" (Kapur's *Elizabeth* films), to those that appropriate Renaissance events and figures (*V for Vendetta*, *The Filth and the Fury*), to television productions (*The Tudors*), popular literature (Faye Kellerman's romance novels), pastimes such as fairs and carnivals, and music (The Sex Pistols), the rich and varied chapters in this collection focus both on how popular culture engages the Renaissance and how our understanding of the Renaissance is influenced by popular culture. To what ends do moderns seek to portray, adapt, or appropriate the English Renaissance? Do most popular engagements of the period tend toward conservativism? How are largely period-specific concepts such as "Reformation" or "humanism" communicated through different media and to different audiences? In what ways have popular adaptations of Shakespeare's plays—say, Zeffirelli's comedies or Welles' tragedies—informed popular ideas about what the Renaissance was "actually" like? Have they promoted an author-centered industry in spite of a largely postmodern scholarship? How have they in turn limited or enabled our teaching and our students' learning about early modern literature and history?

An Age for All Time brings together leading American and British scholars of Renaissance literature and popular culture to begin answering these questions. I have chosen a title for the volume—*The English Renaissance in Popular Culture: An Age for All Time*—that signifies in multiple competing directions. First, as the subtitle's riff on Ben Jonson's famous lines about Shakespeare would suggest, the volume seeks to capture the dynamic by which the specific and often inescapably local histories of sixteenth- and seventeenth-century life have been represented as transhistorically relevant subjects. I am talking here about popular concepts of such disparate subjects as Reformation, witchcraft, carnival, and groundlings, to mention only a few, as they are presented in popular culture. Classic Hollywood cinema (Ken Hughes' *A Man for All Seasons* [1966]), auteur films (Terrence Malick's *The New World* [2005]), Shakespeare films (Zeffirelli's *Romeo and Juliet* [1968]) and adaptations (Greenaway's *Prospero's Books* [1991]), television shows (*Blackadder* and *Monty Python's Flying Circus*), and popular entertainments such as rock music and Renaissance fairs have contributed equally to the establishment of a formidable mythology of what the period was and why it remains relevant to moderns. Second, as the main title would suggest, the volume seeks to be comprehensive in addressing a range of ways in which the English Renaissance is taken up by popular media of various kinds; methodologically speaking, this book works to reconcile the seeming contradictoriness of a popular culture industry in which considerably different media forms—marked by their own unmistakably distinctive vocabularies and technologies—manage, nonetheless, to employ remarkably similar strategies of adaptation and produce similar ideas about the period. In fact, such media often engage in open dialogue with one another. As Thomas Cartelli and Katherine Rowe point out, much contemporary popular art—particularly "new wave cinema"—is defined precisely by a deliberate integration of media forms, which "promiscuously take their visual and audio cues from their vernacular surround…from contemporary advertising, television newscasts, rock video, the stylings and sounds of popular (mainly youth) culture."[4] Since this volume is equally interested in how the Renaissance is depicted *and* perceived in popular culture, such an interest requires attending to the convergence, not merely the distinctiveness, of postmodern media.

Though *An Age for All Time* is the first book to cover ways in which the Renaissance figures generally across popular culture media, numerous previous studies have considered how film portrays or otherwise engages history. In fact, historical film studies is an emerging subfield of history, one dominated mainly by the pioneering work of Robert A. Rosenstone.[5] Rosenstone's unwavering belief is that "visual media are a legitimate way of doing history—of representing, interpreting, thinking about, and making meaning from the traces of the past."[6] Though he recognizes several previous studies devoted to the topic of history on film, he argues that none "has ever taken the historical film on its own terms as a way of seriously thinking the past."[7] More recently, Robert Brent Toplin has expanded the conversation by anatomizing the defining elements of historical cinema as a genre with its own rules—like horror, westerns, and so on—and defends the strategies used by Hollywood directors to present history to massive audiences. Like Rosenstone, then, Toplin seeks to challenge the traditional notion that "*real* history...[is] much more interesting than the 'reel' stuff depicted in Hollywood's myth-based stories."[8] Each chapter in this volume takes seriously the assertions of historians such as Rosenstone, Toplin, and Paul Halsall that popular cultural texts can be "better or at least equally as good [at documenting history] as any academic history."[9]

In addition to expanding this cinematic conversation into considerations of how music, sounds, fairs, popular novels, the web, and other media configure history, this volume rejects the necessity of a binary conception of "real" and representational history. The literary scholars assembled here tend to approach the various historical texts they analyze as thoroughly "performative" interpretations, which Derrida famously defines as "an interpretation that transforms the very thing it interprets."[10] For the types of interpretive texts and traditions studied in this volume, in which certain famous stories are told and retold, "the very thing" Derrida references becomes increasingly more difficult to locate; as Julie Sanders describes this complex dynamic, "One common pattern that emerges...is that hypertexts often become 'hyper-hyper texts,' allusive not only to some founding original text or source but also to other known rewritings of that source."[11] In other words, the impossibility of rediscovering the "real" is heightened in texts that analyze more distant time periods and, perhaps tellingly, most book-length studies of historical films have focused on cinema depicting relatively recent historical events (e.g., civil war, Holocaust, Vietnam).

There are important exceptions. Early Modern literary scholars Barbara Hodgdon, Michael Dobson, Nicola J. Watson, and Julia M. Walker all have written excellent studies of Elizabeth I's modern afterlives, extending their analyses into films about the Virgin Queen.[12] By considering the ideological and memorializing work such texts perform, these scholars have rejected the primacy of the real over the representational. Many Early Modern historians, however, have unfortunately continued to insist on the traditional distinctions. John Aberth's *A Knight at the Movies: Medieval History on Film* (2003) considers the rich Medieval history film legacy. Aberth makes a point, though, to avoid "films that are largely literary," such as those based on Shakespeare's histories, and draws a rigid distinction between representation and "real" history: "I believe that the two realms...should be kept separate."[13] Susan Doran and Thomas S. Freeman recently published *Tudors and Stuarts on Film*, which features sixteen introductory essays by historians on historical films (excluding television productions) about Renaissance kings and queens.[14] Because it is the only book dedicated solely to the subject of

Renaissance history on film, it deserves extended consideration here. While many of the individual essays in the volume provide excellent overviews of the major questions such films raise—and surely will prove useful for humanities instructors invested in teaching the past—the book's approach to the topic is surprisingly conservative since its major aim is, "Above all," to analyze "the accuracy of historical films in dealing with early-modern Britain."[15] Setting out deliberately to challenge the claims of scholars such as Toplin and Rosenstone, Freeman's introduction supports the traditional claim that historical films tend to "distort our perception" of past events, and he dedicates more than thirty pages to showing how films are anachronistic, interpretive, and even "inherently" inaccurate, until he arrives at the following conclusion: "Knowledge of the past is still most effectively conveyed in written words."[16] Much of Freeman's concern has to do with the danger of talking about the past incorrectly: "while audiences accept the principle that historical films are frequently inaccurate, they tend to accept the 'facts' depicted in them uncritically."[17] Upon this completely anecdotal and negative assertion about nonacademic audiences, then, a methodology is founded. I believe it is a deeply flawed one. For every quotable "dummy" out there who doesn't know, say, that Henry VIII was *really* in his forties when he divorced Catherine—as opposed to the twenty-something Henry of *The Tudors*—there are, of course, many other individuals who know this fact or will learn about it *as a result* of their interest in the series. Rather than always beginning with the assumption that film and television viewers are lazy and stupid, scholars should try being a bit more generous.

To sum up, then, what I wish to make especially clear at the outset, *An Age for All Time* explores a historical period that has been relentlessly mediated by popular literary and media hypertexts of various sorts, albeit ones with their own generic, technological, and historical modes of operation. Many of its essays openly reject the primacy of what Nietzsche calls "monumental history," whose motto is "let the dead bury the living," in favor of histories that respect the knowledge gained by "thinking unhistorically."[18] To this end, the sort of "history" this book performs is less concerned with uncovering or understanding the past than understanding our present uses of it. While previous studies of history through film have limited their analyses to a cinematic genre we often label "historical film"—that is, a genre categorizing films such as *JFK* and *Birth of a Nation*, which have a more or less overt interest in telling stories about the past—we gain much by studying texts in which history is appropriated for only secondary or even tertiary purposes. Rather than limiting consideration of the popular culture Renaissance to works such as Kapur's *Elizabeth* (1998), which may be primarily a sixteenth-century tale, this collection also considers films, songs, and written texts whose allusions and references to the period are fragmentary, symbolic, political, or even stylistic. A television commercial featuring Henry VIII—such as the one run by Century Cigarettes in the 1960s—might contribute as much to some people's perception of the Renaissance king as a feature film like *A Man for All Seasons* or an academic text; likewise, the comedic portrait of Elizabeth I in *Shakespeare in Love* might very well emerge as a more influential hypertext for our generation than more "serious" ones such as the award-winning Channel 4 miniseries *Elizabeth I* (2005), starring Helen Mirren.

The pedagogical value of making our students conscious of how adaptation operates lies largely in helping them to recognize their own historically contingent perspectives as readers of historical texts—and, consequently, of the contingent and contextual nature of historiography. Just as "my" generation's *King Lear* has become impossible to read without remembering Jane Smiley's commentary in *A Thousand Acres* (1992), the current generation of college students will likely always know a Renaissance colored by the influence of Kapur's Elizabeth films and the Showtime series *The Tudors*. As Linda Hutcheon has recently argued in *A Theory of Adaptation*, despite "the constant critical denigration of adaptation,...Palimpsests make for permanent change," and we would be wise to avoid claims to the contrary.[19] Questioning our students about the ways in which their understanding of the past is filtered through popular culture—and about the ways popular culture uses the past—causes them to think critically about both historical continuity and difference.

Precisely because of this book's respect for the potential knowledge-making qualities of such representational texts, I have chosen the term "popular culture," rather than "mass culture," in its title. As is well known, both terms are fraught with oversimplified connotative and denotative meanings, but, as Richard Burt has neatly summarized the difference, "mass culture is defined as culture imposed 'on the people' whereas popular culture is culture made by 'the people.'"[20] Burt quite logically chooses the term "mass culture" in his groundbreaking analysis of "the extent to which Shakespeare's heterogeneous cultural presence often cannot be recuperated as so many examples of resistance to hegemony and cultural imperialism"—a necessary counter to the common tendency of we few Shakespeare scholars who tend to see popular Shakespeares as "identical with greater public access."[21] Further, if "mass" and "popular" seem like problematic terms, the term "culture" has become nearly impossible to define. For our purposes, Douglas Lanier's point that "to designate popular culture as popular *culture* (as opposed to popular entertainment) is to make an implicit—and for some a controversial—claim about its artistic nature and value."[22] Lanier's decision to use the term, nonetheless, in *Shakespeare and Modern Popular Culture* (2002) implicitly recognizes the value of many popular appropriations of Shakespeare's work. Likewise, the authors in this volume adopt a mode of intellectual inquiry that is always open to the *potential* value of such engagements, regardless of whether they ultimately are believed to function in progressive ways. Consequently, I have not sought to regularize these terms throughout the chapters, instead allowing the authors to assess how the individual texts they explore function in relation to their specific audiences.

The Renaissance in Popular Culture

In an episode of the acclaimed BBC sitcom *Blackadder II* (1986), the main character, Edmund or Lord Blackadder (Rowan Atkinson), is forced into hosting in one small house two simultaneous parties whose guests must not know about the other party: in one room is his visiting aunt, who is an absurdly rigid puritan, and in the other is a collection of lewd and rowdy fellows who have placed bets on who can consume more alcohol. As Edmund tries to play host, moving frantically between both worlds, his increasingly drunken inability to manage them speaks to the gulf between two familiar, largely incompatible, popular versions of the Renaissance: the bustling sixteenth century and the boring seventeenth century. It should be said that the vast majority of popular engagements of the Renaissance focus on sixteenth-century events and figures, a reality reflected in the contents of this volume. Generally speaking, the sixteenth century, especially the later Elizabethan period, is represented as the English Golden Age, characterized by pageantry, intrigue, and a metaphoric and often literal colorfulness suggesting the vitality and infinite possibility of an England whose future greatness is already clear. Comedic representations of the sixteenth century, such as *Blackadder II*, often feed modern fantasies of a distant world without care, one in which dancin' and prancin' or a good practical joke are possible cures for almost any crisis; in this regard, such representations are generically literary and functionally nostalgic. Dramatic representations of the sixteenth century, such as Ken Hughes' *A Man for All Seasons* and Charles Jarrot's film *Mary, Queen of Scots* (1971), draw out the tensions and the historical stakes of events in a Britain suddenly thrust from relative obscurity into the center of international affairs and the jungle of an increasingly Machiavellian universe. Major literary figures of the sixteenth century also are pervasive in popular culture, both as characters (Thomas Wyatt in *The Tudors*; Sidney in *Monty Python* #36 and Scott and Barnett's historical fantasy, *Armor of Light*; and Marlowe in Neil Gaiman's *Sandman* #13) and as adapted authors (Spenser in Margaret Hodges' children's version of *The Faerie Queene*; and Marlowe in Derek Jarman's film of *Edward II*).

By contrast, the seventeenth century—at least up through the Restoration—is usually depicted as a humorless and apocalyptic age, one clouded especially by the zeal and stereotyped asceticism of the godly. Even in the most secular of seventeenth-century popular narratives, such as Malick's beautiful film *The New World*, the palettes tend to be muted, the sounds faint, the movements controlled. The superior marketability of the popular sixteenth century, with its heaving bosoms, frenetic energy, and (excruciatingly) blaring trumpets, is reflected clearly in the disproportionate number of films, songs, and images focused on the Tudors and the literary world of Shakespeare and his contemporaries. The seventeenth-century Renaissance, on the other hand, is represented by a smattering of works on the voyage to the new world and back (Disney's *Pocahontas* and *Pocahontas 2* [1995, 1998]); the civil war (Nicola Cornick's romance novel, *Lord Greville's Captive* [2006] and the Channel 4 four-part series *The Devil's Whore* [2008]); the execution of Charles I and the rule of Cromwell (*Cromwell* [1970] and *To Kill a King* [2003]); and the occasional oddball production, such as Alex Cox's *Revenger's Tragedy*, Kevin Brownlow's film *Winstanley* (1975), and Monty Python's musical history of the English civil wars. Though a recently published essay collection has been devoted to tracing Milton's relatively massive presence and influence in popular culture,[23] only a few popular works depict Milton in his own time (e.g., Peter Ackroyd's 1996 novel *Milton in America* and the 1974 BBC film *Paradise Restored*). The post-Restoration seventeenth century, in such films as *Restoration* (1995) and *Stage Beauty* (2004), is characterized by the same splendor, busyness, and sensuality we find in engagements of the previous century, providing a bookend of sorts for the boring seventeenth-century Renaissance—which happened, in reality of course, to have been England's most tumultuous age.[24]

Popular engagements of both centuries reflect directly one of the well-known problems of early modern scholarship, which is the dearth of information about common people and the consequent focus on royalty and aristocracy. Unlike scholars, though, who study this problem in an attempt to capture as comprehensive a view of the period as possible, non-scholars, whose understandings of the Renaissance are disproportionately influenced by popular culture, will have at best a highly synechdochic perception of the period. Though comedies tend to focus more on commoners than do dramas, they also efface the harsh realities of sixteenth- and seventeenth-century life for the majority of English men and women. In this sense, they function much like Renaissance comedies themselves. Like Shakespeare's plays, popular culture paints a picture of the Renaissance dominated by the actions of its kings, queens, and courtiers—and also, importantly, by the spaces they occupy. On film, Renaissance London is a relatively narrow space defined by its most constant sites of return, Hampton Court Palace and the

Tower, and, less often, by vaguely constructed stand-ins for Whitehall and Greenwich. As always, there are numerous exceptions to the rule, such as the socially diverse theatrical spaces of Southwark or the cramped interiors of brothels and taverns, but, in popular culture, Renaissance England typically is synonymous with royal England between about 1500 and 1688.

The range of the typical in popular Renaissance historical texts also registers an interest in the period that can be characterized paradoxically as both a looking backward to "lost" ideas and values, and a looking ahead to modernity; it registers the complexity, in other words, of a period some scholars refer to as the Renaissance (usually the domain of comedy) and others as early modern (more the domain of drama). Whereas Madden's *Shakespeare in Love* revels in its nostalgia for a benign sixteenth-century London where even the harshest puritans can be won over by a good play, films such as *The Sea Hawk* and *Cromwell* function as narratives of origin for such modern developments as the expansion of the British empire or the emergence of republican values. As such examples might suggest, however—through, say, the former's new world denouement or the latter's insistence on the dignity of Charles I—most of these texts appeal to a modern curiosity about the past that is always simultaneously nostalgic and teleological. Popular Renaissance texts usually highlight both the seductiveness of the foreign and the comfort of the familiar. This paradoxical feature of Renaissance popular culture is demonstrated best by the preponderance of work imagining the private lives of great men and women. To demonstrate these patterns, I want to consider the cases of three popular Renaissance icons: Henry VIII, Elizabeth I, and Oliver Cromwell.

Popular texts featuring Henry VIII both distance and titillate modern audiences by focusing on the king's barbaric treatment of his numerous wives. While Henry is typically portrayed as a "Renaissance man," an equally able scholar, musician, politician, and athlete, he is almost always also a hothead, a man whose uncontrollable rage, passion, and impulsiveness serve to explain and—in certain cases—even justify his behavior. In Alexander Korda's great 1933 film *The Private Life of Henry VIII*, Charles Laughton plays the king in a tale that begins on the day of Anne Boleyn's execution and ends with Henry's marriage to his sixth wife, Katherine Parr. The film's opening caption goes far in explaining Korda's handling of this extremely, and impressively, compressed narrative:

Henry VIII had six wives. Catherine of Aragon was the first: but her story is of no particular interest—She was a respectable woman, so Henry divorced her. He then married Anne Boleyn. This marriage also was a failure—but not for the same reason.

To begin, Henry VIII's reign is interesting (and marketable) precisely because of his marital woes, and not because of any particularly important political events, such as the break of England from Rome. While Henry is criticized slightly for divorcing a respectable woman, the tone clearly is meant to be humorous, as it is when Anne's execution is explained away by reference to her reputed looseness. Although the film is not entirely comedic, it relies heavily on contemporary comedic conventions, especially in order to explain significant chronological shifts and to transition from marriage to marriage, and the opening caption's lighthearted tone serves to govern audience reactions to the events it depicts.

The use of humor and the contextualization of Henry VIII's acts within a Merry Old England serve often in popular texts to humanize a king who could just as easily be depicted as a monster—especially in a postfeminist age. The pattern is established early in the century, however, and examples are abundant. Murray and Weston's 1910 music hall hit "I am Henery the Eighth, I Am" uses the king's name to celebrate a Wife of Bath-like woman who has bested even the real Henry:

> I'm Henery the Eighth, I am!
> Henery the Eighth I am! I am!
> I got married to the widow next door,
> She's been married seven times before.
> Every one was an Henery
> She wouldn't have a Willie or a Sam...

Harry Champion's version was at one time the fastest-selling song in history, and it has been remade multiple times, by Herman's Hermits in 1965, for example, and by Homer Simpson who plays Henry in a 2004 episode of *The Simpsons*, in which he agrees to undergo marriage counseling with his wife, Margerine of Aragon. The counseling fails, and Queen Margerine files for the divorce. Similar comedic treatments of Henry include Robert Shaw's ridiculous, if terrifying, performance as the king in *A Man for All Seasons* and, more obviously, the 1971 comedy *Carry on Henry*.

Exceptions to this pattern occur mainly in films focused on the experience of Henry's female victims, such as *Anne of the Thousand Days* (1969), in which Richard Burton's behavior toward Anne is anything but humorous. But, unsurprisingly, the most complex portrait of Henry VIII can be found in the Showtime series *The Tudors* (influenced rather directly by *Anne of the Thousand Days*), and only *in part* because it is thirty hours long to date. Despite the show's pitch as an erotic Renaissance soap opera, Jonathan Rhys Meyers' Henry VIII is refreshingly complicated, and this fact is owing mainly to the time the series devotes to developing its female leads. For example, though the audience can be made to feel complicit at times in Henry's and Wolsey's machinations to obtain a divorce from Catherine—the result of our witnessing Henry's passionate relationship with Anne—we also are forced to see Catherine's suffering, and the series suggests clearly that the queen has been wronged by Henry and his counselors. So while Henry is our focal point, our major subject of interest and the inevitable figure with whom we identify, he is also morally dubious at best, which makes for sometimes unsettling viewing. The power of the portrait is, in many ways, grounded in Henry's physical appearance, since creator Michael Hirst chooses to present a twenty-something king rather than the much older figure of history. This boyish and hairless Henry—a far cry from the Holbein-like Henries of earlier generations—exudes a youthful beauty and sexiness that seduces viewers, even as his behavior repulses. Just like other Renaissance popular culture texts, though, *The Tudors'* obsession with the private lives of the king and his courtiers reveals the source of our interest in these texts—as well as the key to their ultimate success—which is their negotiation of the foreign and the familiar.

Just as the scandalous story of Henry VIII's six wives both titillates and alienates modern audiences, the story of his daughter Elizabeth I's virginity fascinates us and provokes our disbelief. Perhaps no English Renaissance figure other than Shakespeare has been more often reproduced in popular culture than Elizabeth, and, unsurprisingly, a great many treatments of her focus on the imagined psychological consequences of repressing the natural human need for sexual and romantic companionship.[25] By emphasizing Elizabeth's sacrifices of personal pleasure and comfort for the public good of England, such works simultaneously humanize and heroize—even as they feminize and disempower—the Virgin Queen. Curtiz's *The Private Lives of Elizabeth and Essex* remains the classic example and the greatest influence on the formula. From the beginning of the 1939 film, Elizabeth (Bette Davis) speaks such tired maxims as "the queen has no hour for love" and "the necessities of a queen must transcend those of a woman," as if trying to convince even herself of their truth. Clearly she is tormented by an inability simply to repress the necessities of a woman, which makes her feel weak. The audience quickly learns, however, that Elizabeth and Essex (Errol Flynn) have not really been able to suppress their love entirely; private scenes between them reveal not only that they have openly declared their love for one another but also may be sexually involved. In any case, the sacrifice here is represented in terms of their inability to marry and live peaceful lives together. Political conflicts between Elizabeth and Essex are represented largely as the result of their mutual struggle to cope with personal pain. In the film's conclusion, it is Essex who *chooses* death, emphasizing the sacrifice of the man—at least equal to that of the woman—for a higher cause (it is no coincidence that Curtiz would direct *Casablanca* just three years later). Unfortunately, in the film's emphasis on heroic male sacrifice, Elizabeth's womanly necessities are shown to trump her monarchal ones; as Essex walks off to the execution-er's block, Elizabeth screams out for him to return: "take my throne, take England, it is yours," but it is too late. Essex is gone. The Curtiz formula—which stretches through such later films as *Young Bess* (1953), *Elizabeth R* (1971), and *Elizabeth: The Golden Age*—clarifies the accuracy of Barbara Hodgdon's claim that popular representations of Elizabeth seek to "rein-scribe her within the binaries of dominant heterosexuality."[26]

The frequent recurrence of such a pattern, especially one that winds up "reinscribing" Elizabeth's power so forcefully, might suggest on the surface only the conservative functions of popular Elizabeths. The point at which such patterns become transparent, however, is also the point when studying them, and teaching them, becomes so potentially interesting and useful. Hutcheon argues that the pleasure of adaptation "comes simply from rep-etition with variation, from the comfort of ritual combined with the pi-quancy of surprise."[27] For sheer originality, Miranda Richardson's portrayal of Elizabeth in *Blackadder II* wins the day. Richardson's Elizabeth is a hilar-ious parody of the popular culture formula, a transformation of the psycho-logically tortured and often depressed queen into a bored and feckless ditz with no concerns beyond the next costume party at court (she goes as Henry VIII), the cleverest tricks to play on her courtiers, or the best places to go skipping in the castle (see figure I.1).

In episode one, she approves of Edmund's marriage to a cross-dressed girl named "Bob," remarking flippantly—and as if she had never considered it before— that "Everyone seems to get married except me," but tellingly, the series never references the topics of marriage or virginity again. The fact that such different works as *Blackadder II* and *The Sea Hawk* are so exceptional in refusing to dramatize the queen's inner struggle to remain a virgin seems helpful: whereas *Blackadder* is able to make Bess familiar simply by reducing her to a silly girl, all too human, the two WWII allegories resist the impulse to bring the queen down to earth altogether—for England is at war and in need of a leader who can perform miracles.

As might be expected, popular portraits of Oliver Cromwell are far more polemical than those of Henry or Elizabeth.[28] But, like portraits of the two monarchs, they bridge the gap between his foreignness, as represented by his godly religious beliefs and practices, and his familiarity, as represented by his modern-seeming republican ideals. Two films created about thirty years apart measure this divide particularly well: Hughes' *Cromwell* (1970)

Figure I.1 Miranda Richardson as a Ditzy Elizabeth I (from *Blackadder II*).

and Mike Barker's *To Kill a King* (2003). In the former film, which begins at the very end of the Personal Rule, a perfectly wartless Cromwell (Richard Harris) emerges from the English countryside to challenge the oppressive actions of a king determined to control both parliament and the spiritual lives of his subjects. Hughes is careful, though, to base Cromwell's heroism less on a display of religious piety and integrity than on a personal conviction about the rights of the common people to follow their consciences. The film traces Cromwell's progressive struggle with, and eventual triumph over, the stubborn and backward-thinking Charles I (played sympathetically, nonetheless, by Alec Guinness). In the final scene, just after the execution of Charles and the dissolution of parliament, an exhausted Cromwell is shown alone in the parliament house, determined still to "give back this nation its self-respect," to "build schools and universities throughout the land," and to "bring the law within the reach of every common man" (See figure I.2).

Then, as if the film still requires clarification about its view of Cromwell, a voice-over concludes it: "Oliver Cromwell ruled the nation as Lord Protector for five years. In that short time, he raised England to be a great power, feared and respected throughout the world. Under his hands were laid the foundation of a truly democratic nation."

Figure I.2   Oliver Cromwell (Richard Harris) the Republican (from Dir. Hughes *Cromwell*).

To Kill a King rests on the interesting premise that attitudes toward the execution of Charles I can be traced through the gradual demise of Cromwell and Fairfax's friendship. Unfortunately, the film's conservative perspective—which at times seems like a lament for the good old days of centralized monarchical power—renders Cromwell a bit of a raving lunatic. The opening scene shows Fairfax (Dougray Scott) looking up at Cromwell's rotting corpse on Traitor's Gate and wondering how things could have gone so wrong. By ending with the same scene, the film provides a sort of Royalist framework for understanding Cromwell's rise to power, one suggesting that in spite of what may have originally been his good intentions, Cromwell winds up doing more harm to England than good. In the film, a very warty and very puritanical Cromwell (Tim Roth) becomes increasingly menacing as he acquires more power, in one scene casually murdering in a London street an innocent commoner who happens to support the king. Unlike the voice-over at the end of *Cromwell*, which seeks to contextualize the Interregnum governments as the foundation for English republicanism, *To Kill a King* offers captions that minimize their importance: "Cromwell's Revolution, though short-lived, changed the course of European history. Nevertheless it would be a further 130 years before the French beheaded their king and brought about the birth of the modern political age.... England has never been a republic since [the Restoration]."

As such diametrically opposed readings of Cromwell might suggest, a polemic largely absent from treatments of Henry and Elizabeth is pervasive in popular assessments of his character and legacy. Elvis Costello's 1979 song "Oliver's Army" references Cromwell's creation of a professional army to criticize the British military's exploitative recruitment of disadvantaged youth in the late 1970s: "Oliver's Army is here to stay / And I would rather be anywhere else / But here today." The irony, however, of Costello's appropriation of Cromwell's legacy to resist the tyranny of state power couldn't be any richer. The popular Cromwell is also captured nicely by Monty Python's song about him, which describes the civil wars and the sensational execution of "that stupid git," Charles I, in so perfunctory and disinterested a manner as to satirize the very absurdity of Cromwell's popular image: "The most interesting thing about King Charles I is that he was 5'6" tall at the start of his reign, but only 4'8" at the end of it…because of…Oliver Cromwell, Lord Protecteur of England, PURITAN, Born in 1599 and died in 1658." Popular renderings of Cromwell differ in ways from those of the Tudors, but in pointing to the modern difficulty of reconciling such seemingly oppositional attitudes as extreme godliness and political progressivism, they nonetheless seek to bridge the gap between the Renaissance and the early modern, the distant and the familiar, the nostalgic and the teleological.

Contents

The thirteen chapters included in *An Age for All Time* offer further suggestions about how the English Renaissance—its major events, figures, concepts, and texts—is reproduced in popular culture, suggesting the myriad ways that serious consideration of the topic can enrich our scholarship and teaching. While the volume is comprehensive in the sense that it covers an array of sixteenth- and seventeenth-century topics and does so across a variety of media, I make no claims for its exhaustiveness, since a foray into this area can only begin to scratch the surface. None of the chapters ask whether these engagements of the Renaissance are good or bad or true or faithful to the "original," questions that Dudley Andrew has rightly described as "tiresome" and unproductive.[29] Instead, they suggest the dynamic ways that modern filmmakers, novelists, musicians, actors, and entertainers approach the Renaissance and analyze their motives for doing so—whether historical, political, or economically driven. While the four parts into which the next twelve chapters are organized will, hopefully, provide a useful taxonomy of sorts for multiple types of Renaissance appropriation, adaptation, parody, and other forms of engagement, they also overlap in important ways, raising similar questions and probing similar themes.

Part one, "Renaissance Icons," centers on popular representations of the Tudors that both extend and complicate my own introductory claims about them. The lead chapter by Ramona Wray eloquently defends *The Tudors'* much-criticized compressions and revisions of "real" history as instrumental to its successful depiction of the early sixteenth century as an unimaginably brutal and chaotic age. Demonstrating the series' resistance to "Golden Age" nostalgia, Wray argues that beneath the sumptuousness of the settings, costumes, and the beautiful eroticized bodies is a "horror-laden" world of danger, paranoia, and hypocrisy. A self-consciously revisionist project, *The Tudors* seeks to rewrite the popular Renaissance by critiquing the obfuscatory effects of shimmery surfaces and glistening bodies.

The other two chapters in this part consider popular presentations of Elizabeth I. Adrienne L. Eastwood analyzes cinematic obsessions with Elizabeth's virginity over the past forty years, arguing that presentations of Elizabeth as defined by her relationships with men have become *increasingly* common, not less so. Eastwood zooms in on cinematic handlings of the Tilbury speech in four films made since 1971, demonstrating the ways in which they systematically dilute the masculinity and androgyny intrinsic to Elizabethan self-presentational ideology. Picking up where Eastwood leaves off, with attention to Kapur's *Elizabeth: The Golden Age*, Courtney Lehmann eloquently observes how "in the midst of its dazzling failure to 'find' the Renaissance, Kapur's film finds 'us.'" Drawing out similarities between the sequel and *Elizabeth* (1998), both of which define the queen in terms of her surrender of the feminine self, Kapur's insistence on artistic control over Elizabeth's image replicates precisely sixteenth-century (and later) male attempts to control that image. Elizabeth's struggle across and against these two films to manage her own representation parallels postmodern negotiations of a world where the survival of the "real" is constantly threatened by simulacra.

Chapters in part two, "Renaissance Fantasies," consider appropriations of figures and practices whose powerful symbolic functions have been almost as important for our thinking about the Renaissance as they were for the early modern minds that invented and deployed them. Here such disparate subjects as the groundling, the witch, the Catholic, and the tournament reveal themselves both as Renaissance fantasies of the real and modern fantasies of the Renaissance. Amy Rodgers looks at a popular historical figure invented by playwrights themselves, the groundling, who has become a seminal figure in historical fiction and film. In part because historical fiction has practically outpaced scholarship in explorations of groundlings, Rodgers sees them as a sort of tabula rasa on which artists can explore questions about audience reactions to Renaissance drama. Most interestingly, though, Rodgers claims that the largely sentimental role groundlings perform in popular culture grows from our desire to situate ourselves as modern members of a past (and thereby authorized) form of mass culture. The next chapter by Melissa Croteau also looks at the ways in which we turn to the Renaissance in order to validate our most problematic desires. The Wachowksi brothers' film *V for Vendetta* appropriates Renaissance figures—the Catholic conspirators of 1605, especially Guy Fawkes—to sanction mass resistance against what the filmmakers see as the tyranny of the post-Bush transatlantic alliance. The film's suggestion that the British government has staged an act of terrorism in order to bolster its power through the spread of fear hinges on this appropriation, since conspiracy theories have always existed regarding the Jacobean government's possible "staging" of the Gunpowder Plot. As Croteau points out, the film's celebration of a Fawkes-like hero who blows up the Houses of Parliament hinges on the notion that some values—especially liberal ones that resist state tyranny—are not ephemeral or contingent so much as they are transhistorical and thus transcendent. Whereas fantasies of the Renaissance groundling and *V for Vendetta* seek to highlight our historical proximity to the period in order to stress continuity, appropriations of the early modern witch point out our distance from the Renaissance as part of a rejection of the past. For Deborah Willis, the primal scene of films about the early modern witch is one in which cruel and unusual punishment, torture, and execution are exacted by the patriarchal authority on the body of a female victim. Unlike films about witches in general, the Renaissance witch cannot be imagined apart from the witch hunter. In the 1960s and 70s especially, when patriarchy and authority were under unprecedented scrutiny, witch films sought to align repressive father figures with a past age of brutality and tyranny. But in extraordinarily ironic ways, Willis points out, they also made viewers complicit with such authorities by subjecting the sexualized, tortured bodies of witches to the male gaze.

The final chapter in this part also focuses on nostalgic recreations of the past, in this case the embodied experience offered by the American Ren Faire. Kevin Wetmore Jr. discusses the deliberately sanitized version of the Renaissance that such Faires offer—lots of funny peasants, unusual products for purchase, and beautiful clothing but no sweating sickness, state-sponsored tyranny, mud, or shit. Wetmore expands his critique by looking at the ways in which the Renaissance portrayed by the Ren Faire actually is an amalgam of medieval and modern phenomena, especially the Faires' presentations of "Renaissance" weaponry and combat. But in pointing out the neo-Medievalism of sixteenth- and seventeenth-century fairs and staged combat—as well as their protomodern, capitalist exchange of novelty items—Wetmore emphasizes that the nostalgia driving Ren Faires is not so different from the nostalgia that characterized fairs in the Renaissance.

The two chapters in the next part, "Renaissance Sounds," follow Wetmore's chapter rather naturally by thinking about extra-visual popular confrontations with the Renaissance. Deborah Cartmell is interested in Renaissance voices, listening for them in Sam Taylor's *The Taming of the Shrew* (1929), the first mainstream Shakespeare "talkie." Carefully considering the original publicity materials that Cartmell claims "fetishized the period" by harping on the film's unprecedented attempt to recover Shakespeare's voice, she reveals the ways in which this recovery actually doomed the film. In spite of the new technology's ability to bring the Shakespearean "text" into the cinema, early responses to the film were negative precisely because of the way that sound was perceived to alter the relationship between the source text and the modern adaptation; suddenly, fidelity to the Shakesperean text became a possibility, but to cineastes, fidelity meant mere mimicry. The recovery of the Renaissance voice figures counterintuitively, then, as a threat to modern art.

Conversely, my chapter centers on punk views of the "English Renaissance" as a primary ideological component of the authorized version of British history. Popular and scholarly treatments of punk and the Sex Pistols, such as Julian Temple's documentary *The Filth and the Fury* (2000), have sought to understand punk anarchism as part of a British tradition of dissent dating back to the early modern period. Their arguments seem more persuasive in light of Johnny Rotten's admission that his punk rock persona was based almost entirely on Shakespeare's Richard III. Contrasting Rotten's musical appropriations of Renaissance history and Derek Jarman's cinematic appropriation of Elizabeth I in England's first punk film, *Jubilee* (1977), I explore what punk can teach us about both the limitations and the potential of a radical Renaissance.

Part four, "Renaissance Cinema," picks up on Richard Burt's recent extended theorization in *Medieval and Early Modern Film and Media* of "analogies between the media of the premodern and early modern past (scrolls, manuscripts, books, tapestries) and the electronic and digital media of the postmodern present."[30] It thus marks something of a shift away from how media respond to the Renaissance on thematic, narrative, characterological, and historical levels, and onto the ways that modern media forms and technologies interact with early modern ones. Burt opens the section by looking at two films by Jacques Rivette: *Paris Belongs to Us*, which features an internal plot about a production of Shakespeare's *Pericles*, and *Noiroit*, which adapts Middleton's *Revenger's Tragedy*. Jacobean plays, Burt demonstrates, serve Rivette's formal and philosophical investment in and departure from the Situationist-inspired concept of the *dérive*, which he engages in order to challenge the dominance of the fidelity-model of textual adaptation. Burt coins the term "dérive-ation" to describe how, in Rivette's two films, various editing strategies cause deviations from the literary texts they derive from, and points to the ways in which the films—and perhaps the Jacobean plays they adapt—offer challenges to definitions of historicism. James Keller also focuses on an adaptation of Middleton's *Revenger's Tragedy*, Cox's 2002 film of the same name. Cox's appropriation of "the Jacobean" is shown to extend beyond textual adaptation and into his linking of a contemporary mind-set about the ascension of James I and postmodern views of human history. According to Keller, the Renaissance play reflects a contemporary view of James' reign as a shattering of the teleological narrative implied by the Tudor myth. For Catholics whom James would reject, and for Protestants whom James would offend by a perceived debauchery, the Jacobean reign represented merely a continuation of the problems associated with the Tudor dynasty and not the occasion of renewal promised by apocalyptic teleology. Cox's post-cataclysmic Liverpool, and post-9/11 West, can be defined by the same foreclosure of apocalyptic teleology; play and film are shown in their very structures to be anti-, not post-, apocalyptic commentaries on the early modern and modern worlds, respectively. The final chapter in the volume, by Donald Hedrick, leaves us with a fairly complex question, and perhaps a challenge to this volume, in asking whether we've allowed film to exercise too restrictive a hegemony over the field of popular interpretation of Shakespeare. He points out early that if Shakespeare has dominated English studies, and if English has dominated other languages, then film's alliance with Shakespeare—especially its "collaboration" with academic Shakespeare—should bring it under greater scrutiny. Has the death of the theater—Shakespeare's natural habitat—really been compensated for by the triumph of the cinema or by film scholarship? Hedrick suggests that the seventeenth-century explosion of entertainment options and concomitant epistemological redefinitions of *choice* expose the relatively limited and limiting potential of film to represent popular or mass Shakespeare. Rejecting the cinema, Hedrick turns to Las Vegas, that Bakhtinian wonderland and postmodern "capitol of capital," as the site of a truly embodied popular experience not far removed from the culture of "sportification" envisioned in much Renaissance literature, and he invites us to embrace a paradigm shift of sorts...to take a gamble. It is my hope that after reading these thoughtful and provocative chapters, you'll be more aware of the potential risks and rewards of doing so, and even experience the thrill and sense of renewal that comes with forgetting your past. What happens in the Renaissance stays in the Renaissance. But what happens to the Renaissance in our own time gives that past new meaning.

Notes

1. See Michael Joseph Gross, "It's God vs. Satan. But What About the Nudity?" *New York Times*, March 4, 2007, AR18.

2. See especially Fareed Zakaria, "Why Do They Hate Us?" *Newsweek*, October 15, 2001, 24; Daniel Henniger, "'Know ye Not Me?' America Sees and Defeats the Face of Evil," *Wall Street Journal*, April 18, 2003, A8; and Ron Rosenbaum, "Degrees of Evil: Some Thoughts on Hitler, bin Laden, and the Hierarchy of Wickedness," *The Atlantic Monthly* (February 2002): 63–68. David Boocker has written on "Milton After 9/11," in *Milton in Popular Culture*, ed. Laura L. Knoppers and Gregory M. Colón Semenza (New York: Palgrave Macmillan, 2006), 177–86.

3. Alex Cox, director of the 2002 film *The Revenger's Tragedy*, argues that regardless of whether particular Shakespeare films can be called progressive, the Shakespeare-on-film industry has systematically *excluded* the reproduction of radical tragedy by Shakespeare's contemporaries; it is an industry, therefore, that should be taken to task for its cultural conservativism.

4. Cartelli and Rowe, *New Wave Shakespeare on Screen* (Cambridge: Polity, 2007), 1.

5. Rosenstone's works include *Lights, Camera, History: Portraying the Past in Film* (College Station: Texas A&M UP, 2007); ed., *Revisioning History: Film and the Construction of a New Past* (Princeton: Princeton UP, 1995); and *Visions of the Past: The Challenge of Film to Our Idea of History* (Cambridge, MA: Harvard UP, 1995).

6. Rosenstone, *Revisioning History*, 3.

7. Ibid.

8. Toplin, *Reel History: In Defense of Hollywood* (Lawrence, Kansas: U of Kansas P, 2002), 1.

9. Paul Halsall, "Thinking about Historical Film—Is it Worth the Trouble?" (November, 2001) http://www.crusades-encyclopedia.com/thinkingabouthistoricalfilm.html (accessed February 1, 2009).

10. Derrida, *Spectres of Marx* (New York: Routledge, 1994), 51.

11. Sanders, *Adaptation and Appropriation* (London and New York: Routledge, 2006), 107.

12. Hodgdon, "Romancing the Queen," in *The Shakespeare Trade: Performances and Appropriations* (Philadelphia: U of Pennsylvania, 1998), 110–70; Dobson and Watson, *England's Elizabeth: An Afterlife in Fame and Fantasy* (Oxford: Oxford UP, 2002); Walker, *The Elizabeth Icon: 1603–2003* (New York: Palgrave, 2004). For other studies of Elizabeth in popular culture, see note 25.

13. Aberth, *A Knight at the Movies: Medieval History on Film* (New York and London: Routledge, 2003), ix.

14. Susan Doran and Thomas S. Freeman, *Tudors and Stuarts on Film: Historical Perspectives* (London: Palgrave Macmillan, 2009), 28.

15. Ibid., 5.

16. Ibid., 1, 20, 22.

17. Ibid., 15.

18. Nietzsche, "On the Uses and Disadvantages of History for Life," in *Untimely Meditations*, trans. R.J. Hollingdale (Cambridge: Cambridge UP, 1983), 72, 62.

19. Hutcheon, *A Theory of Adaptation* (London and New York: Routledge, 2006), 11, 29.

20. Burt, ed., *Shakespeare After Mass Media* (London and New York: Palgrave Macmillan, 2002), 3.
21. Ibid., 7, 5.
22. Lanier, *Shakespeare and Modern Popular Culture* (Oxford: Oxford UP, 2002), 7.
23. See Knoppers and Semenza, *Milton in Popular Culture.*
24. See Ronald Hutton, "Why Don't the Stuarts Get Filmed," in Freeman and Doran, *Tudors and Stuarts on Film,* 246–58.
25. As mentioned above (12), this is actually one of the few topics that has been written about: In addition to the major works noted above (see note 12), see Thomas Betteridge, "A Queen for All Seasons," in *The Myth of Elizabeth,* ed. Susan Doran and Thomas Freeman (New York: Palgrave, 2003); and Renee Pigeon, "'No Man's Elizabeth': The Virgin Queen in Recent Films," in *Retrovisions,* ed. Deborah Cartmell, I.Q. Hunter, and Imelda Whelehan (London: Pluto Press 2001).
26. Barbara Hodgdon, "Romancing the Queen," 112.
27. Hutcheon, *Theory of Adaptation,* 4.
28. John Morrill has recently written about Cromwell on film in "Oliver Cromwell and the Civil Wars," in Freeman and Doran, *Tudors and Stuarts on Film,* 204–219.
29. Dudley Andrew, *Concepts of Film Theory* (Oxford: Oxford UP, 1984), 100.
30. Burt, *Medieval and Early Modern Film and Media* (New York: Palgrave Macmillan, 2008), 1.

Renaissance Icons

Henry's Desperate Housewives: *The Tudors*, the Politics of Historiography, and the Beautiful Body of Jonathan Rhys Meyers

Ramona Wray

The mass of published material that accompanies the highly success-ful Showtime series *The Tudors* includes a collection of shooting scripts written by Michael Hirst (who also wrote the screenplays for *Elizabeth* [dir. Shekhar Kapur, 1998] and *Elizabeth: The Golden Age* [dir. Shekhar Kapur, 2007]).[1] In an arresting display of machismo, finery, and insouciance, the cover prioritizes an image of a seated Henry VIII with three of his wives in a row behind him. The arrangement of selective marital history has been cropped: that is, the wives are visible only from the neck down. Hence, it is impossible to guess at the respective spouses' identities. Each woman is registered only by and through her body—in particular, through the conjunction of cleavage and collar bones, which underscores the series' reliance on twenty-first-century standards of beauty. The empha-sis on nonindividualized forms points up the erotic nature of the televisual enterprise—sexualized bodies will be prominent throughout—while also playing upon popular notions of Henry VIII as the ultimate "S & M" lover (see figure 1.1).

Upping the ante on history, the composition suggestively establishes Henry as the beheader not of two but three family members: the marital timeline is violently and stylishly hyperbolized.

Figure 1.1   A Sexpot Henry VIII (Jonathan Rhys-Meyers from the Showtime Series *The Tudors*).

Positioned in the middle of the implied carnage, sleeves rolled up and muscles flexed, showtime's Henry (Jonathan Rhys Meyers) appears unrepentant. Anticipating events that will extend beyond the polygamous grouping, Rhys Meyers' intense gaze directly meets the consumer: this is a purposefully confrontational Henry devised by a creative team highly conscious of the fact that it is challenging a long tradition of entrenched royal depictions. With each queen headless, the king's is the only face on display, and this works, alongside a simple monochrome costume and controversially short dark hair, to stress both Rhys Meyers' youth and his extraordinary beauty. As Thomas S. Freeman argues, Henry VIII is invariably envisaged on celluloid as a "hearty…rogue," a corpulent and middle-aged figure that brings to mind the iconic contours of the well-known Holbein cartoon.[2] In contradistinction, *The Tudors* breaks with convention by prioritizing a slimline, twenty-something object of desire, with Rhys Meyers clearly placed in the traditional feminine position of, in Laura Mulvey's phrase, "to-be-looked-at-ness."[3] Legs in long leather boots spread wide, shirt undone to the waist, and pelvic ruffles nodding to the Renaissance cod piece—this is Henry the rock-star sovereign, England's sex-god monarch. In this context, as later, Henry retains a sense of hegemonic masculinity only via what Kenneth MacKinnon has described as "disavowal."[4] The royal authority emanates from corporeal confidence, from charisma, and from a latent sense of danger and dominance. Typically in this image, Henry does not wear a crown: the diadem is held casually by the third wife as just another item of jewellery in a bejewelled environment. Instead, it is the chain—with all of its metaphoric connotations of duty and of weighing down—that signifies kingship. Here is a Tudor ruler both committed to a playboy lifestyle and shackled to the responsibilities of his office.

The image recurs on a limited DVD box set edition targeted at the UK market: an additional tagline, "As seen on the BBC," points to a neat reversal of expectation about the ways in which the Renaissance travels (not from England to America but from America to England).[5] Filmed at Ardmore Studios, Ireland, and internationally distributed via Sony Pictures, the Showtime series has attracted exceptional viewing figures, lucrative sales to over seventy "territories," and prestigious Emmy awards. In many ways a market-based response to HBO's *Rome*, the recreation of Henry VIII constitutes "event television"—that is, television characterized by feature-film quality (the series is shot entirely in HDCAM), a budget of tens of millions, and a stellar international cast. The ethos suits the five hundredth anniversary of Henry's ascension to the throne in 2009 and has conceptual links with some of the other creative interventions marketing the occasion. For example, David Starkey's *Henry: Virtuous Prince* consorts with *The Tudors* in its emphasis on youth, apprenticeship, and emergence.[6] Like Starkey's book, the most striking aspect of *The Tudors* is its epic scale: series one (ten hour-long episodes) opens in 1509, the year of ascension, while series two (another ten hour-long episodes) concludes in 1536, the day of the execution of Anne Boleyn. With twenty hours of television devoted to not that many more years of history, *The Tudors* constitutes an unprecedented, rich, and detailed take on the Henrician phenomenon.

One of my arguments in this paper is that *The Tudors* is facilitated by what we might loosely call the "Shakespearean cinema" of the past twenty years. Playing on its most successful precursors (not least *Henry V* [dir. Kenneth Branagh, 1989], Kapur's *Elizabeth*, and *Shakespeare in Love* [dir. John Madden, 1998]), and on the popular historical understandings gleaned from them, *The Tudors* takes these films' successful features and transferable elements and places them in arresting juxtaposition. Yet if *The Tudors'* approach to the sixteenth century is anchored in recent heritage-based reinventions of the past, the series' range and scope takes it beyond the remit and import of earlier productions and into previously uncharted representational territory. Accordingly, this essay argues that *The Tudors* is the most definitive and eloquent expression of a sea change, a radical revision of the ways in which the origins of the Tudor dynasty, the Reformation, and the long-standing ramifications of religious change are explained and understood in the popular imaginary.

*   *   *

Henry VIII's life and times have, of course, been filmed and televised many times: most memorable are the infantilized monarch played by Charles

Laughton in *The Private Life of Henry VIII* (dir. Alexander Korda, 1933) and the mercurial despot enacted by Keith Michell in the BBC television series of 1970, *The Six Wives of Henry VIII*.[7] Following in the footsteps of the recent rebooting of several adventure-oriented Hollywood franchises, *The Tudors* announces itself in relation to these films as a prequel. Unlike most appropriations of history that, as Julie Sanders has demonstrated, rely "upon the reader's awareness…of [the] life and the mythology surrounding it," *The Tudors* asks an audience to abandon preconception.[8] Its central summarizing line appears as a voice-over at the beginning of each episode—"You think you know the story but you only know how it ends: to get to the heart of the story you have to go back to the beginning." The statement posits the importance of a point of departure and highlights an innovative retracing procedure. Inside this schema, a knowing intertextuality allows for *The Tudors* to gesture to the visual expressions of popular tradition, as when Henry "sucks out the fruit [of a pomegranate] with relish" or greedily plunges his hand into the guts of a perfectly baked swan pie: this, of course, is the gourmand of cinematic lore.[9] Via a grammar of appetite, such sequences offer us a context for the more rounded Henrician figure of subsequent history, but, crucially, they do so by insisting on the *precursor articulation*, the moment when a different life trajectory was still possible. Part of the logic of the whole, therefore, depends upon a "what if?" paradigm: hence, the stress upon serendipity and contingency in the narrative draws attention to what might have been, while the periodic insertion of dream sequences plays out alternative possible permutations of history. A striking example of the method occurs when an audience is granted a glimpse of Anne Boleyn being stabbed by an assassin. Only retrospectively revealed as a fiction, the inset operates so as to destabilize spectators' vantage points and sense of hindsight, disrupting linear conceptions of time in the process. The sequence also directs us to the significant place of personality or character in the "what if?" historical scenario. As is characteristic of contemporary U.S. television drama, *The Tudors* stresses personality over narrative, encouraging identification through fast-paced yet intimate camera work. The "heart of the story" is not only the interior life of Henry (in the opening sequence, a series of flashcut images finally pauses upon his forehead, suggesting an intense Hamletian engagement with an individual psychology) but also that of the surrounding players whose internal dynamics are established and developed across three decades.

For Henry, development is underscored in terms of physical, psychological, and monarchical maturation. In the opening episodes, Henry is consistently seen having sex, playing tennis, and jousting, while his kingdom is largely run in absentia—and corruptly—by Cardinal Wolsey (Sam Neil).

Henry's first appearance succinctly states the reign's priorities: Henry swiftly announces his position on the papacy and war with France before asking "Can I play now?" and departing to indulge more epicurean pursuits. The sheer number of the sex scenes (three involving Henry in the first twenty minutes alone) have seen *The Tudors* dismissed by historians as, in the words of David Starkey, a "shameful…bonkorama."[10] But this assessment ignores the ways in which the twin tropes of sex and sport maximize "the erotic potential" of *The Tudors'* visuals, while providing a masculinity-soothing rationale for the un-Henrician body.[11] As Rhys Meyers has explained, "Anyone who hunts, owns a kingdom, wrestles and has that much sex is going to be in shape."[12] The defamiliarization of the monarchical image is here countered by Rhys Meyers as a context-conscious reading of appearance. Moreover, the reinvention of Henry as a young, energetic, and neglectful sovereign allows for many implicit and explicit Shakespearean borrowings (in particular, from *Henry IV* and *Henry V*). Most obviously, in an early conversation with Thomas More (Jeremy Northam), Henry considers the posthumous fame of the youthful Henry V, declaring, "He is remembered because he won the battle of Agincourt…That victory made him…immortal!"[13] Within the fiction of the parallel articulates an anxiety about lineage particular to Henry; beyond its confines, the comparison is predicated upon an idealizing conception of each monarch and a filmic logic that, inspired by Laurence Olivier's *Henry V* (1944), makes of Agincourt a heroic, national achievement.

The determining prospects available to the Henry of *The Tudors* are elaborated in a somewhat schematic fashion: the king is discovered as being well-versed in humanist and Machiavellian thinkers alike. Yet the point is clear: Henry is envisaged as an empathetic figure because of a struggle with competing demands of kingship and because he is drawn between alternative models of contemporary political behavior. Central to the series, then, is the idea of self-creation—the king needs to grow into his part. The construction is tried-and-tested, for, in Branagh's successful *Henry V*, the central protagonist is similarly imagined as, in Kathy Howlett's words, a "boy-king" grappling with uncomfortable "ideological tenets" in the interests of the "security of the commonwealth."[14] It is this youthful drive that serves to mark Henry out from his first wife, the fully and otherwise sympathetically rendered Katherine of Aragon (Maria Doyle Kennedy). Katherine is granted dignity, generosity, and political wisdom, yet the age gap is pointed up in such a way as to suggest that the relationship is severely generationally dysfunctional. Typical here are the scenes in which a black-clad Katherine moves in stately but slow procession through the court in contrast to Henry, who is invariably more colorful and active; the contradistinction betokens a heterosexual mismatch. This instance is indicative of the way in which, in this adaptation, costume functions less as a manifestation of historical reconstruction than as a visual aid (as in Baz Luhrmann's *William Shakespeare's "Romeo + Juliet"* [1996]) to direct interpretation and to facilitate audience response. Across the series as a whole, the process also works to situate social mobility and psychological development: thus, Anne Boleyn's rise from lady-in-waiting to royal mistress is reflected in an escalation of spectacular costumes and a dazzling assortment of "crown-like" headpieces, while Katherine's gradual descent into poverty, obscurity, and illness is registered in her increasingly shroud-like clothing. Most obviously, the relationship between self-becoming and costume is crystallized in the figure of Henry himself. As in the climax to Kapur's *Elizabeth*, where the young sovereign transforms herself into the Virgin Queen, Henry gradually and incrementally grows into the costuming iconically associated with his monarchical counterpart.

Unlike the debate over dress and appearance (which has seen the production team fairly readily conceding purist objections), the unrelenting pursuit of sexual gratification in early modern England has been staunchly defended, not least by Rhys Meyers, who declares that "People had an awful lot of sex [in the Renaissance]...They were much more sexually gregarious in the sixteenth century than we are today."[15] For Rhys Meyers, there is a pragmatic explanation for the period's apparent investment in sexual emancipation: "In England the sun goes down at 4:30 in the afternoon and there are only so many legs of lamb you can eat of an evening. Sex was the highlight...And it helped warm the bed," he states.[16] Over and above the stereotypical Henrician equation between sex and appetite, the comment caters to assumptions about Englishness and implicitly contests viewers' expectations that the period was dominated by working practices of chastity and innocence. Heterosexual sex is an underwritten area in Renaissance studies; however, given Renaissance ideals of virginity and marriage, the kinds of foreplay—heavy, technically-adventurous and clothes-free intimacies—imagined in *The Tudors* seem unlikely. There is no notion in *The Tudors* that the gender inequality, which is seen to affect most aspects of Renaissance women's lives, might also be registered sexually. Rather, women are imagined as emancipated and desiring subjects: the series collapses early modern and modern sexual practices to portray Renaissance heterosexuality as mutually enabling and all too familiar in its soft-porn contours.

In the court of *The Tudors*, Henry's desirability cuts across any question of consent. (An early sequence shows Henry with his arms across the naked breasts of a lady-in-waiting: "Do you consent," he asks, to the breathy and un-ironic response of "Yes, your Majesty.") Involved activity on the part of women is linked as well to destructive forms of sexual politics, since

Henry's liaisons (whether with the peasant, Bess, he has captured in the forest, a lady-in-waiting, like Mary Boleyn, or a visiting Princess, such as Marguerite of Navarre) are invariably politically freighted. The ways in which the series constructs Henry as the exploited object of the Boleyns' ambitions is exemplary: Anne (Natalie Dormer) is used by her father to raise the social status of a *nouveau riche* family. The stratagem helps to explain the otherwise anachronistic fact that Anne appears to have had access to a Tudor version of "The Rules."[17] Knowing that Henry quickly lost interest after sleeping with Anne's sister, the family concocts a plan that prioritizes "playing hard to get" and heavy petting that, stopping just short of consummation, sends the king into a frenzied obsession he mistakes for love. A romantic montage that sees Henry promising to honor Anne's maidenhead until marriage is undercut by a close-up revealing the monarch masturbating into a bowl held by his footman (who carefully wipes him down with white silk afterward). This particular construction of the "groom of the stool" typifies both *The Tudors'* demythologizing take on royalty and its edgy approach to the popularly enshrined details of the historical record.

Inside such a decadent environment, Rhys Meyers' elegantly dissolute and febrile appearance fits to great effect. This is not the actor's first outing as "The King"; he won a Golden Globe for his portrayal of Elvis Presley in the CBS mini series, *Elvis* (2005). Intertextuality, writes Julie Sanders, functions according to "complex processes of filtration, and in terms of…webs or signifying fields."[18] And elements of the Presley mythology certainly animate not only the workings of Henry's retinue of "yes men" and inner masculine circle but also chime with his fears of aging and his incipient insomnia and hypochondria. More broadly, through films such as *Velvet Goldmine* (dir. Todd Haynes, 1998), *Titus* (dir. Julie Taymor, 2000), and *Match Point* (dir. Woody Allen, 2005), the actor brings to the set a reputation for executing enigmatic and disturbed roles. Rhys Meyers' own much-publicized struggles with alcohol are additionally held in play here, along with the cliché of the hard-living Irish actor (the Celtic strain of the music is a constant evocative reminder of Rhys Meyers' roots). What Steve Brennan and Bernadette O'Neil describe as "the sad and certain predictability" of a Hollywood equation between the Irish, the "whiff of alcoholic drink" and the "bad boy" designation operates to imbue the part of Henry with a compelling unpredictability.[19] Hence, Henry breaks off a romantic dinner with Anne to brutally beat an unwelcome messenger: the simultaneity of the two modes demonstrates a temperament explosively mercurial in its everyday incarnations. Rhys Meyers provides an insight into his motivation when he states that the Tudor king "was less of a lad than people believe. He had a lot of very hard, very frightening experiences as a young boy living in that court."[20] Pop psychology notions of childhood are projected into the Renaissance and draw heavily on postmodern realizations of Hamlet (not least Michael Almereyda's cinematic version [2000]) to inflect the production of a damaged, insecure monarch and to grant the Henrician figure a particularly moody and sensitive mien.[21]

Throughout, Henry's moods are intimately linked to his failure to produce a living male child; as a motive for divorce the requirement is inscribed and emphasized as an inheritance, property, and political affair. So far, so conventional. But importantly for *The Tudors*, infertility is also deeply personalized. The theme is read back into *The Tudors* from the context of a modern period with alternative understandings; hence, almost all of the participants reveal the emotional costs involved in the failure to reproduce. For instance, Katherine of Aragon talks with dignity (albeit to a lady-in-waiting already pregnant by her husband) about the trauma of stillbirth: the implication is that personal grief takes precedence over political necessity.[22] By the same token, Henry is frequently depicted as brooding over the couple's failures. An early shot shows him weeping in the confessional, establishing (well before he meets Anne) his guilty fear that infertility is a punishment for marrying his brother's wife: typically, the emotions (emptiness, lack of fulfilment, and a sense of a superficial existence) represented are more in keeping with a twenty-first-century response, with a state of affairs that encompasses individual (rather than dynastic) tragedy.

The pesky fact that Henry is already parent to the living Princess Mary (Sarah Bolger) is glossed over, not least through a romantic representation of the capricious indulgence with which he treats his daughters. Modernity romances paternity and, despite the accompanying humiliation brought to bear upon Katherine, *The Tudors* places Henry's discharging of his duties toward his illegitimate son, Henry Fitzroy, in an affirmative light. Events are telescoped to bring together the 1519 birth of Fitzroy and the 1521 execution of the traitor, the Duke of Buckingham (Steven Waddington). Neatly crosscut with the reluctant march of Buckingham to execution, Henry's delight in the baby boy's penis is constructed as an infectiously celebratory moment. The party to mark the birth is one of the rare occasions on which Henry actually wears his crown: the moment makes clear the series' nexus between concerns of manhood, esteem, and generative power. And in case less attentive viewers overlook the symbolism, Henry responds to the congratulations with a rather ungallant "Thanks—I always knew it wasn't me." At moments such as these, it is possible to see *The Tudors*, in common with successful spin-offs such as the "Shakespeare Re-Told" series, as playing to multiple-taste publics.

The Tudors' sentimental approach to childhood is also seen in the way in which the toddlers Fitzroy and Elizabeth are figured. Fitzroy's death is brought forward to allow for an emphasis on Henry's grief. In the emotive sequence in which the sovereign sheds private tears before a miniature crown, the blond curls of Fitzroy are connected to those of the child Elizabeth (and, by extension, to Anne Boleyn's inset memories of her infancy). Discussing Victorian representations of Elizabeth as a child, Michael Dobson and Nicola J. Watson argue that Elizabeth's "pre-sexual childish body…becomes safely iconic and…returned to its function of representing national progress": *The Tudors* recalls just such a portrayal.[23] But, typically, the series enacts this maneuver by evoking the Elizabeth of modernity as she is mediated through filmic and televisual iconization. Hence, the child is shot bathed in a golden light: she possesses a sense of composure beyond her tender years and an enigmatic, quasi-magical quality. Viewers tutored in filmic intertextuality are able to recognize that the child prioritizes a unique promise of futurity and security and, in this context, Henry's throwaway comment that one day his daughter may "preside over empires" becomes firmly prescient. The idea is illustrated in an arresting exception to the series' customary *modus operandi* of importing and expanding female characters.[24] Henry's sisters (Margaret and Mary) are morphed into one character called Margaret (Gabrielle Anwar), who is presented in the series as childless. This means, de facto, that not only Mary, Queen of Scots (and the entire Jacobean line), but also Lady Jane Grey, and her momentary reign, are wholly written out of existence. Over and above idealizing Elizabeth and projecting forward a fantasy of her contest-free rise to power, the omission operates so as to position the Tudors as the last great kings. With the Jamesian family wiped out and deemed insignificant, it is with the Tudors, in this version of history, at least, that the royal narrative—and the story of England—ends.

*   *   *

If a glossy exterior belongs with the gorgeous and exquisitely attired central players, then this feature is at a considerable remove from the series' vision of the Renaissance itself. In this respect, Jerome de Groot's observation that HBO's *Rome* and *Deadwood* emphasize "a particular gritty reality in order to break with past representations" and showcase a new kind of experiential "authenticity" is particularly relevant to *The Tudors*.[25] In this series' conception of history, the period falls short of an expected "golden age" heritage drama template; instead, a conjuration of the Renaissance is characterized by a sense of upset and brutality, suggesting a disjunction between the personalities and the temporal moment with which they are affiliated. The characters are familiar, but the contexts in which they live their lives are not. Notably, the series pays vivid attention to the unstable materiality of Tudor existence (episodes are frequently punctuated with scenes of horse-drawn carts piled high with dining-chairs and furniture), which points up ideas of enforced mobility, potential dispossession, and the ever-present threat of pestilence. Post-watershed television visuals, including close-ups of corpses, miscarried fetuses, and burning heretics, are instrumental in elaborating the Renaissance as a graphically traumatic and physically immediate event. The doctors who hover about Henry frequently resort to ineffective herbal and/or bloodletting "cures," stressing an impotent medical profession and the isolation of the affected/infected individual. Belonging with this emphasis on a pre-Enlightenment Renaissance are nuanced moments of superstitious dependency and interpretation (particularly concerning pregnancy, disability, and death): vigorously implied is the journey still to be taken toward more rational modes of situating bodily experience. This is reflected in the "dark, low-key look" cinematography of the series—paintings, especially by Caravaggio, are cited as inspiration; lighting is restricted on both set and location; and stock is shot without filters.[26] The effect is to suggest that, for all its splendor and sumptuousness, the Henrician court is dangerous, precarious, and essentially unknown beneath its surface: angled antinostalgically, *The Tudors* situates the past as horror-laden and chaotic, as a period to withdraw from rather than actively embrace.

Matching this unsettling sense of the Renaissance, *The Tudors* constructs a correspondingly quotidian and ever-shifting sense of early modern politics. The series enlists post-EU understandings of countries inside European borders to elaborate an accessible power map. For example, Renaissance nonaggression pacts such as the Treaty of London (1518) and more amiable "foreign policy" outings such as the Field of the Cloth of Gold (1520) are collapsed into one "Treaty of Universal and Perpetual Peace," which Henry and his court travel to France to sign and endorse. The aim of the treaty, as the series envisions it, is not only to cement an Anglo-French alliance but also to create "Pan-European institutions" and ratify a NATO-like insistence upon maintaining peace. The simplification might be seen as indicative of what David Starkey has argued is *The Tudors'* "intention to dumb down…so that even an audience in Omaha would understand it."[27] More charitably, it could be suggested that this reinvention of history allows American audiences, in particular, to take on board not only the threats faced by the English nation over the course of the sixteenth century but also the crucial place of Rome in contemporary debate. One of the strengths of *The Tudors* is that, from its inception, the series establishes politics and religion as codependent, and not least through the central figure of Cardinal

Wolsey. A Cardinal agitating to be the Pope, as well as an English administrator with a tight grasp on domestic and foreign policy, Wolsey operates as the audience's point of reference for European governmental machinations, one effect of which is to spotlight the mutually defining relation between Henry's actions and the contingent nature of international affairs.

In this way, Wolsey is exemplary of a process in *The Tudors* in which representatives of instituted authority are imagined as mirror images of the larger movements that they alternately subscribe to or resist. A centering upon personality thus becomes a means of political revelation. Concentrating on the fortunes of particular characters, indeed, is part and parcel of the series' unfolding of the Reformation, with personalities such as Cromwell, Cranmer, Latimer, Bishop Fisher, and More consistently identified with discrete agendas and perspectives. The process is largely shaped by the accessibility requirement: as writer Michael Hirst explains, the series "is about the Reformation. How do you sell that to a U.S. audience without getting them hooked on the characters first?"[28] Also allowing for accessibility of meaning is the way in which debates are discovered incrementally. Questions related to the intellectual contexts of the Reformation are approached gently before being more stridently developed. For example, in early episodes More talks with the Spanish Ambassador about "his friend" Erasmus and the growth of Lutheranism. Issues around conscience and papal authority are then discussed over quiet dinners between More and Henry and are portrayed as informing considerations in male friendship. As other players enter the discussion, its main themes are finessed, with a greater range of alternatives being introduced and tested. The accumulative procedure allows an audience to retain engagement and to be guided comfortably through a steadily denser construction.

The presentation of Henry in these discussions is distinctive in that he is never wholly identified with any of the multiple shifting sides. A sense of Henry's relative secularity is carefully maintained through costume; in particular, dress (the king's tight-fitting jerkin and boots contrast with the more voluminous robes of religious representatives and advisers) is important for enacting a symbolic separation between the monarch and his theological environment. Moreover, Henry's personal relationship with God remains scored with defensiveness. The first of the sovereign's only two recourses to divinity emerges after the birth of his illegitimate son: drunk with delight at the arrival of Henry Fitzroy, the king rails at his maker: "God, can you hear me? I have a son, God!"[29] Contrary to a portraiture tradition that imaged Henry in terms of his piety, this interlude privileges a remote and antagonistic relation with God: once again, an impression is afforded of a personality distinguished by its contemporaneousness, with doubt and vexation as the defining signifiers. This is not to suggest that the monarch is disengaged from debate, but, rather, that his interest is articulated as essentially intellectual rather than spiritual. In this regard, books are vital: the early conflagration to which Luther's books are consigned notwithstanding, the Renaissance text is valorized and deified in *The Tudors* and imagined as one of the instruments through which the young Henry assumes ownership of his monarchical role. Toward the end of the first series, the "on-the-make" Cromwell (James Frain) passes secretly to Anne Boleyn a copy of William Tyndale's *The Obedience of a Christian Man* (first published in 1528). As envisaged, Anne (typical of a series that points up the significance of women's roles, she is represented as a key reforming figure) shares the gift with her kingly lover: the accompanying cut to Henry reading the volume against a flash of lightning suggests both an earth-shattering conjunction of reader and text and an access to knowledge of "Shakespearean" proportions (in *Prospero's Books* [dir. Derek Jarman, 1991], for instance, books are similarly elevated to forces of transformative authority). From this point on, Henry is distinguished by a greater political verve: his injunctions to council—"Things were done without my approval, and this stops now…We shall reconvene very shortly"—underline the distance travelled from the "Can I play now?" of the opening episode. In part, then, Tyndale's work is constructed as the impetus behind an unprecedented involvement in the running of the state. The call to order establishes *The Tudors* as subscribing, much in the manner of recent detective fiction, to a drive to organize the past, to bring it to a working efficiency that offsets the tendency to political and social unruliness.[30] In many ways, Henry is the man who will perform this function and bring the Renaissance out of the dark into modernity.

The man identified by Cromwell as having secured the Tyndale text for Anne is the author of *Supplication for the Beggars* (first published in 1529), Simon Fish, whom More later puts to the stake. Typical of the martyring scene is the way in which Fish (Martin Murphy) is briefly but empathetically drawn, not least through a quasi-heroic death that works through close-up to suggest the inherently dangerous nature of More's religious zeal. The realization is preempted by an early flashcut of the otherwise idealized humanist privately prostrating himself and revealing a naked patchwork of self-flagellating scars. The flashcut is repeated at later moments of high tension, reinforcing the notion that, despite More's unique role in eschewing hypocrisy, the Utopian *domus* conceals a longer history of self-persecution. Indeed, it is in its conjuration of religious types discovered as fanatics that the series appears most indebted to the ideology and iconography of *Elizabeth: The Golden Age*. In *The Tudors*, early modern fanaticism and twenty-first-century East-West ideological conflicts are brought together. For example, a Jesuit (before the order has even been founded) is told via the discourse of the "suicide bomber" that, if he were to die in the attempt to assassinate Anne, his "family would be looked after and [he] would be welcomed into heaven." Over the course of the series as a whole, More is discovered as joining forces with a number of immoderate personalities who yearn for martyrdom. A sustained series of reaction shots of his wife and daughters rob More of the integrity and honor enshrined in the representation of the protagonist in the film version of *A Man For All Seasons* (dir. Fred Zinnemann, 1966). Instead, the angry pleading of female faces in *The Tudors* highlights More's self-aggrandizement and his particularly gendered refusal to separate out issues of state and conscience.

Given the variations and mutations of world politics in *The Tudors*, it is hardly surprising that individual careers marked by a rise and fall are a constant. Toward the end of the first series, as one aspirant to power fades (Wolsey), another (Cromwell) emerges to assume his place. The repetitive quality of the filling and refilling of key positions is emphasized in the fact that different characters find themselves facing similar ethical dilemmas throughout. At the end of the first series, Wolsey as Chancellor, given the weight of his guilt and corruption, is unable to pray; at the end of the second series, Cromwell as Chancellor, given the weight of his guilt and corruption, is also unable to pray. The notion of history repeating itself works not only politically but also in terms of characters' emotional lives: in the second series, Anne and Henry sit over sullen dinners that Henry and Katherine endured in the first. And, in a moment of barbed irony, Anne arrives at the Tower enunciating to herself the formulation previously associated with Katherine: "I am the King's true wedded wife." What this suggests is a model that privileges the circular nature of history and that underscores the premise that, the more things change, the more they remain the same. Even in the recurring image of the stately duck pond, around which the characters endlessly walk, is a powerful sense of this notion prioritized.

History as circle is cynically conceptualized: however young and fresh (and most of Henry's appointees are exactly that) a particular type may be, power is a pervasively corrupting influence. This orientation is wonderfully exemplified in the presentation of Rome and the figuration of Pope Paul III (Peter O'Toole). Drawing heavily on HBO's rival figure, the mafia don Tony Soprano (James Gandolfini), the charismatic Pope delights publicly in his male grandchild and proffers an immediate solution to the Boleyn problem: "Why doesn't someone just get rid of her?" he asks with casual aplomb. Vatican policy is imagined in terms of an easy pragmatism: monarchs, it is stated, have "soldiers and guns" (hence, they need to be courted), while popes enjoy access only to "beauty and truth." And, in the callous world of

Rome, there is no debate over which is more useful. Interestingly, the secular calm of O'Toole's Pope connects him with Henry's distance from England's religious fervor. Intertextually, the two are further linked by their Irish "hell-raiser" reputations and the recollection of O'Toole's famous performance as Henry II: casting here lends an additional layer to metaphorical understandings of the conflict between England and the Papacy as a familial separation between father and son. The prioritizing of two star personalities—Rhys Meyers and O'Toole—helps to articulate with a particular force the paternal-filial construction of the church and ensures that the break with Rome takes on appropriately seismic proportions.

There is only one problem: it is the wrong pope. The Pope who refused the divorce and excommunicated Henry was Pope Clement VII, not Pope Paul III. The error has been seized upon as indicative of poor research, but this is an assumption that betokens a patronizing reading of television drama and a conservative view of historical recreation. Instead, *The Tudors* is often self-conscious about its envisaging of history as a purposefully imaginative process. For example, while it is generally accepted that Wolsey died (in 1529) of natural causes, the expiry is imagined here as a powerfully climactic suicide. Yet what is important is the scene immediately following, in which Henry orders that the suicide be covered up—"No one must ever know." The construction of an alternative story allows "conspiracy theories" of history to be ventilated (earlier, the attempted assassination scene is reminiscent of *JFK* [dir. Oliver Stone, 1991]) and gestures again to competing interpretations of the historical record and the role of mediation in the reading of its core events. Inside this schema, it is not the particular pope that matters; rather, it is the narrative function the pope executes as a personification of the consistently oppositional forces of Rome.

Henry is not only a rewriter of history but also a poet, actor, composer, and patron; in this sense, he is seen to inhabit a world similar to that explored in *Shakespeare in Love*. Court musicians, writers, and artists are drawn as characters in their own right and emerging from their largely lower-class social affiliations is a marked impression of a creative meritocracy. Present throughout is Thomas Wyatt (Jamie Thomas King): his poems enter the story-line as voice-overs, with such lines as "They flee from me, that sometime did me seek" furnishing a wry, diegetic commentary. Similarly, the career and bisexual love life of Thomas Tallis (Joe Van Moyland) is consistently pursued: his status as artist bestows upon him a choric position, while his music is envisaged as being directly shaped by the Renaissance court. In Rome, a figure such as Michelangelo is comically realized: the Pope is almost knocked over as the artist exits the Sistine chapel in a rage. "Not like that, asshole," he shouts over his shoulder, "Moses looks like a pile of crap." The cynicism of the Pope's response—"We forgive him because he is a genius…Whatever that means"—is undercut when an accompanying vista of the Sistine Chapel invokes recent films concerned with painterly inspiration (including *Girl with a Pearl Earring* [dir. Peter Webber, 2003]) exactly to reveal that "genius" in modernity.

Throughout the series' contemporary filtering of cultural practice, political praxis is never far away. Wolsey's suicide sequence is intercut with scenes from a court masque satirizing his life; his death is literally spliced with the counterpointed representation on stage of the same event, facilitating a keen sense of the topicality of drama. A related scene shows Cromwell electing to sponsor the writing of "a Mr. Bale" as a propaganda push. Both moments represent, to adopt a recent formulation, "an extension of the impulse to read between the lines" of canonical writing while also providing insight into the relation between state power and production and into the evolution of "literature" as a discrete representational category.[31] Early in season two is a sequence during which Cromwell shows off a newfangled piece of machinery toiling in the palace: "It's called a printing press," he states, "And it will change the world." The implication is not only that this is the conduit through which the Reformation will emerge into public consciousness but also that the invention marks the onset of modernity. As an example of technology, the printing press was the precursor of other, more familiar forms of mass communication, including television itself. Here, in a knowing glance at its own practices and appeal, *The Tudors* acknowledges its place as another rewriting, as an articulation of history on an international scale, and as medium of understanding made available via multiple interpretive domains.

*   *   *

Earlier parts of this chapter drew attention to the series' status as a prequel, yet *The Tudors* might also be constituted as a sequel in that it comes after the glut of "Shakespeare" films of the 1980s and 1990s and builds upon their example. Within circulating constructions of the Renaissance, *The Tudors* draws upon what has established itself as marketable and acceptable. "Shakespeare" on screen comes to the aid of the popular explanation of history, and history defers to an elaboration of "Shakespeare" in the search for a ready style and grammar of representation. The continuing alignment in the popular imaginary between Shakespeare and Elizabeth is also facilitative. "Henry…gave us Elizabeth I, a kind of founding feminist," Rhys Meyers states, and in many ways the king's newfound respectability and "film-ability" are authorized by his being the queen's father.[32] The notion of

Elizabeth as "her father's daughter" is essential to contemporary constructions of the virgin monarch: in many ways, then, Henry's dominant display of masculinity is made possible by his daughter's androgyny, his heterosexuality affirmed through the popular articulation of her single status.

Jerome de Groot has argued that while "historians wish to mark history out, to control and boundarise it…it is in the transformations and transgressions of the historical that culture's desires, innermost workings, and underlying assumptions might be seen."[33] Certainly, at those moments where *The Tudors* manipulates the historical, compressing time-lines, amalgamating personages, debunking familiar notions, and leveling hierarchies, the pressures of the post-modern are particularly in evidence. This chapter has argued that prominent among contemporary investments are anxieties centered upon extremism and infertility, fanaticism and faith, masculinity and heterosexual desire, communication and the status of the book. *The Tudors'* "transgressions of the historical," then, speak to an age caught up in questions of multiculturalism, technology, ethics, and the power of established and emergent religions.

In contradistinction to largely defunct arguments over the importance of "fidelity" and "authenticity" in the adaptation of literary texts, discussion of how best "history" might be screened, revised, and rewritten is still largely unresolved.[34] *The Tudors'* depiction of the Renaissance is revisionist—it breaks clear from an expected "golden age" heritage-based template to move into as yet untested arenas. The unpalatable nature, in academic terms, of such a move is reflected in responses to *The Tudors*, as earlier parts of this chapter have demonstrated. Arguing against simplistic understandings of "dumbing down," and recognizing the ways in which *The Tudors* works inside more inclusive notions of accessibility, this chapter posits the importance of understanding religious and cultural change through layered modalities of telling and via the central contribution of emotion, personality, and celebrity. Moving between different polarities, Rhys Meyers exceeds the frame of the story, his omnipresence in global media forms allowing him to take on the role of cultural commentator and even public historian. A production that spans national interests and institutions, *The Tudors* summons numerous bodies of knowledge and explanation on the part of viewers and assumes a sophisticated, collaborative, and even transnational interpretive ability. In *The Tudors*, no single version of history is ultimately privileged: the events and transactions of the past alternately appear as assimilation, imitation, and bricolage. The question asked by *The Tudors'* publicity—"What would *you* do if *you* were Henry?"—emphasizes a linear direction that can alter or founder at any point. The "real story," with which we are tantalized, concerns flexibility and unpredictability—the capacity for reinvention that is in essence the series' "heart."

Notes

1. Michael Hirst and Michael Wilder, *The Tudors: It's Good to be King* (New York: Simon Spotlight, 2007). This image is also reproduced on publicity initiatives. Accompanying the series are two novels: Anne Gracie, *The Tudors: The King, the Queen, and the Mistress* (New York: Simon Spotlight, 2007); and Elizabeth Massie, *The Tudors: King Takes Queen* (New York: Simon Spotlight, 2007).

2. Thomas S. Freeman, "A Tyrant for All Seasons: Henry VIII on Film," in *Tudors and Stuarts on Film: Historical Perspectives*, ed. Susan Doran and Thomas Freeman (Basingstoke: Palgrave, 2009), 43, 30.

3. Laura Mulvey, "Visual Pleasure and Narrative Cinema," in *The Film Studies Reader*, ed. Joanne Hollows, Peter Hutchings, and Mark Jancovich (London: Arnold, 2000), 243.

4. Kenneth MacKinnon, *Representing Men: Maleness and Masculinity in the Media* (London: Arnold, 2003), 116.

5. *The Tudors* was made by Peace Arch Entertainment for Showtime, in association with Reveille Eire (Ireland), Working Title Films (UK), and CBS (Canada). The series was originally shown on Showtime in April 2007 before being broadcast by the BBC in October of that year.

6. David Starkey, *Henry: Virtuous Prince* (London: Harper, 2008).

7. See Freeman, 36–37, 30.

8. Julie Sanders, *Adaptation and Appropriation* (London and New York: Routledge, 2006), 143.

9. Hirst and Wilder, 46.

10. David Starkey "The Tudors is gratuitously awful," *The Daily Telegraph*, October 16 (2008), 5.

11. MacKinnon, 111.

12. Francesca Bibb, "Jonathan Rhys Meyers in *The Tudors*," *Red Magazine*, November (2007), 183.

13. Hirst and Wilder, 56.

14. Kathy M. Howlett, *Framing Shakespeare on Film* (Athens: Ohio UP, 2000), 101, 109, 114.

15. Gabrielle Donnelly, "His Majesty's Pleasure," *The Daily Mail: Weekend*, September 15 (2008), 22.

16. Chris Sullivan, "Mock Tudor," *The Mail on Sunday: Live*, July 27 (2008), 15.

17. Ellen Fein and Sherrie Schneider, *The Rules: Time-Tested Secrets for Capturing the Heart of Mr. Right* (New York: Warner Books, 1995).

18. Sanders, 24, 159.

19. Steve Brennan and Bernadette O'Neill, *Emeralds in Tinseltown: The Irish in Hollywood* (Belfast: Appletree, 2007), 161.

20. Sullivan, 15.

21. See Mark Thornton Burnett, "'To Hear and See the Matter': Communicating Technology in Michael Almereyda's *Hamlet*," *Cinema Journal* 42.3 (2003): 56–57.

22. Female-female relations are uneasy and subject to quick betrayals: the series brings to mind recent female-led television dramas, including *Desperate Housewives*.

23. Michael Dobson and Nicola J. Watson, *England's Elizabeth: An Afterlife in Fame and Fantasy* (Oxford: Oxford UP, 2002), 169
24. In general, women's roles are amplified and, in particular, wives are introduced and given major roles.
25. Jerome de Groot, *Consuming History: Historians and Heritage in Contemporary Popular Culture* (London and New York: Routledge, 2009), 199.
26. Louise Bishop, "Regarding Henry," *Producer: The Digital Production Magazine*, Summer (2007), 8–9.
27. Starkey, 5.
28. Michael Hirst, "Off with his head?," *Radio Times*, September 29–October 5 (2007), 19.
29. Hirst and Wilder, 134.
30. See de Groot, 201.
31. Sanders, 147.
32. Michael Deacon, "King of the Swingers," *The Daily Telegraph: Television and Radio*, September 29 (2007), 3.
33. de Groot, 250.
34. See Imelda Whelehan, "Adaptations: The Contemporary Dilemmas," in *Adaptations: From Text to Screen, Screen to Text*, ed. Deborah Cartmell and Imelda Whelehan (London and New York: Routledge, 1999), 3.

CHAPTER 2

The Secret Life of Elizabeth I

Adrienne L. Eastwood

In popular culture today, representations of Elizabeth I tend to oscillate around a central and gendered duality. On the one hand, they visually reference the "Gloriana" of her most frequently reproduced portraits: the image of royal authority in the tradition of kings, splendidly and powerfully arrayed; and on the other, they supply romantic and sexual narratives that attempt to explain Elizabeth's identity as an unmarried woman.[1] The interplay between these two perspectives in popular film versions of Elizabeth creates a fractured portrait of female authority: masculine regality in some degree of conflict with feminine emotionality. Rather than functioning, as some critics have suggested, as a "quasi-feminist heroine" or a "feminist icon," twentieth- and twenty-first-century representations of Elizabeth increasingly present her as defined and circumscribed by her relation to men.[2] Perhaps this is why discussions about Elizabeth almost always include a debate on the question of her virginity—in spite of the fact that the debate will never be resolved. The myth of the Virgin Queen continues to tantalize modern imaginations, begging for an explanation of the Queen as a woman. The continuing abundance of fictional representations of the Queen and her family in literature and on film testifies to the persistent interest in the secret lives of the Tudors.[3]

Cinematic representations proffer such narratives, and in doing so, they mediate, or diminish, the effect of the queen as imperious, autonomous, or authoritarian. Audiences are enticed into investing more deeply in the romantic narratives because the act of supplying details, however fictional, about the queen's identity invites imaginative involvement. Cinematic representations of Elizabeth I "make history" by transforming the open and ambiguous discourses of Elizabeth's reign into closed ones that make sense to popular audiences.[4] Such discourses presume to explain what Elizabeth thought or how she felt, her frustrations and her triumphs, packaging her identity for popular consumption. This process humanizes her, but it also dilutes the powerful, masculine aspect of Elizabethan ideology, bringing out feminine foibles that diminish the presentation of monarchal authority. By analyzing recent cinematic representations of the famous Tilbury speech, this chapter traces the way in which representations of Elizabeth reduce her strength as a ruler and emphasize her emotional life, suggesting that women in power can be strong, as long as they are not too strong.

In some ways, this popular investment in the emotional and sexual life of the queen derives from historical accounts. Elizabeth's habit of advancing her favorites (and also punishing them if they disappointed her) is well documented. But it is perhaps the portrayal of the queen as a "Virgin" that lies at the heart of the matter. Kathryn Schwarz argues that "we have invented not an Elizabeth for our own times but a reiterative animation of early modern concerns" about gender and sexuality.[5] Although virginity is—and was—a complex category that is ultimately defined by men, this changes, Schwarz observes, when "virginity speaks for itself."[6] "Ideology," she asserts, "may have invented the Virgin Queen, as it certainly invested in a cash crop of less exalted virginal bodies. But it is a strangely permeable ideology, not so much contested or subverted as porous to unexpected positions of articulation."[7] The trope of virginity is persistently vulnerable to patriarchal "permeability." But, whereas Schwarz sees early modern and popular ideas of virginity as essentially the same, I suggest that there is a cluster of meanings attached to "virginity" that is not available to popular audiences.

The *OED* lists as its primary definition of "virgin" the following: "An unmarried or chaste maiden or woman, distinguished for piety or steadfastness in religion, and regarded as having a special place among the members of the Christian church on account of these merits." This definition, in use from the eleventh century through the seventeenth, indicates Roman "vestal virgins"—a religious rather than a secular category. It is this meaning, expressing impenetrable power, that the Elizabethan ideological machine accessed in the sieve portraits.[8] In modern dictionaries, the primary definition is sexual: "a person (esp. a woman) who has had no sexual intercourse."[9] How, then, can today's audiences imagine a woman (who is not depicted as a nun), as a member of the first category? The effect is that when popular audiences imagine a "Virgin Queen," explanations are required.

In *Of Chastity and Power*, Philippa Berry articulates the ways in which Elizabeth's formulation of virginity worked both to produce political control and to open up the queen and her government to a coded and complicated critique.[10] As deployed by Elizabeth and her regime, virginity stands for impenetrability—in the person of the queen and England itself. In this, it adopts a masculine resonance: capable of penetration, but itself impermeable. Instead of virginity being ultimately construed as a sexual category, it becomes part of the larger discourse of kingly power to which Elizabeth laid claim. As Susan Frye details in *Elizabeth I: The Competition for Representation*, Elizabeth employed a "representational strategy" comprised of both masculine and feminine traits.[11] Frye argues that Elizabeth used the medieval doctrine of the king's two bodies to indicate that though "her natural body was inevitably female, constructed through cultural norms that placed her below men in the cosmic and social hierarchies," her "political body was constructed within a masculinist legal tradition and thus was often represented as male."[12] Elizabeth's appropriation of masculine traits appears in various ways in her speech rhetoric and the manner in which she attempted to represent herself at public ceremonies and entertainments.[13] As Frye notes, an androgynous construction would be "the strongest possible representational position" for the queen.[14]

In her speeches, Elizabeth similarly deploys both genders, casting herself both within and above her culture's gendered expectations. Her rhetorical strategy acknowledges her culture's normative ideals of female weakness or frailty, and then asserts a superseding masculine authority derived from her lineage as the daughter of a king. To cite one example, in 1566, Elizabeth is reported to have said to a delegation of lords and commons: "and though I be a woman, yet I have as good a courage answerable to my place as ever my father had. I am your anointed queen. I will never be by violence constrained to do anything."[15] The queen effectively reframes the "problem" of her gender by inscribing herself in the traditionally masculine discourse of kingship derived from her heredity. In this way, Elizabeth rejects attempts to define her as merely female and asserts herself instead as what her contemporary George Buchanan deemed "*mascula vis*," or "manly character," as a position from which to rule.[16]

In cinematic depictions of the queen, her masculine character drops out. Since Sarah Bernhardt's performance in 1912, Elizabeth has been portrayed specifically in relation to the men who were her favorites: Robert Dudley, Walter Ralegh, and Robert Devereux. Barbara Hodgdon argues that these and other early representations of the queen (including Bette Davis' *The Private Lives of Elizabeth and Essex* [1939], and Glenda Jackson's *Elizabeth R* [1971]) feminize her in order to "reinscribe her within the binaries of dominant heterosexuality."[17] Popular Elizabeths, according to Hodgdon, tend to produce "a particular truth about the Queen's sexuality."[18] The idea that one might have access to Elizabeth's inner life is at the core of this "truth," and the effect of such narratives is to reduce the queen to being defined primarily by her natural body and its relation to men.[19] Following Hodgdon, I argue that recent cinematic representations of the queen subordinate her political prowess and strength as a ruler to the fantasy of her emotional and sexual life as a woman. In doing so, they come close to reproducing the discourses favored by Elizabeth's detractors, suggesting that very little has changed regarding Western attitudes about female power in over 400 years.[20]

Elizabeth's most infamous detractor, the Catholic in exile, Cardinal William Allen, exemplifies anti-Elizabethan rhetoric in his vitriolic *Admonition to the Nobility of Rome*, written to incite Catholic unrest on the eve of the Spanish Armada. Allen's diatribe covers the range of arguments against her rule, accusing Elizabeth of being a "pretender" and "usurper" of the throne as well as an "incestuous bastard, begotten and borne in sinne."[21] Most tellingly for my purposes here, Allen also accuses her of having indiscriminate sex:

> With the forsaid person [Dudley] and divers others she hathe abused her bodie, against God's lawes, to the disgrace of princely majestie & the whole nations reproche, by unspeakable and incredible variety of luste, which modesty suffereth not to be remembered, neyther were it to chaste eares to be uttered how shamefully she hath defiled and infamed her person and cuntry, and made her Courte as a trappe, by this damnable and detestable arte, to intagle in sinne and overthrowe the yonger sorte of the nobilitye and gentlemen of the lande, whereby she is become notorius to the wourlde...[22]

Allen claims to have knowledge of Elizabeth's sexual life, which he uses to discredit her claim to the throne. As Carole Levin argues in "Gender, Monarchy, and the Power of Seditious Words," much of the seditious discourse against the queen focused on "the sexual behavior of the sovereign."[23] Levin concludes by noting that "as a woman ruling alone Elizabeth represented deeply felt concerns about rule, stability, women's roles, and sexuality," and that seditious statements characterizing the queen as a "whore and an incompetent female" enabled them to express their dissatisfaction with the situation of female rule.[24] What I would emphasize is that sexualizing the queen insists on the fact of her natural and therefore penetrable body, which necessarily undermines the masculine or androgynous constructions adopted by Elizabeth herself. Popular cinematic representations do the same thing.

Shekhar Kapur's 1998 film *Elizabeth* presents a young Elizabeth who is unequivocally sexually active. The film takes shape around the queen's self-conscious (though not historical) transition into the mythic Virgin Queen. In the penultimate scene of the film, a tearful Elizabeth, played by Cate Blanchett, submits to a severe hair cut and the laborious application of white makeup as she assumes the role of Virgin. Her emergence as mythical being is set up specifically as the rejection of the sensuous indulgences that the film assumes she has enjoyed. Flashbacks of the young queen in the arms of the dashing Robert Dudley play behind the images of her transformation, suggesting that as she assumes the role of the Virgin Queen, adopting the iconography of the Virgin Mary, she rejects her sexual life. At the conclusion of the haircutting scene, a close-cropped, androgynous Elizabeth delivers the line: "I have become a virgin." She then emerges at court, every inch a queen, regally costumed in a dress evocative of the Ditchley portrait.[25] The movie presents an Elizabeth who must be either sexually active or powerful, but not both, essentially the same demand made by Cardinal Allen. Rather than viewing Kapur's Elizabeth, as some critics have, as a "post-feminist" queen assuming control of her own identity, we should interpret her as forced by her culture into sexual self-sacrifice, a situation that paves the way for the emotionally and psychologically distressed queen so often referenced in popular culture today.[26] And because the idea that she "become" a virgin—or more accurately *The* Virgin—originates in a suggestion made by Francis Walsingham (played by Geoffrey Rush), the potential for this transformation as a self-defining "feminist" moment is diluted.

In more recent representations, the romantic narratives that characterize Elizabeth's subjectivity and femininity continue to be enhanced, as the queen's secret life takes center stage. As the feminine elements of the queen's personality are highlighted, the masculine qualities that she herself adopted in her speeches are displaced onto the ever-present men of Elizabeth's court and council. This occurrence is most clearly illustrated by the screen versions of the queen's famous 1588 speech to the troops at the Tilbury camp because here Elizabeth reportedly wore armor, uniquely appearing as visually androgynous.

The Tilbury speech itself similarly presents the queen as possessing both masculine and feminine qualities. As in other speeches, it derives its rhetorical power from Elizabeth's clever recasting of gender:

> I know I have the body of a weak and feeble woman, but I have the heart and stomach of a king and a king of England too—and take foul scorn that Parma or any prince of Europe should dare to invade the boarders of my realm.[27]

In a familiar rhetorical move, the queen assumes qualities of both genders by referencing her natural female body and her political male one. Louis Montrose has argued that "this speech gains rhetorical force from Elizabeth's identification of corporeal and geographical boundaries, from her subtle application of the land/body trope to herself."[28] This casts the potential invasion of England's borders as an attempted "rape"—a transgression of the "boarders" of both land and body. According to this reasoning, the queen's person is vulnerable to attack, but because she claims the support of her subjects, her lineage, and her

God, she will ultimately prove to be impenetrable. She references the trope of virginity that was being deployed with increasing intensity in the 1580s to project power and invincibility.[29] As this oft-quoted speech is delivered on screen, we see the feminine body, variously exposed to, and protected by, the men who were her subjects—members of her council, her court, and her army. Instead of conveying the speech's sense that a monarch transcends the corporal body, the filmed queen comes across as being limited by her body.

In the miniseries *Elizabeth R*, which ran in 1971, the height of "women's liberation," Glenda Jackson's Elizabeth is more historically grounded than other versions. As her character develops, this Elizabeth seems more powerful and authoritarian than any who has appeared before or since. This may be because, as Hodgdon notes, this miniseries attempts to reclaim Elizabeth from earlier productions that focused almost exclusively on Elizabeth's relationship with Essex. However, Hodgdon argues that even this carefully historicized representation of the queen tends to focus attention on Elizabeth's emotional and sexual life as characterized by her relationship with Dudley.[30] While Dudley (by now the Earl of Leicester) is absent from the Tilbury sequence, the scene nevertheless undermines Elizabeth's masculine power by presenting her in tension with her soldiers.

At Tilbury, Jackson's Elizabeth is stern and distant. The scene opens not on the queen but on two soldiers (one young and one old) expressing discontent over the quality and quantity of rations, and in an exchange resonant of Shakespeare's *Henry V*, debating what duty a soldier owes his monarch. They see her from afar, but she can barely be heard as she begins her speech. The camera cuts to Elizabeth, on horseback, unaccompanied and dressed elegantly in a maroon gown and tall hat, holding a golden staff. She wears a collar of armor. She scarcely moves as she delivers her speech, and the camera cuts several times back to the soldiers as they continue to argue about proper soldierly behavior. A faint murmur of voices can be heard, suggesting that many soldiers are involved in their own conversations. They seem to pay very little attention until the queen mentions the "rewards and crowns" that they are owed for their service; then they cheer halfheartedly. After her speech, she bursts into a tent, swearing about the uncomfortable gorget.

In this version, as envisioned by director Roderick Graham, Elizabeth is presented as a leader, almost mundanely doing her job, delivering a speech and perhaps shrewdly deciding to mention remuneration to manipulate her audience's response. However, this rendering of the Tilbury speech is not exactly the rousing rhetorical success that historical accounts describe. This Elizabeth struggles to be heard, and only achieves limited success in her effort to rally the troops. Elizabeth's presence is further diminished in this sequence by placing her in competition with the soldiers, and her effectiveness as a ruler is undermined by the partial failure of the speech. The effect of these choices is to present a queen who is at least partially dependent on her male subjects. The indifference of the soldiers to her speech, while presenting a sly transhistoric comment on political rhetoric in general, causes the queen to struggle for their attention, an act that diminishes the presentation of authority.

By 2005, Elizabeth's speech at Tilbury has taken on a different emphasis. That year saw the airing of two critically acclaimed series about Elizabeth I made for the small screen. In both *The Virgin Queen* with Anne Marie Duff (Masterpiece Theatre Series, directed by Coky Giedroyc) and *Elizabeth I* starring Helen Mirren (directed by Tom Hooper), Elizabeth appears commanding, but a softer, more emotionally volatile side also emerges. *The Virgin Queen*, like most visual representations of Elizabeth I, makes ample use of the more famous portraits (the Ditchley, Armada, and Rainbow portraits, for example) in costuming—a move that, like the portraits themselves, marries iconic images of power with femininity. Duff's Elizabeth, like the state-sponsored portraits that doubtless informed the production, is emotionally volatile and passionate, while visually magnificent. The queen arrives at Tilbury atop a white horse, being led by Leicester. Her gown is a light color, and she wears an armored breastplate with a cross of red ribbon on it. She is greeted by smiles and shouts of enthusiasm: "It's the Queen!" She shares a meal in a tent with Leicester, with whom she flirts playfully by tossing a morsel of food at him. Leicester warns her that her safety might be at risk—that her soldiers, among whom there were likely Catholic sympathizers resentful of the recent execution of Mary Queen of Scots, might attack her. The way in which the queen relates to Leicester, as protector, advisor, and playmate, constructs her as perhaps more human than the Glenda Jackson version, but also as emotionally vulnerable to him since she so clearly craves his attention.

As the apparently ailing Leicester falls asleep, the queen muses about the horrid details of the execution of her cousin, and as if suddenly struck by a thought, she takes out a quill and begins to compose the now-famous speech. As she writes, she pauses to consider her words, and in a voice-over, reads the beginning of the speech. There is a cut to her privy council and a male voice takes over, reading to the councilmen. The camera cuts again to Elizabeth on horseback before her troops just as she delivers the lines: "I know I have the body of a weak and frail woman, but I have the heart and stomach of a king! And a king of England too!" Her soldiers answer with enthusiastic applause. As she goes on, the camera lingers on the faces of the soldiers, who watch her with rapt adoration.

This version of the Tilbury speech emphasizes the queen's attempts to shape her persona via her speeches, but it also makes the point that they were carefully constructed, approved by a male council, and rehearsed before they would have been read to the people. Showing the queen, quill in hand, concentrating on speech writing, presents her as firmly in control of both her political policies and her persona. If the scene had been left here, perhaps fading into the scene before the troops, it would have presented Elizabeth I as powerful and authoritarian indeed. But on screen, Elizabeth's own voice is literally replaced by a male voice possessed by a member of her council who takes up reading the speech. By the time she appears before her soldiers, her authority appears diluted, weakened by its side-trip through the masculine space of the council chamber.

The Channel 4 series with Helen Mirren, with its tagline "The hardest thing to govern is the heart," presents the most emotional, and in some ways the least effective, version of Elizabeth. The series plays up the idea of sexual sacrifice—constantly showing the queen, with bosoms heaving, fending off the passionate advances of Leicester played by an increasingly grim Jeremy Irons. The female body is emphasized from the opening scene in which Elizabeth's physician (Dr. Lopez) conducts a gynecological exam and announces that the now forty-year-old queen is "*vagina intactica*," and therefore eligible to proceed with the marriage negotiations with Alencon. This depiction forces the viewer to perceive the queen as corporal body first—and I would argue we never quite see her emerge as the impenetrable political body portrayed by the Elizabethan ideological machine.[31] Instead, this version constructs a vulnerable and emotional Elizabeth, defined by her relationship to prominent men: first Leicester, and then Essex, both of whom are present at Tilbury.

The Tilbury sequence in *Elizabeth I* begins with a shot of the queen surrounded by her council, pointing to a huge map and strategizing about troop deployment. A powerful figure, but one literally encircled by men. She rejects their concerns about her safety—insisting on her intention to be with her troops. But in a private moment before they leave for Tilbury, she anxiously asks the ever-present Leicester, "What should I say to the soldiers who are willing to die for England?" Leicester, suited in armor, holds the queen's hand and offers his assurance and courage. In one of the most revealing moments, it is Leicester who tells Elizabeth that she has "the heart and stomach of a king." The image of a commanding monarch is diluted here either by the presence of men or by the fretful anxiety of an uncertain woman. Apparently this queen is so distracted that she needs to be gently reminded of her own lineage.

She arrives at Tilbury on a white horse being led by—you guessed it—Leicester. Wearing a breastplate, which she chides Leicester for "convincing" her to wear for her safety, she beams at her soldiers and talks to them from atop her horse. There is a makeshift throne on the battlefield—a rostrum with a chair on it. She does not, however, choose to be seated. Instead, she begins her speech standing next to the throne on the rostrum. By staging this option and choice, this version tries to construct the queen as charismatic—a woman of the people, not necessarily descended from kings. She quickly abandons even this raised platform. The men are absolutely silent, and she walks among them shadowed in every frame by a protective Leicester. As she says, "I am come among you at this time but for my recreation and pleasure, being resolved in the midst and heat of the battle to live and die amongst you all, to lay down for my God and for my kingdom and for my people mine honor and my blood even in the dust," she reaches down and grabs a handful of earth for emphasis. She beams at her soldiers and seems to gain momentum from their positive response. As the music builds to a crescendo, she brushes away a tear and a soldier kneels and kisses her gown. As she raises him up, she touches his cheek and lovingly smiles at him.

This Elizabeth makes the most of this speech as a dramatic moment; she is presented as possessing charisma (in fact it appears as though she improvises the entire speech) but not the grandeur of an anointed monarch. Her vulnerability and emotion are emphasized in this scene, not her power or stateliness. In short, she is presented much more as a woman relating to a field of men than as a powerful political leader. Perhaps this lack of dignity stems from assumptions about the intended American audience—more accustomed to the chauvinism and violence of the Sopranos than the stateliness of the English monarchy.

In 2007, Shekhar Kapur brings back Cate Blanchett's version of the queen in *Elizabeth: The Golden Age*, a performance that earned her an Oscar nomination.[32] This film, which ostensibly focuses on the latter part of Elizabeth's reign (though none of the leading figures appears to age), seems inevitably to lead to Tilbury as the culminating and defining moment of the queen's reign. Movie trailers and posters feature an image of Elizabeth, red hair flowing and in full armor, clearly evocative of this historic moment. But the film incessantly selects Ralegh (played by a dashing Clive Owen) as its focus, relegating Elizabeth to the margins, obsessive and jealous, often collapsing in fits of tears. In one scene, a spectacularly costumed Elizabeth faces down a potential assassin in a church: she rises up and turns to him, splendid and powerful with an ethereal lighting, and literally stares down his attack. But this scene is undermined by several that feature the queen in hushed, passionate conversation with Ralegh, actually begging in one scene "just one kiss." Ralegh literally appears to be the center of Elizabeth's world—a prominence he most certainly did not enjoy historically. This Elizabeth is fractured: split between the iconic beauty and majesty of the public Gloriana, and the private, emotionally needy, sexually deprived woman we have come to recognize as the popular Elizabeth.

At Tilbury, Kapur's Elizabeth is visually spectacular. She appears as she does in the trailers: red hair flowing (in the iconic style of a virgin maiden), on the back of a beautiful white horse and in full armor, all alone. She faces her troops, and the men appear astonished but pleased. However, Kapur chooses not to

include the text from Elizabeth's famous speech. Instead, we get an approxima-
tion of the speech's content, but avoidance of its gendered ambiguity:

> My loving people, we see the sails of the enemy approaching; we see the
> Spanish guns over the water; we will meet them face to face. I am resolved to
> live or die amongst you all. While we stand together, no invader will pass; and
> when this day is over, we will meet again in heaven or on the field of victory.

This watered-down version of the Tilbury speech basically reiterates the idea
that the queen intends to fight alongside her subjects. The lack of rhetorical
power present in these lines subjugates the political aspect of this moment
to the visual spectacle. In the ensuing scenes, however, the speech at Tilbury
is all but erased by the astonishing display of a swashbuckling Ralegh, who
appears almost single-handedly to defeat the Spanish Armada. Elizabeth's
most powerful rhetorical and political moment is overshadowed, if not
erased, by Ralegh's military prowess.

In each of these filmic representations of the Tilbury speech we see an
Elizabeth who is, in varying degrees, mediated, and politically reduced, by
her relationship to men. The relatively commanding queen in *Elizabeth R*
dwindles into the emotional and vulnerable one in the most recent Channel
4/HBO series, but in each case her authority is subordinated to her emotions and displaced onto her male subjects. These "reduced" Elizabeths do
not present the queen as a prisoner to her turbulent emotions, as the earliest
screen versions tended to do, but they do subtly feminize her by deflecting
attention from her—at one of her most powerful historical moments—and
training it instead onto her male subjects. The films shift the focus from
the ruling woman to the men in her life. She is not the overtly sexualized
Jezebel featured in Cardinal Allen's diatribe, but she does appear subordinate to male pleasure. By turns, she attempts to seduce (or struggles with
the impulse to try) a male audience of soldiers, her council, or her favorites,
while her effectiveness as a ruler is acknowledged only visually, if at all.[33]

Notes

1. The work of Francis Yates and Roy Strong established the idea of a "cult of vir-
   ginity" constructed through portraiture and pageantry. See Yates, *Astraea: The
   Imperial Theme in the Sixteenth Century* (Harmondsworth: Penguin, 1977); Roy
   Strong, *The Cult of Elizabeth: Elizabethan Portraiture and Pageantry* (London:
   Thames & Hudson, 1977); and *Gloriana: The Portraits of Queen Elizabeth*
   (London: Thames & Hudson, 1987). More recently, Louis Montrose has chal-
   lenged the notion of a monolithic image of the queen successfully controlled
   by the Elizabethan government. See, for example, "Idols of the Queen: Policy,
   Gender, and the Picturing of Elizabeth I," in *Representations* 68 (1999): 50–101.

2. David Grant Moss refers to twentieth-century Elizabeths as "quasi-feminist" (798), and Thomas Betteridge notes that representations of Elizabeth correspond "directly to the way the status of women has changed during the twentieth century" (248). See "A Queen for All Seasons: Elizabeth I on Film," in *The Myth of Elizabeth*, ed. Susan Doran and Thomas Freeman (Basingstroke, England; and New York: Palgrave, 2003).

3. In addition to the screen representations I discuss in this essay (Kapur's *Elizabeth* [1998] and *Elizabeth: The Golden Age* [2007], *Elizabeth I* [with Helen Mirren, 2005], and *The Virgin Queen* with Anne Marie Duff [2005]), a multitude of historical fictions about the Tudors exist, and Kathryn Schwarz references *Elizabeth I CEO* among other texts in her article, "The Wrong Question: Thinking through Virginity," *Differences: A Journal of Feminist Cultural Studies* 13.2 (2002): 1–34.

4. The concept I borrow here is outlined by Michel DeCerteau in *The Writing of History*, trans. Tom Conley (New York: Columbia UP, 1988). DeCerteau argues that history is constructed by individuals who translate what he calls "scenarios" into a "currently intelligible discourse" (6).

5. Schwarz "The Wrong Question: Thinking Through Virginity," 5.

6. Ibid., 8.

7. Ibid., 7.

8. Louis Montrose, "Idols of the Queen," *Representations* 68 (1999): 50–101. See also *The Subject of Elizabeth: Authority, Gender, and Representation* (Chicago: Chicago UP, 2006).

9. "Virgin." *Chambers Dictionary.* 1st ed. 1993.

10. Philippa Berry, *Of Chastity and Power* (New York: Routledge, 1989). See especially Chapter 6: "Rewriting Chastity: Representations of the Unmarried Queen by Chapman, Shakespeare, Ralegh, and Spenser."

11. See Susan Frye, *Elizabeth I: The Competition for Representation* (Oxford: Oxford UP, 1993).

12. Ibid., 12–13.

13. Frye notes that the representation of the queen was by no means under her control. As it was with her sister Mary, Elizabeth's gender became the site where her detractors attacked her (17–21).

14. Ibid., 36.

15. *Elizabeth I: Collected Works*, ed. Leah Marcus, Janel Mueller, and Mary Beth Rose (Chicago: Chicago UP, 2000), 97.

16. Buchanan's epigram, written in Latin, appears in Camden's *Remains Concerning Britain*, ed. R.D. Dunn (Toronto: U of Toronto P), 306.

17. Barbara Hodgdon, *The Shakespeare Trade: Performances and Appropriations* (Philadelphia: U of Pennsylvania P, 1998). See Chapter 4: "Romancing the Queen," 110–70, 112.

18. Ibid., 112.

19. Hodgdon traces the story of Elizabeth and Essex, the most referenced relationship in the earlier popular representations of the queen's reign, to a 1680 "pseudo-memoir" titled *The Secret History of the Most Renowned Queen Elizabeth and the Earl of Essex, by a Person of Quality* (120–22). The Essex narrative dominates the

popular representations that Hodgdon examines, including: *Queen Elizabeth,* 1912 (starring Sarah Bernhardt); *The Private Lives of Elizabeth and Essex,* dir. Michael Curtiz (Warner Brothers, 1939); and *Elizabeth and Essex: A Tragic History,* serialized in *Ladies Home Journal,* November 1928.

20. See *Dissing Elizabeth: Negative Representations of Gloriana,* ed. Julia M. Walker (Durham: Duke UP, 1998).

21. *English Recusant Literature* 1558–1640, ed. D.M. Rogers, vol. 74 (New York: Scholar Press, 1971), xi.

22. Ibid., xix.

23. Carole Levin, "Gender, Monarchy, and the Power of Seditious Words," in *Dissing Elizabeth: Negative Representations of Gloriana,* ed. Julia M. Walker (Durham: Duke UP, 1998), 77–95; 78.

24. Ibid., 91.

25. David Grant Moss argues that "The Ditchley portrait has in effect become the standard image of her in popular culture." See "A Queen for Whose Time?," *The Journal of Popular Culture* 39.5 (2006): 796.

26. This position is taken by Thomas Betteridge in "A Queen for All Seasons," in *The Myth of Elizabeth,* ed. Susan Doran and Thomas Freeman (New York: Palgrave, 2003), and by Renee Pigeon in "'No Man's Elizabeth': The Virgin Queen in Recent Films," in *Retrovisions,* ed. Deborah Cartmell, I.Q. Hunter, and Imelda Whelehan (London: Pluto Press 2001). Additionally, Barbara Hodgdon argues that Lytton Strachey's *Elizabeth and Essex: A Tragic History* (1928) "puts Elizabeth on the analyst's couch"; this depiction of the queen as emotionally scarred from her unusual childhood has fueled many of the popular representations of Elizabeth.

27. Marcus, et al., *Elizabeth* I, 325–26.

28. Montrose, "Idols of the Queen," 149.

29. In the 1581 court entertainment, "The Four Foster Children of Desire" (attributed to Philip Sidney), the queen residing in "the Fortress of Perfect Beauty" is besieged by four men, who are characterized as "driven to see the furie of Desire" (71). Here, courtiers stage a sexual assault to display England's power before the French ambassadors. See Jean Wilson, *Entertainments for Elizabeth I* (Woodbridge, England: Rowman & Littlefield, 1980).

30. Hodgdon, *The Shakespeare Trade,* 151.

31. On the ideology of the queen's two bodies, see Marie Axton, *The Queen's Two Bodies: Drama and the Elizabethan Succession, Studies in Fiction* 5 (Atlantic Highlands, NJ: Humanities Press, 1977).

32. Judy Dench received the Oscar for her portrayal of Elizabeth in *Shakespeare in Love* (1998).

33. I am grateful to the students at San Jose State University in my graduate seminar on Renaissance Literature (ENGL 217, Fall 2006) and my upper-division class "The Age of Elizabeth" (ENGL 143, Spring 2008) for their insights regarding popular Elizabeths.

CHAPTER 3

Where the Maps End: *Elizabeth: The Golden Age* of Simulacra

Courtney Lehmann

You have adventures. You go where the maps end.
—Elizabeth to Ralegh, *Elizabeth: The Golden Age*

But what becomes of divinity when it reveals itself in icons, when it is multiplied in simulacra? Does it remain the supreme authority.... Or is it volatilized into simulacra which alone deploy their pomp and power of fascination...? This is precisely what was feared by the Iconoclasts, whose millennial quarrel is still with us today.... [T]heir metaphysical despair came from the idea that the images concealed nothing at all....
—Jean Baudrillard, "Simulacra and Simulations"

Shekhar Kapur's sequel to his highly acclaimed film *Elizabeth: The Virgin Queen* (1998), aptly titled *Elizabeth: The Golden Age* (2007), is, from its opening credit sequence, visibly scarred by the nine years separating it from its predecessor. Though the former is a classic period film, based on inquiry into and intrigue over Elizabeth's personal life and political ambitions, *The Golden Age* is irrevocably steeped in the ontological crises that characterize the post-9/11 world: specifically, the rise of religious fundamentalism, the place of unlawful detainment and torture in an ostensibly enlightened society, and the imperative to restrain leaders who claim to have "God" on their side. But at least at first glance, Kapur's film is not a straightforward allegory of "us" versus "them," freedom versus fundamentalism, Christian (Protestant) versus Muslim (Catholic) "other." Quite the contrary, *Elizabeth: The Golden Age* represents the "bad guy"—Philip II—as a megalomaniac whose Armada plot clearly invokes the Powell Doctrine of "Overwhelming Force," whereas the "good guys"—the moderate, English Protestants—maintain suspected "enemy combatants" in obscene, Camp X-Ray-style conditions while reveling in truly medieval forms of torture. Indeed, the singular irony of *this* period film is the fact that no matter how far back Kapur's lens stretches in search of the glory of the "Golden Age," the camera consistently represents only competing cadrés of evildoers who patently reject Renaissance humanism's insistence on the dignity of man. However, despite the film's dazzling failure to find the Renaissance it goes in search of, Kapur finds *us*—along with a very contemporary problem that the real Elizabeth seemed to know far too much about—surviving a "society of simulacra" in which the *real* war on terror is the terror of losing "the real" itself.

Elizabeth: The Golden Age is provocatively iconoclastic in its evocation of contemporary political crises. But for many audiences, Kapur's film proved to be too iconoclastic—in the Renaissance-specific, Reformation sense of the term—as the director found himself rebuffing accusations that the film was expressly anti-Catholic. These charges stem from the hyper-"Catholicized" representational milieu in which the fanatical Philip (who looks uncannily like Mel Gibson) is situated. Every scene featuring Philip abounds in icons of Christ, along with waves of incense and holy water, proliferating prayer beads, and stained-glass Saints. Similarly, at the end of the film, the slow-motion drowning of these same relics, which now include not only the sacrosanct mission bell but also an exquisite white horse—an allusion to the four horsemen of the apocalypse and, more specifically, the white horse that allegorizes "conquest"—appears propagandistic to even the most agnostic spectator. Eager to respond to outraged critics who accused him of "church-bashing," Kapur jumps at the bait, tearing the film out of its Renaissance context and inserting it into a society all too familiar with religious warfare. Indeed, for Kapur, *The Golden Age* is "actually very, very deeply non anti-Catholic. It is anti extreme forms of religion.... It's anti an interpretation of the word of God that is singular, as against what Elizabeth's was, which was to look upon her faith as concomitant. The fact is that the Pope ordered her execution; he said that anybody who executes or assassinates Elizabeth would find a beautiful place in the kingdom of heaven. Where else have you heard these words?" Kapur asks, immediately answering his own question: "Salman Rushdie?" With surprising candor, the director shows his hand, indicating that the film's so-called anti-Catholicism is, in fact, a statement against Islamic fundamentalism.[1]

This is precisely the lure of the period film: it is the escapist genre *par excellence*. And what title could be more illustrative of the genre's nostalgia-inducing effects than *The Golden Age*—a title that sends the audience hurtling back to the Renaissance where we can collectively forget or, more accurately, project the present geopolitical travesties in the Middle East onto the palimpsestic figure of Elizabeth I, a queen in whom the personal and political have historically converged. In fact, Kapur explains that *The Golden Age* revolves around Elizabeth's inner-conflict between "true Divinity" and "Mortal feelings," a crisis that can only be resolved when she recognizes that in order to rise above the misguided, mortal passions that drive Philip's Holy War, she must become "truly Divine," which means, quite simply, that she "cannot have *any* Mortal feelings." However, despite Kapur's desire to cultivate a radically "tolerant," even "zen" philosophy of "true Divinity" (Cate Blanchett characterized Kapur's personal mission as an attempt "to tell the story of Buddha through Elizabeth"), the film falls prey to the familiar cliché of reassuring Western audiences that "God" is, in fact, on our side, in addition to reifying other disturbing myths perpetuated by the patriarchal theology of global capitalism.[2]

Despite planning a third film in what would thus become the first period-film version of a Lucas-style trilogy, Kapur shies away from characterizing *The Golden Age* as a sequel to *The Virgin Queen*, as if he recognized that sequelization is tantamount to simulation, or, in Robin Wood's terms, the "same formula [as the original], with variations."[3] Nevertheless, *The Golden Age* is remarkably similar to *Elizabeth: The Virgin Queen*, as both films hinge on a love story and a tale of religious turmoil, with "variations" in which Dudley is replaced by Ralegh as Elizabeth's love interest, Philip II replaces Norfolk as Elizabeth's nemesis (the Pope is a consistent enemy in both films), and Mary, Queen of Scots, replaces both Bloody Mary and Mary of Guise as the "bad" Mary whom Elizabeth must reluctantly execute. Thus, Kapur insistently frames *The Golden Age* less as a sequel to and more as a continuation of *The Virgin Queen*. In a conspicuous effort to establish continuity between the two films, Kapur introduces Elizabeth as a doll, clasped loosely in the hands of the child princess Isabella of Spain; examined closely, the doll is an *exact* replica of the regal figure in whom Kapur's first film culminates. This, then, is the point from which our analysis must begin, for it is this moment in the original film that Elizabeth reinvents herself as a virgin, creating a simulation of her former self *sans* desire.

At the start of this pivotal scene, Elizabeth asks: "must I be a stone, and be touched by nothing?" Although her words are addressed to Walsingham, the queen's eyes are directed up at the enormous statue of the Virgin Mary, beneath which she kneels and whimpers. Walsingham, who has served less as her personal advisor than her puppeteer, replies: "All men need something greater than themselves to look up to and worship. They must be able to touch the divine—here on earth." Wistful, Elizabeth responds by referring to the statue now in a sympathetic vein: "She had such power over men's hearts. They *died* for her." Walsingham cues her accordingly: "They have found nothing to replace her." Walsingham's remark suggests the English people's longing for a simulacrum of the Catholic cult of Mary, which the Protestant Elizabeth will deliver by becoming, quite literally, a born again virgin queen. Hence, the ensuing scene shows Elizabeth reminiscing about the various men in her life (both good and bad), as she at last acknowledges that she must settle for having sacred rather than secular power over men's hearts. Meanwhile, her waiting women perform an extreme make-over on their queen, sobbing as tresses of her strawberry blonde hair fall to the floor; reluctantly, they stay the course, completing the ordeal by covering Elizabeth's face and extremities with heavy white plaster. Looking ill and yet otherworldly, Elizabeth exclaims: "I have become a virgin," as a lone tear cascades down her cheek. But since the real thing—Elizabeth's hymen—cannot be restored, to "become a virgin" is apparently to seal oneself off from anything resembling the *human*. Thus, emerging cyborg-like from pure, white backlighting, Elizabeth wears a white wedding dress with a frock, wig, and heavy white facial plaster, announcing to the stunned audience, "Witness, Lord Burleigh, I am married—[she raises her ring finger to his lowered eyes]—to England." Suturing the divide, Elizabeth's "body natural" marries her "body politic" and, appropriately, the final shot is a close-up that makes her face resemble a death mask, signaling the conclusive demise of her former desiring self.

Although I have argued elsewhere that this outcome is a deeply socially conservative move on the part of the director, who hereby reduces the most important decision of the queen's life to the inevitable consequence of her failed love affair with Lord Robert Dudley, there are other possibilities that, in light of the sequel, emerge to offer competing perspectives on this scene.[4] Indeed, when compared with *The Golden Age* in which Elizabeth is, at best, a sex-starved spinster, this climactic moment seems more meaningful as a display of "virginity as a patriarchal trope inhabited by sovereign female *intention*."[5] In other words, this scene could be read as an instance of Elizabeth taking charge of her own representation—indeed, her own simulation—and, therefore, an example of "women perform[ing], knowingly, the conditions that lend them social value" in patriarchal culture.[6] In a brilliant reading of *Elizabeth: The Virgin Queen*, Kathryn Schwarz goes one step further to contend that "[i]n reversing this seemingly natural teleology [of sexuality], *Elizabeth* presents virginity as an aggressive fiction which, projected backward, becomes history" and, in turn, proves Elizabeth's "mastery both of signification and monarchical authority."[7] It is this notion of virginity as an aggressive, self-directed performance that biographer Susan Frye refers to as the queen's "self-possessed virginity," a phrase that she opposes to the patriarchal ownership of Elizabeth's so-called marriageable virginity, which commodifies the queen, quite literally, according to her exchange value.[8] Hence, the crux of *The Golden Age* is the ongoing battle over the queen's two bodies—"real" and hyperreal—and Elizabeth's concomitant struggle to retain her "self" as it deceives and, at times, recedes into the endless play of simulacra that others would have her inhabit.

But why, the question might be raised, is the matter of simulacra relevant to Elizabeth I, beyond her long history of simulation in film? Because Elizabeth was the first of the English monarchs to insist that her portrait be derived *not* from a template, as all others before her had, but from "live" sittings; I would argue, in other words, that Elizabeth insisted on the *reality* of images—a concept well ahead of its time—and a form of transubstantiation that she refused to have blasphemed. As Nanette Salomon observes, rather than attributing the absence of an official court painter "as a sign of Elizabeth's lack of funds…as has been suggested," this phenomenon "may best be understood in terms of Elizabeth's own determined avoidance of a powerful 'master' to shape her image artistically, just as she had assiduously avoided a master as a mate."[9] Importantly, then, whatever the claims of the numerous studies of Elizabethan iconography, Salomon argues that not the painter, but Elizabeth herself, must be considered the "director" of the simulation.[10]

When we are first introduced to Elizabeth in *The Golden Age*, she is unquestionably in charge as she presides over a meeting with members of her Privy Council, many of whom are urging her to punish all the Catholics in England. She responds, however, by explaining that "I will not punish my people for their beliefs, only their deeds. I am assured that the people love their queen." Poised, confident and, above all, *self*-assured, this is the Elizabeth we recognize from the concluding moments of *The Virgin Queen*; as such, Kapur succeeds, thus far, in managing Elizabeth's image in a way that is consistent with his "original" map, despite the fact that *The Golden Age* is, in Baudrillard's terms, a map of a map. Nevertheless, Kapur is a classic example of Baudrillard's optimistic "cartographer," who is fully invested in "his mad project of an ideal coextensivity between the map and the territory."[11] In other words, Kapur approaches his film as the map that *is* the "territory" or, the "real" Elizabeth, when, in fact, his sequel is an example of *second order* simulation in which we see "the generation by models of a real without origin or reality: a hyperreal."[12] But what is actually at stake in *The Golden Age* is the threat of inaugurating a shift from second to *third order* simulation, wherein iconoclasm—no matter who the "director" may be and what image is being contested—is no longer possible because there are *only images*. Accordingly, if we substitute "monarch" for "God" in the following Baudrillard quotation, we can see this problem as it applies both to Elizabeth's legacy and Kapur's mission: "But what if God himself can be simulated, that is, to say, reduced to the signs which attest his existence? Then the whole system becomes weightless; it is no longer anything but a gigantic simulacrum... *never again exchanging for what is real, but exchanging in itself, in an uninterrupted circuit without reference or circumference.*"[13]

In *The Golden Age*, his problem is precipitated by the fact that, in the 1580s—precisely the decade featured in the film—the queen was at a crossroads in her representation, situated ambiguously between the "marriageable virgin" of the 1560s and 1570s and the figure of abstract iconography of the 1590s, when the Goddess-worshipping "cult of the virgin" was at its peak. (By then, of course, Elizabeth was well past childbearing years and the marriage issue was essentially moot.) In other words, the 1580s was the critical decade in which the queen had to work particularly hard to keep her iconicity, her self-simulation, from becoming a complete abstraction—from becoming, as Baudrillard attests above, a sign of a sign—based on its total lack of connection to her *real body*. Throughout this challenging period, Elizabeth maintained a posture of self-mastery while remaining, as her biographers note, in a state of quiet, often desperate, longing. Specifically, as "her closest male associates and advisors [including Lord Robert] made decisions independent of the queen's authority, threatening the very ground upon which she shape[d] her public image as increasingly divine and magical,"[14] she experienced an affliction akin to what Alain Badiou calls "the passion for the Real."[15] One of the defining characteristics of postmodern society, this state of pathological expectation, as Žižek explains, stems not only from a hyper-mediated and mediatized culture that is, thereby, systematically deprived of the Real, but also from the West's experience of "the basic sameness of global capitalism...."[16] Yet even in the protocapitalistic world of early modern England, Elizabeth's relationship to her own body was nothing if not mediated, as Frye notes, by men whose "perform[ances] and [other] representations...attempted to define her within *their* anxieties and concerns."[17]

The first indication in Kapur's film that Elizabeth is longing for the Real—whatsoever violence it may entail—is her expression of this passion in its purest form: transgressive sexual desire. Immediately following her opening silencing of the Privy Council, for example, Elizabeth is shown in a small flotilla with her ladies-in-waiting and Walsingham, who raises the issue—or, rather, her lack of "issue"—deriving from the queen's refusal to marry. When he suggests available suitors from European countries like Austria and France, Elizabeth is quick to invoke the feared "other," adding "Turkey, China," to the list. When Walsingham answers her with his quietly aghast expression, she explains, "that's the difference between you and me, Francis: I find the impossible far more interesting." In this instance, the word "impossible" may be easily replaced by "real," for what Elizabeth yearns for is something other than the ordinary, the usual, the expected—available to her now, it would seem, only in the form of imagined encounters with exotic, Eurasian, "others." Her question to Bess, her waiting woman: "What would you look for in a husband?" is similarly indicative of her longing; whereas Bess offers the modest answer of "honest eyes," Elizabeth adds "and good legs, so you wouldn't tire of looking at him."

Hence, despite having given herself over to the "truly Divine" in the final scene of *The Virgin Queen*, Elizabeth appears to be showing signs of having "Mortal feelings" in *The Golden Age*. Or is this just a ruse on Elizabeth's part, as her bodily territory simulates sexual desire to outsmart her politically conservative cartographer, the inscrutable Walsingham? Significantly, as Maria Parry observes, any "[a]ttempts to restrain her or to influence her policy were [considered] dissimulation or underhanded dealing;"[18] in fact, when Elizabeth prepared to sign a subsidy-granting act (which, before she scrutinized it, contained a subtle clause promising that she would marry), she exclaimed: "I love so evil counterfeiting and hate so much dissimulation."[19] The distinction between dissimulation and simulation is critical here: "To dissimulate is to feign not to have what one has. To simulate is to feign to have what one hasn't."[20] Elizabeth was a masterful simulator of a male power; so convincing was her ability to feign to have what she didn't—crudely put, a penis—that a lexical change in English law was precipitated by her performance, as the definition of the monarchy was modified to accommodate the seeming paradox of the "female prince."

As we have seen in *The Virgin Queen*, Kapur largely abandons this particular matter of simulation and instead focuses on the issue of the queen's virginity, boldly stating that Elizabeth *feigns* to have the maidenhead that she no longer had. But the issue grows more complicated in *The Golden Age*, which, as a simulation of a simulation, presents us with the queen at another remove. Her representation in this film is, therefore, in danger of lapsing into *third order* simulation, wherein, paradoxically, "the territory," that is, Elizabeth's body, "no longer precedes the map, nor survives it. Henceforth, it is the map that precedes the territory.... In this passage to a space whose curvature is no longer that of the real, nor of truth, the age of simulation thus begins with the liquidization of all referentials," thereafter "substituting signs of the real for the real itself."[21] Indeed, in *The Golden Age* it is not Kapur's map, but Ralegh's, that performs this meta-cartographic function, unmooring Elizabeth and forcing her to lose her bearings in her own body. Thus, through his "mad project" of conflating reel and real, Kapur—with the help of his internal cartographers—inserts himself into the history of men who have attempted to control what we might think of as Elizabeth's "sequelization," that is, the battle to define her "second self," or, the persona beneath—and beyond—the crown, the "twenty-seven dresses," and the other prostheses that define the Royal "We." In so doing, however, Kapur ultimately seeks not sequelization but, rather, a reversion to the reassuring fiction that characterized his previous film: the notion that behind every good woman is a better man.

*   *   *

> [Sequels] are obviously very skillful in…their knowing deploy-
> ment of the most familiar narrative patterns…. essentially those
> "good old values" that…[the film is] designed to re-instate: rac-
> ism, sexism, "democratic" capitalism… [and] the individual hero
> whose achievements somehow "make everything all right"…every
> man can be a hero—even, such is the grudging generosity of con-
> temporary liberalism, every woman.
> —Robin Wood, "Papering the Cracks"

Such is Robin Wood's take on the socially conservative function and features of sequels, wherein *reassurance*, above all else, "is the keynote."[22] Surprisingly, the formal bookends of *The Golden Age*—the introduction of the child princess Isabella (who, in reality, would have been twenty-one in 1585) and the culminating image of Elizabeth holding a child—unexpectedly satisfy the first criterion of sequelization, which is "childishness," or, the "widespread desire for regression to infantilism" in order "to evade responsibility."[23] Even more interesting is Ralegh's attempt to test Elizabeth's maternal sensibilities upon first meeting her, while also preying on her barely sublimated passion for the Real. Ralegh's initial appearance at court is a classic example of his ability to use competing maps to disorient the queen, as he proposes *his* sequel to Elizabeth's current persona in the form of "Virginia." With a highly seductive tone, he announces: "I have claimed the *fertile* coast in your name and called it Virginia—in honor of our *Virgin* Queen." Leaning on both the words "fertile" and "Virgin," Ralegh begins to drive a wedge between Elizabeth's "body natural" and her "body politic"; indeed, that she is already conscious of her age and potential sterility is made clear at the outset of the film, when she impatiently orders her doctors to "proclaim that the queen is still fertile," even though she would have been fifty-two in 1585. A similar divide is created by the gifts with which Ralegh presents her: a potato and tobacco. When Ralegh offers her the potato, he refers to it as "very nourishing," eliciting her desire to be "fertile" by calling upon her maternal instinct; when he offers her the tobacco, he all but winks at her while describing it as "very stimulating," clearly questioning her status as a virgin. That Ralegh has made Elizabeth self-conscious of her internal contradictions as a "nourishing" mother to her people and as an aging Virgin Queen desperately in need of "stimulation" is evident in the subsequent scene involving the queen and Bess, the queen's chief lady-in-waiting. As Elizabeth examines the lines on her face with a quizzical expression, Bess explains: "Smile lines, my lady." "Smile lines…" the queen murmurs, somewhat bemused, then suddenly serious, she adds: "When do I ever smile?" Hardly the young, at times giddy, self-confident monarch of *The Virgin Queen*, Elizabeth is deeply troubled by the specter of her own mortality in this film, and she often resembles a dour old crone with a schoolgirl crush.

When Elizabeth has her first formal audience with Ralegh, she wears a dress in the style of a virgin—with her bust pushed up to the point that her nipples nearly show. In fact, *The Golden Age* features approximately thirty-three incredibly sumptuous dresses—nearly one for every scene in which the queen appears—corresponding to another formal function of sequelization: spectacle, or, as Wood elaborates, "the sense of reckless prodigal extravagance; no expense spared…."[24] Indeed, in 2007–2008, when signs of the global economic slowdown were already painfully visible, the gilded extravagance of *The Golden Age* followed hard upon reality. Prophetically, Wood argued in the nineties that "as capitalism approaches its ultimate breakdown, through that series of escalating economic crises prophesied by Marx well over a century ago, its entertainments must become more dazzling, more extravagant, more luxuriously unnecessary."[25] But for all the glam and glitter, Elizabeth cannot catch Ralegh's eye the way she once ensnared Lord Robert, for in this film the Wizard of Oz-style shoe is on the other foot: Ralegh's. Indeed, fascinated by Ralegh's tale of the New World, Elizabeth listens with heaving breasts, hanging on his every word as he roguishly conjures his seductive vision of a "fair wind" and the sight of "land" as a "pure—naked—fragile—hope." She then asks Ralegh to carry on "hoping…" when, in truth, her giggling waiting women know that she has *really* seized upon the word "naked," and therein lie "hopes" of her own. Shortly thereafter, they walk together; turning a corner, she proceeds to tell Ralegh—with a flirty thwack of her feathery crop—that she likes him, and he replies candidly "and I like you." Suddenly, the queen appears vulnerable, blushing as her body natural betrays her discomfort with the truth of her attraction.

But, if anything, Ralegh has a profoundly *un*natural effect on Elizabeth, leading her to say and do things that strike the audience as distinctly out of character. For example, Ralegh is shown frequently lounging about in Elizabeth's Privy Chamber, regaling her with his adventures while they study maps—*without* her Ladies present—until she implies that she'd like to travel with him. Calling her bluff, Ralegh replies: "Why don't you?" "Oh do not tease me, Mr. Ralegh," she chortles, catching Bess arriving out of the corner of her eye. Offering to have Bess board the ship in her place, Ralegh is quick to state that "men have needs—a beautiful woman on board would drive us all mad." Practically an invitation to her bed, the queen repeats to herself, "men have needs," adding, with an eye directed toward Ralegh, "let them satisfy their needs on land." Unfortunately for the queen, Ralegh will do so, but with *another* "Elizabeth"—Bess—who, until she became the queen's head waiting woman, was known by her given name of Elizabeth. A kind of simulacrum in multiple respects, Bess is literally the "next best thing" to Elizabeth herself, for she is the person whose favor men must court before they can gain access to or an audience with the queen. Subsequently, Bess is shown in a graphic lovemaking scene with Ralegh, which is cleverly intercut with images of Elizabeth, naked, staring at her body despairingly in the mirror. Through this tableau, Kapur uses Bess in ways that are similar to her Renaissance suitors—in this case, as a means of providing the film audience with access to the queen's real person—"pure, naked, fragile"—indeed. Moreover, Kapur's provocative juxtaposition of the three nude bodies suggests both the intimacy and the disturbing entanglements that will soon govern the relationships among and between these characters.

In the wake of Elizabeth's failure to "find herself" in the mirror—ironically, at the very moment that Bess and Ralegh find each another—the queen visits her astrologer, another reader of maps. Though he knows nothing of her unrequited affection for Ralegh, Dr. Dee reads her face and declares disapprovingly, "something has weakened you." Thus, after her meeting with Dr. Dee, Elizabeth is emboldened and, playing the power card, she denies Ralegh's request to leave for the New World. Interpreting the sojourn he seeks as a personal affront, Elizabeth tells Ralegh that he is needed in England and, impulsively, knights him as "Captain of her Royal Guard" in order to keep him close by, under her watchful eye. When she expects gratitude from him, Ralegh's silence flouts and befuddles her, as she once again becomes the stammering schoolgirl, storming: "Am I so hideous that you can't even look me in the face?" Ralegh replies, "Why do you speak like a fool when you're anything but a fool?" Prepared to argue with him, she suddenly relents, and agrees: "Yes I am—a vain and foolish woman. You—you come here as if from another time and I've—I would follow you there if I could…" she cries, sighing dramatically as she collapses on the floor. But which "I" would she follow, when she has completely lost sight of herself amidst Ralegh's dubious charms? Ralegh has now managed to inscribe the word "fool" upon territory that is becoming increasingly alien to Elizabeth.

Worse still, when she begins to catch on to Ralegh and Bess's clandestine affair, Elizabeth shrinks progressively into a figure that is unrecognizable to even the most perceptive of her biographers. In a matter of seconds, for instance, she devolves from hanging playfully on Ralegh's arm to violently rebuking him for his candid assessment of her as someone who "eat[s] and drink[s] control." Consequently, she proves him right by forcing him to dance the *volta* with Bess, actually taking his hand and placing it near Bess' crotch to demonstrate the proper hold. Clearly, having played the fool, Elizabeth will now recover her lost agency through self-sabotage, torturing herself with the sight of the couple's barely masked attraction. She stares at them as they dance and, when Walsingham enters, she commands: "Leave us. I want them left alone." Here, the royal "We" ("Leave us") is conflated with the lowercase "us" ("them") of personal memory, as Elizabeth becomes lost in reverie; splicing scenes from *The Virgin Queen* into Elizabeth's mind, Kapur shows the queen performing her sensual *volta* with Lord Robert. When the live court music grows silent, however, it is Elizabeth who appears to splice Ralegh's face onto Robert's, creating her own film in the process. But as Elizabeth's "film" abruptly disappears into the present moment of *The Golden Age*, she seems at last to understand that she cannot lay claim to the former territory, only the new map, which painfully etches desire back onto her mortal body.

Hence, the juxtaposition of this scene with the Babington plot to kill Elizabeth is pivotal. Dressed like a bride, in virginal white, Elizabeth—it would appear—has chosen to re-sanctify her relationship with God *despite* the recent reawakening of her "Mortal feelings." Before she can consecrate this decision, however, her would-be assassin enters and screams "Elizabeth!— Whore!" Upon hearing the *second* of these words, Elizabeth turns and opens her hands as if to expose her Christlike stigmata; now that any hope of a love affair with Ralegh is dashed, she greets her death like a lover. Subsequently, the gun fires directly at Elizabeth's bosom and no one really understands what has happened until Walsingham reveals that the assassin has been double-crossed, for the gun was loaded with blanks. What is critical about the moment that the gun fires is that *this* should be understood as the climax of the film, for this is the point at which Elizabeth indulges her "passion for the Real." Indeed, Kapur's Elizabeth doesn't need mass media or digitalization or virtual reality to translate her existence into a tangle of simulacra, for her very life was, in fact, always mediated by semblances that she was expected, alternately, to shun, dissemble, or resemble. After all, the queen herself famously exclaimed: "We Princes are set on stages, in the sight and show of all the world."[26] Hence, the significance of the assassination attempt is that it is *not* a "staged fake," as Slavoj Žižek argues of the inertia of life within postmodern culture or, our "capitalist utilitarian despiritualized universe," wherein "'real life' itself" is always at risk of undergoing a "reversal into a spectral show."[27] Quite the contrary, martyrdom is perhaps the one performance that cannot be co-opted by such forces—postmodern, early modern, or otherwise. Simply put, Elizabeth experiences a pure, naked, fragile encounter with the Real of death.

What is so important about the placement of this scene is the fact that for Kapur, it is the *decoy* for Elizabeth's encounter with the (pseudo) Real of life—Ralegh's lips. For Kapur, it is not Elizabeth's resignation of desire, but her indulgence of it, that is the real climax of his film, functioning structurally as the beginning of the apocalyptic battle that will decisively humiliate Philip and his almighty Armada. But in order for Elizabeth to rise to this occasion, she, too, must first be humiliated. Reduced to a reassuring vision, in Robin Wood's words, "of helplessness and dependency,"[28] Elizabeth asks Ralegh if "in some other world, in some other time, could you have loved me?" He replies: "I know only one world, and in this world, I *have* loved you." Underscored with swelling music, this scene features Elizabeth begging Ralegh to do "one thing" for her—something she "ha[s] not known in a long time—a kiss." Leaning toward each other, the two engage in a slow but restrained jointure of their lips, and Elizabeth sighs, "I die," foolishly flopping her head into his lap. The importance of the line "I die" cannot be wasted on the attentive viewer, because Elizabeth *really* "died" in the previous scene—when the gun fired in the Church and, for all she knew, she *was* dying—whereas here, she dies, possibly, only in the Renaissance bawdy sense of "the little death," or, an orgasm. But her plaintive, shrinking stature suggests rather that she would give up everything simply to die here and now in Ralegh's arms.

Predictably, upon her discovery of Ralegh and Bess's secret marriage, Elizabeth sinks to an unimaginable low by engaging in a one-sided catfight with Bess—another classically "reassuring" moment as women are shown dividing and conquering each other over a man. As usual, Ralegh brings out the worst in Elizabeth; for when he arrives at court she repeatedly strikes Bess and demands his imprisonment, screaming: "My bitches wear my collars!" The queen here is a petulant child and, despite Walsingham's request that she remember her "dignity, Majesty," and Ralegh's protestations that she has veered from his map—"This is not the queen I love and serve"—all Elizabeth can do is scream "Get out! Get out! Get out!" eventually collapsing by a wall in grief. Hence, a new cartographer must intervene and, appropriately, it is Dr. Dee, shown poring over his cosmological maps, who apparently inspires Elizabeth's decision to combat the Spanish forces by sea, hinting at how some "spread their wings and soar." In other words, not only must she fly away from Ralegh, which she does, by freeing him from prison and commissioning him to command the Royal Fleet, but also by setting her sights on a "pure, naked, fragile, hope" that a fair wind might indeed scatter the Spanish ships as they head toward the treacherous shores of Tilbury.

That she should reappear now in full command, wearing a complete set of armor and her long hair down—in the style of a virgin in beautiful, lilting, curls—thus signifies Elizabeth's identificatory journey from wayfaring to warfaring Christian, as she rallies her troops by telling them that she is determined to "live and die" with them on the field. This statement is much more evocative of the queen's well-known declaration stating her determination to "liv[e] and di[e] a virgin" (and, therefore, more in keeping with the preoccupations of Kapur's Elizabeth), than it is of what the real Elizabeth said at Tilbury, which, aside from being her most famous speech, stresses her *mastery* of her paradoxical gender as one who has "the body of a weak and feeble woman but…the heart and stomach of a King, and a King of England too."[29] This verbal and oft-printed inscription whereby Elizabeth reclaims both herself and her map of England as a singular, indivisible territory simply does not square with Kapur's map of Elizabeth. Why? Because the sequel cannot rely on a woman as its ultimate dispenser of reassurance. Rather, as Wood explains, the sequel's unique ability to dispense reassurance is founded in a fundamental conflict—in this case, Philip's apocalyptic Holy War—and its resolution in the sequel's final gesture: the "restoration of the father."[30]

This process begins when Elizabeth learns from Dr. Dee that a war is coming in which one world power will defeat another. His prediction as to who will win, however, is perfectly ambiguous. Apropos of this juncture in the film is Wood's contention that the climactic conflict must generate a "widespread sense of helplessness—that it's all out of our hands, beyond all hope of effective intervention, perhaps already predetermined." This sensibility, in turn, leads to the imperative "to believe" even if only to arrive at the conclusion that, in the end, "God" was on our side all along.[31] Hence, as the brown-skinned and wild-eyed Catholics roll out their flotilla of superstitious practices—chanting over a multitude of candles, fingering their beads, and hoisting flags that picture The Passion itself—Kapur's Spaniards are "heavily signified as foreign,"[32] ostensibly preconditioning the audience to accept their eventual annihilation at the hands of Ralegh's English "fire ships."

In fact, although English fire ships (pioneered chiefly by Sir Francis Drake, *not* Ralegh) played a role in the defeat of the Armada, it was really a mysterious storm that scattered the majority of the fleet off the coast of Ireland, an event that was interpreted as Divine Intervention on the side of the "elect," Protestant nation. Predictably, however, it is not capricious Fortune but the charismatic Ralegh who must stand in as the would-be father of the English victory, for not only is his wife pregnant with his child, but also he is the one shown making the cartographic decisions to scatter the Armada's formation with fire ships. As Ralegh lights his ship on fire, he swings—in a scene that hearkens back to Errol Flynn in *The Sea Hawk*—across the boat and is subsequently shown swimming out of harm's way amidst the relics of the exploding enemy flotilla, as the famous Catholic mission bell, along with many crosses, beads, and an ethereal white horse, all go overboard in an effort to escape the fire. Here, we see the world that Protestants fear most—a world literally swimming with icons that acquire a life of their own—yet this scene is ultimately reassuring because these fetishes live only to drown in the murky depths of the North Sea. Elizabeth, victorious, appears at the cliffs in her "stigmata" pose, with oversized, gossamer angel wings sewn onto her exquisite white wedding gown. Blowing in the windy aftermath of the storm, the wings are not gratuitous ornament in this otherwise sumptuous film; rather, they embody Dr. Dee's prophecy that Elizabeth will "spread [her] wings and fly." But as Kapur's camera dollies around her in a dizzying fashion, what is most interesting about this, as well as the film's closing image, is that Elizabeth is steadfastly reemerging as her own cartographer. Indeed, despite Kapur's attempt to restore her to the statue with which his prequel ends, Elizabeth's iconography more convincingly evokes "The Rainbow Portrait" (c. 1600), in which she is shown as the sun who makes the rainbow possible—a perfect pictorial statement following the storm that scattered the Spanish Armada and foiled Philip's effort to rule the world (see figure 3.1).

Although, as in *The Virgin Queen*, the screen fades to a shimmering white with which we expect the film to end, the scene proceeds to a shot of Elizabeth making amends with Ralegh, as she appears again with her bosom pushed up in the style of an eligible maiden in a gorgeous silver gown. Aware that his child has been born and that it is a boy, she says to him "You must be proud"—"and fulfilled," she adds—clearly intimating that her sacrifice for her people is to remain sexually *un*fulfilled and, of course, childless. As if on cue, Bess appears and hands the child to the queen to receive her blessing. With this final tableau, Elizabeth condenses all the threats featured in the film into the reassuring image of the Virgin (Mary) Queen, emphasized by the vision of Elizabeth standing with the babe at her breast. At this moment, Elizabeth turns toward the camera as the lighting changes from natural sunlight to a heavenly white, and exclaims: "I am called the Virgin

Figure 3.1 Cate Blanchett Posed as Elizabeth I, after the "Rainbow Portrait" (from Dir. Kapur *Elizabeth: The Golden Age*).

Queen. Unmarried, I have no master. Childless, I am mother to my people. God give me strength to bear this mighty freedom. I am your Queen, I am myself."

As the camera cranes high, we see her cape blowing in the wind—a symbol of her God-granted, mighty "freedom"—and the same elemental force that defeated the Armada. Hence the *final* reassurance that the film dispenses is that Elizabeth's so-called freedom is, in fact, her ability to renounce it; for clearly, she is a mere agent, indeed, prisoner, of God's will. With Kapur's help, then, Elizabeth is hereby shown consenting to the restoration of the ultimate father: "God." But even as she does so, another inscription—something closer to what she herself might have wished for— emerges. For as the camera rises, we see Elizabeth standing triumphantly *on a map*—a recollection of the famous "Ditchley portrait" (1592) wherein, as Susan Frye explains, Elizabeth sought to materialize her Divine Right as a "heavenly intermediary."[33] Inspired by a speech she gave at Oxford in 1592 in which she claimed her subjects' love for her was a kind unknown "among friends" or "even among lovers," for it "is of such a kind as has never been known or heard of in the memory of man,"[34] the Ditchley portrait shows her standing over Oxfordshire itself, with a verse that renders her provocatively androgynous: "The prince of light. The Sonne." As Frye observes, "[i]n claiming from her people a sacred, binding love that acknowledges her chaste isolation, the queen creates herself as a figure standing, as in the Ditchley portrait of 1592, between England and God."[35]

Perhaps the *most* reassuring function of the period film is to create nostalgia for the *present*, and, therefore, a sense of complacency with the way things are. This is why the period film is the most conservative of genres. Yet why would a film about a monarch who ruled the world without a man be "reassuring" in 2007? Because this was precisely the period in which Hillary Rodham Clinton was in the thick of her bid for the most powerful political office in the world, and the resulting anxiety was tangible. The way in which *The Golden Age* works, then, is to *exorcise*—proleptically—the demon of female control by creating a superfluous sequel to *The Virgin Queen* in which not one but three controlling women figure prominently: Elizabeth herself; Isabella, future Queen of Spain; and Mary, Queen of Scots. If the latter two replace Elizabeth's role in *The Virgin Queen* as the modulator of the virgin/whore dichotomy, then the Elizabeth of *The Golden Age* is forced to come to grips with the mother/spinster dialectic, culminating in a film that engages every stereotype that Hillary Rodham Clinton would encounter in the mass media. That the film became a retroactive success after wins at the Oscars in 2008—after Hillary found herself in a neck and neck battle for the democratic nomination—suggests the cultural force of the film's reassuring fictions indeed. And just as the spirit of Elizabeth R. seems to break through the diegesis in the end to claim some piece of the map, so, too, the resilient Hillary R. received her "Ditchley" moment in becoming Secretary of State. Nevertheless, for those of us interested in more than just "papering the cracks" of the dominant patriarchal ideology, as Barack Obama's presidency represents the "same formula, with variations," we will continue to wait for Elizabeth: the sequel.

Notes

1. I wish to thank Gregory Semenza for the tremendous humanity he exercised as I worked to complete this chapter. Kapur's remarks may be found on the director's personal Web site: shekharkapur.com/blog/welcome.htm.
2. Kapur's exact words are "Divinity is Absolute is the moral stand of the film. To be truly Divine you cannot have *any* Mortal feelings" (emphasis mine). shekharkapur.com/blog/archives/my_films/golden_age/. Last accessed March 9, 2009.
3. Robin Wood, "Papering the Cracks: Fantasy and Ideology in the Reagan Era," in *Movies and Mass Culture*, ed. John Belton (New Brunswick: Rutgers UP, 1996), 203–28, 204.
4. See Lehmann, "Crouching Tiger, Hidden Agenda: How Shakespeare and the Renaissance Are Taking the Rage Out of Feminism," *Shakespeare Quarterly* 53.2 (2002): 260–79.
5. Kathryn Schwarz, "The Wrong Question: Thinking through Virginity," *Differences: A Journal of Feminist Cultural Studies* 13.2 (2002): 1–34, 6.

6. Ibid.
7. Ibid., 9.
8. Susan Frye, *Elizabeth I: The Competition for Representation* (Oxford: Oxford UP, 1999), 77. "Marriageable" is a term used throughout discussions of Elizabeth I in relation to her age and the acquisition of a spouse—conversations that stopped occurring with intensity only in the 1590s, when she was in her sixties.
9. Nanette Salomon, "Positioning Women in Visual Convention: The Case of Elizabeth I," in *Attending to Women in Early Modern England*, ed. Betty S. Travitsky and Adele F. Seeff (Newark: U of Delaware P, 1994), 64–95, 65.
10. Ibid., 67.
11. Jean Baudrillard, "Simulacra and Simulations," in *Jean Baudrillard: Selected Writings*, ed. Mark Poster (Stanford, CA: Stanford UP, 1988), 166–84, 167.
12. Ibid., 166.
13. Ibid., 170 (emphasis mine).
14. Frye, 96.
15. This phrase occurs throughout Alain Badiou's *Le Siécle* (Paris: Éditions du Seuil, 2005).
16. Slavoj Žižek, *Welcome to the Desert of the Real!* (London and New York: Verso, 2002), 7.
17. Frye, 97 (emphasis mine).
18. Maria Perry, *The Word of a Prince: A Life of Elizabeth I* (Rochester, NY: Boydell Press, 1999), 144.
19. Qtd. in Perry, 144.
20. Baudrillard, 167.
21. Ibid., 166–67.
22. Wood, 204.
23. Ibid., 207
24. Ibid.
25. Ibid., 207–8.
26. Qtd. in Perry, 200.
27. Žižek, 14.
28. Wood, 215.
29. Qtd. in Perry, 209.
30. Wood, 213.
31. Ibid., 209.
32. Ibid., 210.
33. Frye, 111.
34. Ibid., 113.
35. Ibid., 114.

PART II

Renaissance Fantasies

Looking Up to the Groundlings: Representing the Renaissance Audience in Contemporary Fiction and Film

Amy Rodgers

In an article on the Los Angeles-based improvisational comedy group, The Groundlings, founder Gary Austin explains how he arrived at the troupe's name: "I picked the name based on Shakespeare's description in *Hamlet* of the people who watch plays while sitting on the ground."[1] Austin's rationale regarding his choice contains some interesting paradoxes. As he acknowledges, the term "groundlings" refers to the audience, but as the name of the company it also stands in for the performers. In addition, the reference in *Hamlet* to which Austin refers makes no note of the theatrical space that the groundlings occupy; rather, it marks Hamlet's unreserved contempt for them: "O, it offends me to the soul to hear a robustious, periwig-pated fellow...split the ears of the groundlings, who for the most part are capable of nothing but inexplicable dumb shows and noise" (3.2.7–11).[2] But like any good paradox, it contains a germ of truth. The concatenation of audience and performer, reverence and derision that Austin implicitly raises addresses something intrinsic about how contemporary scholarly and popular discourse constructs the groundling and the work this figure does in these arenas. Although "groundlings" refers to actual historical subjects, the term has accrued multiple meanings over four hundred years. Coined by early modern playwrights, the groundlings connoted a spectatorial type defined largely by boisterous behavior, a preference for low comedy and bombastic acting, and a tendency to snack during performances.[3] In current parlance, the term stands as a somewhat vexed signifier, ranging from the crude spectators originally invoked by early modern playwrights to a group of idiot-savant-like interpreters whose existence was only possible in the golden age of Renaissance theater.

Why, I want to ask, is the groundling such a seminal figure in popular representations of the early modern theater, particularly those found in historical fiction and film? In addressing this question, I hope to push beyond the idea that the groundling is simply part of the historical *mise-en-scène* and therefore a requirement in contemporary thinking about what Renaissance theater was like "back then." Rather, I suggest that the groundling fills a sentimental as well as a historical lacuna in the Western cultural imaginary, invested as it is in early modern dramatic traditions. While much of the period's veneration has been run through Shakespeare (and to a lesser degree Marlowe and Jonson), depictions of their audiences play a critical, yet under-theorized, role in the manufacture and maintenance of popular mythologies about Elizabethan England (as in the title of Shekhar Kapur's 2007 film: *Elizabeth: The Golden Age*). And, while we have little definitive information about those who stood in the amphitheater yards to watch plays, the groundling has almost as significant a presence in scholarship as in fiction, suggesting that this figure is created as much through exposure to popular representations as historical data. As scholars we may know that, historically speaking, the "groundlings" were made up of people of diverse occupations, classes, and nationalities, but it's still hard to forget the gap-toothed lumpkins that people the audience in Olivier's *Henry V* (1944) or John Madden's *Shakespeare in Love* (1998).

Of greatest interest to me, however, is how twenty-first-century viewers situate themselves in relation to the figure of the groundling. In the examples that follow, I explore some of the historical and mythological narratives about Renaissance audiences that recur in contemporary film and fiction. The vast majority revolve around nostalgia, a type of desire as slippery and inchoate as are notions about the groundlings themselves. Sociologist Fred Davis argues that nostalgia's meaning has shifted from the longing for a particular place to that for a particular time, thereby offering an emotional investment in our proximate and distant past.[4] Conversely, it can also push that past firmly away, by postulating a "better time" that is now irretrievable. Janus-faced, nostalgia works to fortify a sort of ideological paralysis. As Susan Bennett puts it, "nostalgia is constituted as a longing for certain qualities and attributes of lived experience that we have apparently lost, at the same time it indicates our inability to produce parallel qualities and attributes which would satisfy the particularities of lived experience in the present."[5] In fictional treatments of the early modern stage, the groundlings are often the reliquary for such sentiments, the site where longings for our interpretative past and anxieties about its present and future begin to coalesce into legible forms.

Before turning to popular treatments of the groundling, I want briefly to review the way early modern scholars have defined and theorized it. Early scholarship on Renaissance audiences tended to place this figure squarely in the middle of debates about the intellectual capabilities of the average early modern spectator. For some, the groundlings were "wretched beings" who kept Shakespeare's genius from reaching its fullest florescence, but more often they were seen as savants, possessed of the "imagination and the power to sink [their] soul[s] in the essence of drama."[6] Later work by such scholars as Andrew Gurr and Ann Jennalie Cook has challenged the concept that early modern amphitheater audiences were made up primarily of London's lower (or even middling) classes.[7] However, "the groundling" still performs as shorthand when scholars want to invoke an early modern audience with immediacy and/or tactility.[8] In addition to theater historians, the groundlings hold a certain allure for projects invested in reproducing early modern spectatorial conditions, such as London's reconstructed Shakespeare's Globe Theatre. Despite the Globe's aim to provide an "authentic" theatrical experience, it has no compunctions about mixing proto- and late-capitalist terminology for audiences: those who purchase yard tickets are called "groundlings," while those who purchase seats are "customers."[9]

Unburdened by a surplus of historical detail, it seems logical that the groundlings would provide a sort of tabula rasa on which fiction authors, seeking to strike a balance between historical verisimilitude and creative license, could exercise their imaginations. More often, however, such descriptions revolve around certain constants. One prevalent version depicts the groundlings as living self-contradictions. Grubby, malodorous, and loud, they also happen to be highly attuned spectators and astute judges of drama, as depicted in this passage from Faye Kellerman's romance *The Quality of Mercy* (1989):

> [T]hey were pure of heart, these vulgar groundlings. They laughed, cried, cheered the hero and booed the fiend, and if the play was wretched the actors would know about it. The nobility in the upper seats were very well-mannered, but not an honest emotion passed through their bodies, not a true passion pierced their hearts. Twas better to stand with the groundlings, smell their foul breath, their sweat, piss and vomit.[10]

Kellerman's description reads like a theatrical take on the idea of the noble savage. The groundlings' vulgar exterior masks an interpretative purity; they are the spectatorial id to the nobility's superego. The idealization in which Kellerman's heroine indulges does not reflect the intellectual currents of the early modern period, but one prevalent in the eighteenth century. Fascinated with the concept of "natural man," sentimentalists such as the Earl of Shaftesbury advised moralist authors to promote "that simplicity of manners, and innocence of behavior, which has oft been known among mere savages before they were corrupted by our commerce."[11] However, just as Shaftesbury's prelapsarian world reveals more about the intellectual traditions and prejudices of the eighteenth century than about the past he laments, Kellerman's prelapsarian theater reflects certain preconceptions that survive in our own historical moment. In singling out the groundlings as the better part of the audience, *Mercy* privileges an entertainment experience that is immediate, tactile, and unmediated; this theater heats the blood rather than passively engages the eye. As such, it creates an overwhelmingly *embodied* experience. Kellerman's version of the early modern stage suggests a then-and-now division put forth by theorists of the Frankfurt School, where certain twentieth-century mimetic technologies (such as photography and film) function to distance their audience from lived experience, an alienation that helps produce the passive spectator culture of the twentieth century.[12] While Kellerman does not state this case directly, such sentiments are underscored by the terms through which *Mercy's* heroine describes and ultimately divides the audience. The "sophisticated" nobility are portrayed as bloodlessly two-dimensional and disengaged from what they see, a characterization that raises twin specters of modern visual technologies and audiences. The groundlings, however, are almost ekphrastically corporeal: scent and sound construct them as a visceral, vital presence. When combined with their innate and passionate connection to drama, the groundlings here serve as a material and sentimental artifact of early modern drama, that Eden of embodied entertainment to which we in the twenty-first century can never return.

Even more prevalent in historical fiction than nostalgia for a theater of the past is that for an author of the past. In Shakespeare-driven fiction, the groundlings often function as a proof-text for the playwright's transformative genius. Unlike Kellerman's portrayal, where the groundlings have an instinctive sense of drama, bardolatry narratives tend to portray them as crude spectatorial templates that Shakespeare refines, even emancipates. In her biographical novel *Will* (2004), Grace Tiffany imagines the inaugural performance of *Julius Caesar*:

When the first players appeared, a deafening roar greeted them, and they could not be heard for a full minute. But Will walked to the lip of the stage and raised his hands, and the audience suddenly calmed, like rough seas before a wizard's spell…In the tiring house Will clasped hands with Burbage. "I redeemed them!…They came in like animals and go out like folk who are thinking."[13]

It is uncertain which is more unflattering here—the portrayal of the subhuman groundlings or of an arrogant, messianic Shakespeare. Hagiography is a commonplace in most Shakespeare-driven fiction, but Tiffany's novel provides a particularly acute example of the groundlings' role in recontextualizing and reifying Shakespeare's place in contemporary culture. While the groundlings are almost always described *en masse*, here they dissolve into mass consciousness, interpellated and controlled by the playwright a là Godard or Hitchcock. One could read this take through a glass darkly: Tiffany's groundlings are automatons held by the sway of what seems like theatrical fascism. However, as the rest of the narrative does not present Shakespeare as an egomaniacal ideologue, this scene likely contains another variation on the authenticity theme. The fervent groundlings may reflect a deeply felt cultural desire to approximate and be proximate to Shakespeare, to construct an experience that seems tangible and possible. Rather than depicting this theatrical past as something historically remote, Tiffany constructs it as an experience that mimics modern celebrity-spectator dynamics. Her Shakespeare is not just the man behind the curtain at the Globe; he is the original mass-culture entertainment celebrity, an early modern rock star. The desire to commune with the Renaissance theatrical past in *Will*, then, is assuaged by imagining it as proximate, similar, *contemporary*. And, although clearly "we" (bardolaters today) are not like "them" (the groundlings) in staging this scene as resembling the concert arena or movie premiere, Tiffany implicitly makes such a connection. In displaying the groundlings against a transhistorical spectatorial continuum of which we ourselves are a part, *Will* suggests that, although temporally separated, we all are connected by Shakespeare's genius.

But the most widespread type of nostalgia expressed in novels depicting the Renaissance stage is that for a sort of public agency, one that can be expressed and enacted with immediacy. For the most part, this agency is imagined as circulating only within the jurisdiction of the theater, such as when Kellerman's groundlings broadcast their opinions of the play as it is performed. Occasionally, however, forms of theatrical and political agency become imbricated. Mostly this conflation is one of suggestion, such as in Mary Gentle's novel of Jacobean political intrigue, *A Sundial in a Grave: 1610* (2005). In it, her protagonist, Valentin (a French assassin), attends a Jacobean revenge tragedy in order to "steal a plot to kill a king."[14] Sometimes, however, these novels portray the realms of the political and the theatrical as so closely aligned, however, that they become indistinguishable. Toward the end of *Sundial*, James I appears upon the Rose's stage, in a play entitled *The Viper and Her Brood*.[15] His throne having been usurped by the earl of Northumberland and his life in danger, James uses the stage as a platform to inform his subjects that he lives and to gain their support to overthrow the pretender. At first, the groundlings only notice what they assume is ham-handed acting: "Some men jeered. His accent was not particularly intelligible" (439). However, they soon discern a shift in the stakes of stage action, from that of an actor trying to create a convincing performance to that of a king whose life and power hangs in the balance of their response:

> James Stuart strode with his limping gait up…to the very edge of the stage…Gazing out into the vast space of the theater, he shouted, "Will you suffer this to happen? Will you suffer a vile male witch to rule your land? The Prince is deceived. His father is not dead. Here I stand. *Am I not your King?*"
>
> A roar went up all around, sudden and deafening.
>
> I stepped back, involuntarily, bringing my back up against another of the painted stage pillars. Sound hit like a blow. Only in war have I heard men's voices with such impact—and here, the higher voices of women screamed out their approbation also, in counterpoint. (441)

Enhanced by the theatrical setting, James' speech is not merely a set-piece of state politics but a genuine negotiation of power. Gentle translates the sort of theatrical agency imagined by Kellerman, whose groundlings can alter the life of a play, to a political agency that determines the future of a nation. The reversal of power between ruler and ruled is summed up most succinctly in Gentle's choice of phrasing: James does not say "I am your king," but instead *asks* "Am I not your King?" In presenting what is fact (James is, after all, the anointed monarch) as conditional, Gentle portrays this moment as proto-democratic, and the early modern theater as a form of an early public sphere.[16]

Gentle's example provides an interesting case, for it is unclear whether her portrayal yearns for the past or whether it imagines continuity with the present. Like Kellerman, Gentle depicts the groundlings and their engagement with what they see through terms that evoke proximity, spontaneity and intense sensory experience. In doing so, she portrays a political action that is immediate and palpable. This system is not a democracy of staged debates and malfunctioning ballots; it is a real, tactile, face-to-face negotiation with power.[17] However, like Tiffany, Gentle describes a dynamic (the circulation and realization of political will) quite familiar to us in the twenty-first century. More questionable is whether it would have been even imaginable to a large portion of a seventeenth-century audience at the Rose. By claiming it was, Gentle suggests parallels between the political spirit of early modernity and modernity, as if democracy were a social energy generated and cultivated on the playing field of the Renaissance stage.

At the nexus of these two facets of nostalgia (that which pushes away and that which draws near), we are perhaps closest to capturing the sort of work it does in these novels and hence in the larger cultural construction of the Renaissance. Scholars tend to imagine nostalgia through the binaries of lost/found or absence/presence, or at best as the unstable middle ground between these terms. I would argue that nostalgia is as much an attempt at self-definition in the present as it is a revitalization of the past. This identificatory process is not unlike Lacan's mirror-stage analogy, where there is an outward recognition of what one should be, but also an inability to sense that one fully inhabits an idealized subjectivity. Even when it is a longing for the past, then, nostalgia always carries that original sense of place—not necessarily the physical space of "home," but the subjective one of identity. The nostalgia surrounding the groundlings seems to spring from a desire to situate ourselves as audiences of a past form of mass culture, one still exercising tremendous influence on scholarship and entertainment today. Complicating this attempt to know "where we are" as audiences is the sliding scale of "high" and "low" culture on which the Renaissance is widely distributed. Early modern drama both is and is not popular; rather, it is not popular in the way that it was in its own historical moment. Such intersections and indeterminacies make it almost impossible to grasp a clear interpretative position with regards to Renaissance drama. How are we supposed to interpret and behave when sitting at a production of *Doctor Faustus* at the RSC? What about when watching *10 Things I Hate About You* at a multiplex in Detroit? At home on TV? When we watch early modern plays at the Globe or in a high school auditorium do we "commune" with audiences of the past (both proximate and remote), or does the arsenal of habits learned from modern visual technologies obscure such connections?

To further explore these questions, I want to turn to two films set in historical periods other than the early modern: Richard Eyre's *Stage Beauty* (2004) and Al Pacino's *Looking for Richard* (1996). While there are numerous films about Renaissance England that feature groundlings, these two examples demonstrate that even when not physically present, the groundlings provide a means of gauging our relationship to the early modern spectatorial past. Both films involve Shakespeare, the figure that still dominates contemporary cultural interest in early modern drama. But the portrayal of the audiences in these films raises a host of other associations that pertain to the larger field of early modern theater and the Renaissance more generally.

Stage Beauty is the story of Ned Kynaston, a Restoration stage sensation famed for his portrayal of women, particularly Desdemona. Egged on by his mistress (the sometimes-actress Nell Gwynn), Charles II issues a proclamation that women's parts must be played by women, and Ned's career vanishes overnight. But thanks to the seductive charms of his former dresser and new star of the stage, Maria, he "discovers" both heterosexuality and how to act "like a man." The film ends with the pair united onstage in a blockbuster performance of *Othello*, done (the film seems to want to say) as it should have been all along. *Stage Beauty* depicts two types of Restoration audiences: a court audience and a hall audience.[18] Needless to say, there are no groundlings. The hall audiences shown in the first and penultimate scenes of *Stage Beauty* are an admixture of nobles and *bourgeoisie*—everyone is seated, well-dressed, and well-behaved. There is something groundling-like in the audience's interruption of the play after Desdemona dies, where shouts of "Bravo, Kynaston" interrupt the action for several minutes. While this intrusion mimics the groundlings' spontaneity, it pales in comparison with the tossing of dead cats, rotten produce, and raucous outbursts often depicted as part and parcel of the Renaissance theatrical experience. The audience in *Stage Beauty* already operates at another level of remove; they seem guided more by conventions of behavior than by pure emotional response. Whereas the groundlings usually are shown as glued to the stage action (such as in the performance of *Romeo and Juliet* in *Shakespeare in Love*), in *Stage Beauty* the audience members look at one another at moments of dramatic crescendo, as if more concerned with their own performances than with what is happening onstage. Even in the final Ned/Maria performance of Desdemona's death scene (which the film clearly marks as a you-should've-been-there moment) the audience members twitch and gasp in horror and then continue to look at how others are reacting.

This moment in the film depicts an audience not only far from the ground-lings, but actually somewhat distant from what we know of Restoration audiences. *Stage Beauty* begins with an epigraph: "In his diary for 1660, Samuel Pepys wrote that the most beautiful woman on the stage was named Kynaston." Pepys also wrote in this diary that "a very pretty lady that sat by me, called out, to see Desdemona smothered," a far cry from the audience's response to the graphically enacted murder in *Stage Beauty*.[19] While several ladies make polite sounds of distress, no one calls out anything, a particularly noteworthy event considering that Maria/Desdemona looks at the audience while being strangled and screams, "Help! He's killing me!" The historical Restoration audience, then, may have been closer in behavior to the groundlings than the film indicates. Since *Stage Beauty* shows the passing away of old conventions of early modern staging (going so far as to suggest that Shakespeare can be really moving once you get all that gender confusion stuff out of the way), perhaps a new audience seemed in order as well.[20] However, even as *Stage Beauty* anticipates a new, more sophisticated audience, it glances nostalgically over its shoulder at the ghosts of spectators past. Right after Desdemona has been brutally strangled onstage, Emilia runs on from stage left meeting the audience's horrified silence. She looks at her mistress's crumpled body, then slowly turns her tear-filled gaze onto the audience, as if to say "How is it that none of you stopped this?" There is a reverse shot of the audience and the camera pans over them, mimicking Emilia's gaze. Paralyzed and uncomfortable, they look blankly back at her; they have no answer to give. Although this moment seems to recall encounters between the groundlings and actors often depicted in fiction and film as moments where they almost breathe together, it contains a kernel of disillusionment that the film does not (or cannot) explicitly acknowledge. For although the long-awaited end of the play is finally performed, the audience's "civilized" restraint goes hand in hand with a suppression of spectatorial agency and energy. The friction generated by the proximity of audience and performer in depictions of the early modern stage does not, in *Stage Beauty*, ignite with quite the same spark; without it, the play here is entertainment-making but not potentially world-making.

Al Pacino takes up this gauntlet in *Looking for Richard*. The film's premise is relatively simple: Pacino wants to bring Shakespeare back to "the people," who have become estranged from their dramatic heritage. He knows they have become so because he conducts a series of interviews on the streets of New York, which are intercut with the film's main action, the staging of *Richard III*. These interviews fall into two categories: formal conversations with those who "know" Shakespeare (actors, directors, and academics) and impromptu ones with those who don't (random individuals). While the rapid crosscutting mostly succeeds as a form of textual editing, a cinematic compression of the play to a postmodern crucible, it does not quite pull off the *ciné verité* feel that the interviews seem designed to provide.[21] Pacino uses select outtakes to construct a montage of unflattering sound bytes that supposedly sum up American popular culture's relationship (or lack thereof) with the Bard. With few exceptions, the interviewees seem either indifferent or hostile toward Shakespeare, their opinions summed up by such phrases as "it's too confusing," "it sucks," and "it's boring." One is left with the feeling that most New Yorkers (who function as synechdoche here for all Americans) don't know or don't care about Shakespeare, or at least that those who do care ended up on the cutting room floor.

But Pacino does find an exception to the ignorance and indifference that permeates the American public:[22] an individual who appears to be a homeless man.[23] Unlike his fellow New Yorkers quoted in the film, he speaks passionately about Shakespeare:

> When we speak with no feeling, we get *nothing* out of our society. We should *speak* like Shakespeare. We should introduce Shakespeare into the academic. Know why? Because then the kids would have feelings. (Pacino: "That's right.") We have no feelings. That's why it's so easy for us to take a gun and shoot each other. We don't feel for each other. (Pacino: "That's right.") But if we were taught to *feel* we wouldn't be so violent to people. (Pacino: "And do you think Shakespeare helps us with that?") He did more than help us. He instructed us.

These sentiments coming from this person surprises, even moves, Pacino, as suggested by his softly encouraging repetition of "That's right" into his subject's commentary. Within the film's structure, this encounter is the first place that Pacino finds some of what he is looking for: the vital, authentic, still-breathing Shakespeare. However, in depicting the homeless man as the one who "gets" Shakespeare, Pacino echoes a bias that extends to the two hermeneutic traditions he most wishes to challenge: academia and traditional British theater. Assigning the greatest interpretative acuity to the individual who appears to be the least privileged, Pacino unwittingly resurrects a figure that has been and continues to be constructed from such contradictions: the early modern groundling.

While all of these texts to some extent share the fiction of the noble spectator, Pacino's modernization highlights a particular problem with that fantasy. Waxing nostalgic over the figure of the groundling or the homeless man not only reduces the issue of class to a whisper, but also imagines the disadvantages associated with this subject position as almost a prerequisite for attaining this Zen-level of insight. In the terms that *Looking for Richard* suggests, it's a bummer to be hungry and poor, but it's so *real*. This romanticization threatens to obscure the fact that most of the people creating and consuming popular novels and films about the Renaissance are those who have access to the sort of material and social resources that Pacino's idealized spectator is denied. Perhaps the tendency to portray the groundlings as interpretatively distant offers a means of minimizing these "unpleasant" realities for an interest group that consists mostly of the middle class and upper class.

This story can, however, be read another way. Although *Looking for Richard* designates itself as a search for one of Shakespeare's most complex antiheroes, it is also about a nonacademic interpreter of one of his plays. It's about a guy from the South Bronx who grew up to be an actor and film producer and who wants access to Shakespeare, but of a different sort than is proffered by academics and knighted British actors. The film is so focused on Pacino's desire to decipher *Richard III* for audiences that feel alienated by its canonicity and historical distance that it obscures the fact that he is a part of the very audience he is trying to reach—or at least, he used to be. In imagining an audience for his Richard, Pacino must first begin with himself, someone who has been reading *Richard III* for six months, and who, despite having already performed the role a number of times, "can't get on with it."[24] Rather than making Pacino's struggle with Shakespeare's text an impediment to his understanding of his work, the film celebrates it, ultimately claiming that the only Shakespeare that really matters is one able to communicate with the many rather than the few. This embodied, vital sort of drama/author is, I believe, what many of the interpretations herein analyzed want to touch through the figure of the groundling, that most embodied and vital of early modern spectators. In doing so, they articulate another sort of link to the early modern dramatic past, one that is not reliant on foreknowledge or education but is tangible, immediate, and, well, popular. It is exactly this sort of presence that Pacino invokes in the scene that bookends his film. The camera moves slowly, almost lovingly, over the sides of a Gothic cathedral, accompanied by a voice-over of Prospero's "Revels" speech.[25] It is an eerie, albeit beautiful, moment, rendering Shakespeare as a wisp of smoke rising from a spectral past: untouchable, ineffable, enigmatic. Then the scene shifts. We no longer see the intricate spires of the cathedral, but the concrete monotony of a New York City housing project. The camera tilts downward, revealing a teenaged African-American man playing basketball on a deserted blacktop and another, older man, dressed in black and walking toward the camera. After a moment, it becomes apparent that this is Pacino himself, already out looking for Richard. But the juxtaposition of these two shots, one ethereal, the other gritty, tells us something more: Shakespeare has been brought back to earth, his words made flesh through the bodies of the young man and the actor. It is here, the film says, that you will find Shakespeare, not in the past or in the clouds, but here in the present and on the ground.

Notes

1. Carl Kozlowski, "Laughing on Solid Ground," *Arriviste Press* (November 2004). http://www.arrivistepress.com/November04/ckozlowskilaughingonsolid-ground1104.shtml (accessed July 10, 2008).

2. *The Norton Shakespeare*, ed. Stephen Greenblatt, Walter Cohen, Jean E. Howard, and Katharine Eisaman Maus (New York: W.W. Norton & Company, 1997).

3. The *OED* cites *Hamlet* as the first use of "groundlings" to refer to the audience.

4. *Yearning for Yesteryear: A Sociology of Nostalgia* (London: Collier Macmillan, 1979), 4.

5. Susan Bennett, *Performing Nostalgia: Shifting Shakespeare and the Contemporary Past* (London: Routledge, 1996), 5.

6. Citations from Robert Bridges, "On the Influence of the Audience," in *The Works of William Shakespeare*, Vol. 10 (Stratford-on-Avon: The Shakespeare Head Press, 1904), 334; and A.C. Bradley, *Oxford Lectures on Poetry* (London: St. Martin's Press, 1955), 392.

7. See Andrew Gurr, *Playgoing in Shakespeare's London*, 3rd ed. (Cambridge: Cambridge UP, 2004); and Ann Jennalie Cook, *The Privileged Playgoers of Shakespeare's London, 1576–1642* (Princeton: Princeton UP, 1981).

8. For example, W.B. Worthen, in a brief meditation on the prologue to *Henry V*, references the audience as "the stinking crowd." See "Staging 'Shakespeare': Acting, Authority and the Rhetoric of Performance," in *Shakespeare, Theory and Performance*, ed. James C. Bulman (London: Routledge, 1996), 18.

9. See http://www.shakespeares-globe.org/theatre/boxoffice/frequentlyaskedquestions/.

10. Faye Kellerman, *The Quality of Mercy* (New York: Ballantine, 1989), 122.

11. Anthony Ashley Cooper, 3rd Earl of Shaftesbury, *Characteristicks of Men, Manners, Opinions, Vol. 1* (London: 1758), 237–38.

12. See Max Horkheimer and Theodor Adorno, "The Culture Industry: Enlightenment as Mass Deception," in *The Dialectic of Enlightenment: Philosophical Fragments*, ed. Gunzelin Schmid Noerr, trans. Edmund Jephcott (Stanford: Stanford UP, 2002); and Walter Benjamin in "The Work of Art in the Age of Mechanical Reproduction," in *Illuminations*, ed. Hannah Arendt, trans. Harry Zohn (New York: Schocken Books, 1969).

13. Grace Tiffany, *Will* (New York: Berkley Publishing Group, 2004), 255–56.

14. Mary Gentle, *A Sundial in a Grave: 1610* (New York: HarperCollins, 2005), 222.

15. This is a fictional play, of course. Within *Sundial*'s diegesis, it is written by Aemilia Lanyer, who has a large and salacious role in the novel.

16. Jürgen Habermas identifies the rise of the public sphere as taking place in the eighteenth century, born out of such burgeoning sociocultural phenomena as news periodicals, the coffee house, and an established *bourgeois* class. While, recently, scholars have been revisiting the idea of whether or not there was an early modern public sphere (specifically the Making Publics Project at McGill University), of greater interest here is that, in the popular imaginary, the early modern theater could be a place for the sorts of expression Habermas envisioned taking place among the eighteenth-century *bourgeoisie*.

17. Twentieth-century film also has a history of suggesting a social impulse toward democracy in historical recreations, from *The Adventures of Robin Hood* (1938) to Trevor Nunn's 1986 *Lady Jane*.

18. There is a brief glimpse of an audience at some sort of impromptu pub theater, but it occurs too quickly to get a sense of the audience's composition.

19. See Gāmini Salgādo's *Eyewitnesses of Shakespeare: First Hand Accounts of Performances 1590–1890* (London: Sussex UP, 1975), 49.

20. One of the most significant changes to staging in the Restoration was the widespread adoption of the proscenium stage. *Stage Beauty's* more "modern" spectators may tacitly acknowledge the sort of two-dimensional (hence proto-cinematic) effects of this development.

21. Neil Sinyard says that "Pacino...find[s] that people either know nothing about Shakespeare or profess themselves baffled by his language" (60). It would be more accurate to say that Pacino finds people who know nothing about Shakespeare, as the film does not indicate how many interviews were performed or discarded. See "Shakespeare Meets *The Godfather*: The Postmodern Populism of *Looking for Richard*," in *Shakespeare, Film, Fin de Siècle*, ed. Mark Thornton Burnett and Ramona Wray (New York: St. Martin's Press, 2000), 58–72.

22. The other exception to this general indifference is an Italian gentleman who unabashedly explains his unfamiliarity with Shakespeare by saying "I no study."

23. Critics have assessed the man's class status variously. Sinyard merely calls him "a black American" (61), while Thomas Cartelli acknowledges the tacit reality of his social condition, calling the subject "a panhandler." See "Shakespeare and the Street: Pacino's *Looking for Richard*, Bedford's *Street King*, and the Common Understanding," in *Shakespeare the Movie II*, ed. Richard Burt and Linda E. Boose (London and New York: Routledge, 2003).

24. Pacino has performed the role three times on stage: at the Actor's Studio in New York City, with David Wheeler's Experimental Theater Company in Boston, and on Broadway.

25. The shot is of Saint John the Divine in New York City.

CHAPTER 5

London's Burning: Remembering Guy Fawkes and Seventeenth-Century Conflict in *V for Vendetta*

Melissa Croteau

Popular culture commonly upchucks the passions of history in distorted form as story panels and chunks of technicolor.[1]

While the claim above by scholar Lucius Shepard specifically and accurately applies to the Wachowski Brothers' film *V for Vendetta*, the historical detritus the film heaves onto our screens is provocative for a scholar of the early modern era. This 2005 film, set in the near future of the 2020s, begins and ends with a depiction of the Gunpowder Plot of 1605: opening with Guy Fawkes being arrested in his cellar of explosives, then skipping ahead to his public hanging (a two-minute sequence), and closing with the Parliament building going up in a glorious pyrotechnic spectacle. Famously, the latter event did not take place on November 5, 1605, because the former did. Although the destruction of Parliament in *V for Vendetta* is set in our future rather than a revision of early Stuart history, this denouement inevitably portrays an alternate history and forces the question "What if?" From 1605 to the present, an incalculable number of pages have been written on what the Gunpowder Plot was and what it meant. To tell their story in *V for Vendetta*, the Wachowski Brothers tap the ambiguity, multivalence, and efficacious mutability of the history surrounding the Gunpowder Treason and the subsequent annual celebrations to commemorate England's deliverance on the fifth of November. So why did the Wachowski Brothers choose this historical framework and what did it mean to them? To discover the answers to these questions, one must look at their equivocating depictions of and allusions to the Gunpowder Plot, at their own clear political agenda, and at the primary source material for this film.

The Wachowski Brothers had encountered the striking graphic novel *V for Vendetta* before embarking on *The Matrix* series of films, and, at that time, they envisioned a film adaptation of Alan Moore and David Lloyd's 1980s "comic" masterpiece. Moore and Lloyd launched the serialized graphic novel in 1981 and completed it in 1988. From the start, it was intended to be a political commentary on the evils and corruption of the Conservative government in their native Britain. *V for Vendetta* is an anti-Thatcherite polemic. Moore and Lloyd were deeply disturbed by what they saw as a narrowing of rights, disempowerment of minorities, and fear-based politicking. In his introduction to the first DC Comics edition of *V for Vendetta*, Moore despairs of his country and warns of an approaching dystopia:

> It's 1988. Margaret Thatcher is entering her third term of office and talking confidently of an unbroken Conservative leadership well into the next century.... [T]he tabloid press are circulating the idea of concentration camps for persons with AIDS. The new riot police wear black visors, as do their horses, and their vans have rotating video cameras mounted on top. The government has expressed a desire to eradicate homosexuality,... and one can only speculate as to which minority will be the next legislated against. I'm thinking of taking my family and getting out of this country soon.... It's cold and it's mean spirited and I don't like it here anymore. Goodnight England. Goodnight Home Service and V for Victory. Hello... V FOR VENDETTA.[2]

Moore describes an England resembling the world of George Orwell's *1984*. His graphic novel was to be a cautionary tale, as its near-future (1990s) setting indicates, as well as a compendium of current governmental iniquities. He and Lloyd alighted upon the idea of Guy Fawkes as a model for their protagonist as they were brainstorming about their nascent political narrative. In an early letter to Moore, Lloyd suggests, "[W]hy don't we present [our protagonist] as a resurrected Guy Fawkes, complete with one of those papier maché masks, in a cape and conical hat? He'd look *really* bizarre *and* it would give Guy Fawkes the image he's deserved all these years. We shouldn't burn the chap every Nov. 5th but *celebrate* his attempt to blow up Parliament!"[3] And thus the masked, revolutionary antihero V was born. The immediate impetus for modeling V after Fawkes was clearly the authors' antipathy toward the current Conservative government. The thought of blowing up the Parliament sitting in England in the 1980s inspired these co-creators to conjure an anarchic spirit, or at least righteous indignation, through the appropriation of the figure of a historical "terrorist." The cliché "One man's terrorist is another man's freedom fighter" is embraced wholeheartedly in Moore and Lloyd's dark comic, which is illustrated by the fact that the "avenger" V uses some of the very same tactics of grotesque violence and torture as does the fascist regime he is attacking.

The plot of the graphic novel *V for Vendetta* takes place in a postapocalyptic 1990s Britain. Africa has been blown off the map, the European continent seems to be missing, and the United States is in dire straits. This is truly a Cold War tale. The Tory government has moved from conservatism to fascism in the wake of the global and local chaos. Abuses of power like labor exploitation, government corruption, complicity with crime networks, prison camps, and the use of torture abound in this world. The comic has a *noir*-like, cinematic feel, eschewing the use of thought bubbles and even captions below frames, allowing dialogue and strikingly dramatic visuals to control the narrative. The book opens with the female protagonist, sixteen-year-old Evey, attempting to find a client for her sexual services in the Westminster district. She has never done this before and naively approaches corrupt police officers, called Fingermen, who try to rape her. V swoops into the frame and saves her, killing a few officers in the process. He then blows up Parliament before her eyes and takes her home to live in his underground lair, a crypt or undercroft filled with banned art, music, books, and film, his "Shadow Gallery" (a possible reference to seventeenth-century Protestant, and particularly Puritan, hostility toward art and festivities). While such a narrative will certainly be recognizable to viewers of the film, this opening also highlights a few of the most significant differences between the graphic novel and the film. First, there is no opening Guy Fawkes sequence in the book, which bespeaks the expanded significance of the figure of Fawkes and the Gunpowder Plot narrative in the film. Concomitantly, the historical Plotters' goal, the incineration of Parliament, is accomplished in the first chapter of this 265-page piece; the grand explosion concluding the comic takes place at Number Ten Downing Street. Moore and Lloyd's agenda leads them directly to Thatcher's address in the end.

In contrast, the film's narrative tension is maintained by the expected Parliamentarian conflagration at the conclusion. Will a "terrorist" plot to blow up Parliament be thwarted again? Will the head investigator, Detective Finch, figure it out before it is too late? Do we want him to? The Brothers W do an excellent job of keeping the audience riveted to *their* Gunpowder Plot.

Another major alteration in the film is the character of Evey, who in the novel is a sweet, blonde teenage would-be prostitute from an average middle-class background. To play this unlikely heroine, the Wachowskis hired the eminently intelligent and contemplative brunette Natalie Portman. This Evey had activist parents who were abducted and killed by the government and a brother who died in the St. Mary's plague, which had been clandestinely created by the government. She also spent five years in the government's Juvenile Reclamation Project, something like Hitler Youth, so she has much cause for anger and vengeance. Unlike the novel's politically and intellectually naïve protagonist, this Evey has the extraordinary family connections and troubled childhood requisite for greatness. In the film, her character is empowered and, like much else in the graphic novel, Evey is sanitized for the viewing audience. She is certainly not out soliciting johns on the night in question; although the opening scene is quite similar to that in the novel, Evey is on her way to a date with her coworker and is caught by the Fingermen simply because she is out past curfew. Overall, Moore, and Lloyd's novel has a distinctly Brechtian, *Threepenny Opera*-esque narrative, mise-en-scène, and tone. Everyone and everything is vitiated and meretricious.

The Wachowskis' cinematic vision is starkly different. There are good guys—for example, nice middle-class families, Evey, various governmental victims, and even V—and there are bad guys—for example, anyone involved in or with the government or established church. Although there has been a war, no nuclear holocaust predates the events of the film. In fact, the British government has manufactured crises in order to push the people into acquiescing to extreme authoritarian rule. The most important of these crises is the St. Mary's plague, named so because it supposedly began at a Catholic school (a reference to Reformation anti-Catholicism, surely). It killed 80,000 people. One of the mysteries solved in the film is the cause of this "plague": the British government. The conservative party's utterly unscrupulous and sinister fear-based politicking put them in power. Even a cursory look at *V for Vendetta* reveals that it is a very thinly veiled critique of George W. Bush's administration in the United States, and the genocidal St. Mary's incident clearly alludes to the conspiracy theories after the 9/11 tragedy that officials in Bush's government either had something to do with the planning of the atrocity or at least knew about it beforehand and allowed it to take place. The idea is that the administration wanted to force the United States into war and encourage the nation to sanction legislation, such as the Patriot Act, that restricts civil liberties.

Alan Moore did not appreciate this appropriation of his text and consequently decided to remove his name from the film before it was released, declaring that his work had been "turned into a Bush-era parable by people too timid to set a political satire in their own country.... [The film] is a thwarted and frustrated and largely impotent American liberal fantasy of someone with American liberal values standing up against a state run by neoconservatives."[4] Indeed, whereas Moore's V resembles a Hegelian or Nietzschean "Great Man," an amoral individualist who effects change in history via his own Herculean efforts, the Wachowskis' V is a leader of a liberal revolutionary movement. In no place is this more evident than in the final chapters of each text. In the graphic novel, V is killed by the establishment "baddies" and Evey takes on his identity, donning the mask and costume and sending V's body off in the subway car to obliterate Downing Street. She now has her own rescuee, a young man, whose training she will commence, as V had schooled her. Before dying, V tells Evey that England "is not saved...do not think that...but all its beliefs have come to rubble, and from rubble we may build."[5] Evey continues V's anarchic work to provide people with the freedom to create a "better world" from the rubble. At this point, the populace is still involved in large-scale, violent rioting in the streets of London. In contrast, the V of the film sends out thousands of Guy Fawkes masks and costumes to his fellow Englishmen, encouraging them to heed the symbol of rebellion and join the movement of the masses. The final scenes of the film feature peaceful crowds gathering around Westminster, all dressed identically. There is obvious irony in a movement that is fighting for civil and personal freedoms and human rights, respect for diversity and individual choice, arraying itself identically. The crane shots of the burgeoning masses of anonymous Guy Fawkes masqueraders do not read as an argument for embracing heterogeneity, but they are meant to portray the groundswell of popular support for V's antifascist views. Unlike the chaotic rabble in the novel's narrative, these people take an organized, active, and united stand against oppression. This is precisely the "liberal fantasy" denounced by Moore. However, this choice reflects another way in which the film resembles the historic Gunpowder Plot.

* * *

Although Guy Fawkes has become the "poster child" and most likely combustible for November 5th celebrations, it is widely known that Robert Catesby was truly "[t]he prince of darkness at the centre of the Gunpowder Plot."[6] Born in 1573, Catesby was one of a group of angry young gentlemen in the 1590s who had experienced the tightening of restrictions on English Catholics during their youth. The Act of Supremacy and the Act of Conformity, both instituted in 1559, made it illegal to celebrate Mass and required those who chose not to attend Anglican services to pay a weekly fine, and also forced citizens to confess the monarch as the head of the Church. From the 1570s through the 1590s, fines for recusancy rose sharply and further restrictions on the civil liberties of Catholics were imposed. For instance, in 1579, "in an effort to weed out closet Catholics, the obligation to swear the Oath of Supremacy was extended to a wide range of officials and professionals, including schoolmasters, lawyers, and justices of the peace," effectively shutting Catholics out of these positions, as they were already prevented from getting a university degree.[7] The English government passed legislation in 1586 allowing the government "to seize a recusant's goods and two-thirds of his lands until he paid the fine he was attempting to evade, converted, or died"; and in 1593, a new Act "required Catholics to stay within five miles of their homes."[8] Elizabeth I's reign is marked by rampant anti-Catholicism for myriad reasons, one of the most salient being her government's disastrous political relations with Spain, the Catholic superpower, which led to Spain's attempted invasion of England and the subsequent defeat of the Armada in 1588. In addition, Elizabeth's excommunication from the Catholic Church by Pope Pius V in 1570 sanctioned (and perhaps encouraged) Catholics to rebel against their queen, which spawned a deep distrust of English Catholics. Furthermore, the Catholic Mary Stuart's claim to the throne was dangerously supported by some prominent noblemen, leading to Mary's execution in 1587 due to alleged assassination plots against Elizabeth on Mary's behalf. In 1601, the Earl of Essex mounted an odd and abortive "Rebellion" against the Queen's Council, aided by several prominent young Catholics, including the charismatic and magnetic Robert Catesby, who hoped to convince Elizabeth to grant the Catholics some relief. While Essex was summarily hanged for his sedition, Catesby escaped with his life and a calamitously exorbitant fine.

When the protestant James VI of Scotland, Mary Stuart's son, succeeded Elizabeth on the throne of England in 1603, Catholics maintained hope that the offspring of a Catholic martyr would surely relieve their sufferings. Their high hopes were encouraged when James I of England released some of the imprisoned priests who had been severely tortured during Elizabeth's reign and even suspended recusancy fines for a year in the wake of a Catholic plot (the Bye Plot) against his life, which was described to his Privy Council by the Jesuit priest Henry Garnet, who ironically would later be assassinated for his knowledge of (not participation in) the Gunpowder Treason. However, James perceived the threat that powerful Catholic gentry could pose to his monarchy and pushed forward to sign the Treaty of London with Spain in August of 1604, ending decades of war and ensuring that Spain would not intervene with England's anti-Catholic policies or attempt to aid English

Catholics. Indeed, the English Catholics were crestfallen, and James' government went on to reinstate the recusancy fines with a vengeance. It is at this point that Catesby, who was related by blood and marriage to a large network of Catholic gentry, began to plan the Gunpowder Plot. By the summer of 1605, thirteen people were involved, and the Plot had grown into an elaborate scheme to establish James' young daughter Elizabeth as a puppet monarch controlled by powerful Catholic aristocrats. The plotters had no desire, therefore, to foment chaos and create anarchy in England but, rather, wished to escape oppression by immediately constructing their own Catholic government (one that might prove as intolerant of Protestants as Mary I's had been). This was certainly a rebellion and a revolution, but they did not, in the immortal words of the Sex Pistols, "want to be anarchy."

Only three of the thirteen conspirators were not a part of the familial Catholic gentry network, and Guy Fawkes was one of them. Born in 1570, Fawkes was the son and grandson of ecclesiastical lawyers living in the northern city of York. Fawkes was raised Protestant, but his father died when the boy was only nine, and his mother remarried a Catholic gentleman, Denis Bainbridge, who lived in a predominantly Catholic region of Yorkshire. Although the details are not known, it is evident that Fawkes converted to the "Old Faith" during his later youth and made contacts, if not friends, in the powerful Wright, Wintour, and Percy families, members of which would be involved in the Plot. At the age of twenty-one, Fawkes, like many young Catholic men of his age, went to the Netherlands to fight with the Spanish Army of Flanders against the Protestant Dutch troops, which England was both supporting and supplying. This military training ground for English Catholic troops was yet another constant source of anxiety for the monarchy. Guy Fawkes, by all accounts, was an "eminently honourable" and "very devout" Christian soldier, a generally cheerful man "of exemplary life and commendable reticence."[9] As he was known by the larger, influential English Catholic families and had become something of a munitions expert, Fawkes was drawn into the "Powder Treason" almost from its inception in 1604. Although he was never the leader amongst this group of angry young men, he seems to have been in charge of the explosives throughout the process. That is why, in the wee hours of November 5, 1605, the King's Guard discovered Guy Fawkes alone in a cellar below the Parliament building (David Cressy calls him "the man with the match"), accompanied by enough gunpowder to demolish essentially two city blocks (thirty-six barrels). Fawkes was interrogated and tortured for several days before he finally broke and told all. Each of the thirteen conspirators either was executed or died in the process of capture, but it is Guy Fawkes, the name and the effigy, who is most remembered today.

What seems to have given the Plot away to the authorities was a cryptic, anonymous letter sent on October 26, 1605, to William Parker, Lord Monteagle, a young peer preparing to attend Parliament on November 5. It contained a warning to avoid Parliament because "God and man hath concurred to punish the wickedness of this time"; therefore, "they shall receive a terrible blow this Parliament."[10] To this day, there is much speculation about who actually wrote this letter, ranging from Lord Monteagle's sister to one of the plotters to whom he was related, or perhaps it was one of their servants. Tantalizingly, conspiracy theorists, both then and now, have posited that the letter could have been written by Robert Cecil, Earl of Salisbury, James' head of security, or Lord Monteagle himself, in order to promote their political careers and standing with the King. Within this school of thought, there are scholars who believe the entire Plot could have been a fabrication of the government for reasons of political promotion or possibly to justify their anti-Catholic policies. Historian Antonia Fraser divides Gunpowder Plot scholars into two groups: "Pro-Plotters," who believe there was a treasonous Catholic conspiracy; and "No-Plotters," who believe it was a government propaganda tool.[11]

In *V for Vendetta*, the Wachowski Brothers play with this four-hundred-year-old controversy by making the "Christian" fascist government the "only begetter" of the St. Mary's plague virus that causes what amounts to genocide in England. They blame "the terrorists," but the true terrorists are those in government perpetrating these atrocities in order to scare the populace into sanctioning an oppressive military dictatorship. Again, the Brothers W are alluding directly to George W. Bush's administration in this narrative. Nevertheless, in the cases of the Gunpowder Plot and the 9/11 attacks, it seems evident that England and the United States were indeed attacked by terrorist enemies of the state. However, it is also clear that the politics of fear was used after these terrorist conspiracies to make significant governmental and legislative changes that effectively restricted the rights of its citizens (or at least a portion thereof). The connections the Wachowski Brothers are trying to make break down when one deduces that the early modern analogue for the character V is the extremist Catholics who were indeed planning to blow up every member of the Houses of Lords and Commons plus the royal family at the opening of Parliament—not a symbolic empty building at nighttime as in the film—and in regard to the September 11th tragedy, V must represent the extremist Muslim members of Al Qaeda, who were certainly not trying to liberate the United States from their "oppressive" government.

It is peculiar and amusing that some reviews of *V for Vendetta*, like Owen Gleiberman's in *Entertainment Weekly*, describe Guy Fawkes as a "17th-century

British anarchist hero," mistakenly reading history through the lens of the film. Indeed, Guy Fawkes is no such creature. The Plotters were far from anarchists, as I have argued, and Fawkes himself was not even a leading figure in the conspiracy. Furthermore, in contrast to Evey's indomitable fortitude under torture in *V for Vendetta*, Fawkes broke when tortured and named names, giving up the rest of the group, which, while understandable, does not conform to most notions of heroism. In addition, the thirteen members of the group were most definitely perceived by the majority of England as traitors who had frighteningly jeopardized their nation, their religion, and perhaps their very lives. Soon after the foiling of the Gunpowder Plot, the government declared November 5 an annual holiday commemorating God's providential deliverance of England. Early modern historian David Cressy explains, "The plot was interpreted as further proof of the relentless evil of Roman Catholicism, and its discovery as a renewal of the promise that God would deliver England from its enemies. The mercy of 1605 confirmed the covenant of 1588."[12] Gunpowder Treason Day, as it was called, reminded the English that they were a nation providentially preserved by God, and the annual sermons preached all over the country on November 5 tended to focus on offering thanksgiving to God for his deliverance, as well as ranting against popish perfidy. As for the populace, bonfires were lit and bells were rung to celebrate the day. No effigies were burnt during James' reign; in fact, this practice was rare until the 1670s, when the Catholic James Stuart, Duke of York, appeared to be the successor to his heirless brother King Charles II. On November 4, 1677, the Dutch Protestant prince William of Orange and James Stuart's daughter Mary wed, and the next day proved to be one of the most ardently celebrated Powder Treason Days in decades, including the burning of effigies of the Pope and the devil.

Between 1679 and 1681, Parliament tried to pass several "exclusion bills" to prevent James, or any other Catholic, from taking the throne. Charles II and the Tories would not permit the passage of any such legislation. Throughout the 1670s and 1680s, it became increasingly common for the Pope and other Catholic icons to be burnt in effigy on November 5. Celebrations were transformed, particularly by the anti-James Whigs, into organized community pageants with parades, printed programs, and costumes. Cressy describes these events as "angry partisan presentations…living tableaux as political cartoons."[13] The phrase "political cartoons" vividly reminds me of both incarnations of *V for Vendetta*, but particularly of that final scene in the film featuring the hordes of identical Guy Fawkes masks, creating the look of organized, uniformed, collective political protest—which could not be more different from the graphic novel's conclusion. Not surprisingly, in the 1680s, Gunpowder Treason Day began to degenerate into chaos and violence in the streets as well. As the Royalists and the Parliamentarians had fought over the meaning and possession of November 5 a generation before, the Restoration English factions of the Tories and the Whigs fought rabidly over the holiday, each group using it to promote its own political agenda. James II took the throne in 1685 to the consternation of many, but his short reign ended abruptly when William of Orange landed in England to much rejoicing on November 5th, 1688. The outcome of the Glorious Revolution added further fuel to the Protestant providentialist reading of England's history, and it was perceived as another merciful deliverance from Catholicism.

Throughout the eighteenth century, however, the holiday became increasingly secularized, moving away from memorializing providentialist history and toward propagandizing political partisanship. Civil unrest in the form of "lawless mobs," some calling themselves "guys," who ran riot through towns and cities stealing, breaking windows, and threatening or perpetrating physical violence, began to be a staple feature of November 5 celebrations.[14] The local authorities responded by setting up trained response units, reminiscent of the riot police of today and those that appear in the film. By the end of the eighteenth century, the Pope and the devil had faded in popularity as effigy material, and "Guy Fawkes had emerged as the principal figure to be displayed and burned."[15] By the early nineteenth century, the holiday was known as "Guy Fawkes Day." Cressy elucidates, "As anti-Catholic agitation and historical memory subsided, Guy Fawkes took on the roles of all purpose bogeyman and carnival grotesque."[16] The holiday had become the possession of the people rather than the government (it was officially taken off the Church calendar in 1859), and as such, it had become an occasion on which to vent antigovernment sentiments. In the 1980s, some British citizens used November 5 as on opportunity to incinerate Maggie. Now, you would not be hard-pressed to find Britons burning Blair and Bush.

* * *

It is clear from the brief chronicle above that the Wachowski Brothers are remembering the Gunpowder Plot and its commemoration as it evolved in popular history, particularly from the late eighteenth century to the present. They seem to ignore or dismiss the seventeenth century's perception of the event as a day of profound thanks and a remembrance of God's awesome and providential deliverance of his "chosen" and enlightened Protestant English nation. However, the political rhetoric of the preamble to the legislation establishing November 5 as a day of celebration, while introducing the pious tone and focus of this "holiday," could promote the kind of self-congratulatory and hegemonic nationalism presented in the film:

> Forasmuch as almighty God hath in all ages showed his power and mercy in the miraculous and gracious deliverance of his church, and in the protection of religious kings and states, and that no nation of the earth hath been blessed with greater benefit than this kingdom now enjoyeth, having the true and free profession of the gospel under our most gracious sovereign King James, the most great learned and religious king that ever reigned therein...: [against] which many malignant and devilish papists, Jesuits, and seminary priests much envying and fearing, conspired most horribly...an invention so inhuman, barbarous and cruel, as the like was never before heard of.[17]

One can see parallels between this rhetoric and that of the English government and its emissaries in *V for Vendetta*. This government exploits real and manufactured crises as it pushes toward a "Christian" fascist state, in which "Articles of Allegiance" must be signed, a clear reference to the Oaths of Allegiance and Supremacy used by Tudor and Stuart monarchs to control their Catholic citizens. An example of such religiously charged political rhetoric appears in the second scene of *V for Vendetta*, immediately after the opening Guy Fawkes vignette. We begin the plot of the film with an extreme close-up on the face of Lewis Prothero, a Rush Limbaugh-esque conservative talk show host who calls himself "The Voice of London" and preaches the Head Chancellor's motto: "England prevails!" In this scene, Prothero is shown on television railing against the United States to highlight the righteousness of England's administration in comparison to the chaos and debilitation of the previously decadent and now decimated United States, which is sending wheat and tobacco to England in hopes of receiving badly needed medical supplies in return. Prothero declares that "it's high time we let the colonies know what we really think of them," by dumping "that crap where everything from the Ulcered Sphincter of Ass-erica belongs!"[18] He goes on to explain the cause of the formerly great nation's fall, clearly issuing a warning to his own audience about the perils of a profligately tolerant society:

> [H]ere was a country that had everything, absolutely everything, and now, twenty years later is what? The world's biggest leper colony. Why? Godlessness....It wasn't the war they started. It wasn't the plague they created. It was judgment. No one escapes their past. No one escapes judgment. You think He's not up there. You think He's not watching over this country. How else do you explain it? He tested us and we came through.

> We did what we had to do.... I saw it all: immigrants, Muslims, homo-
> sexuals, terrorists, disease-ridden degenerates. They had to go! Strength
> through unity; unity through faith. I'm a God-fearing Englishman and
> I'm godammed proud of it![19]

The Wachowski Brothers' script obviously indicts the extreme religious right of the United States through Prothero's speech, while sending an apocalyptic warning to those who might allow such an oppressive regime to come to power by succumbing to media manipulation. In the England of this film, all those who stray from the profile or conventions of the white, Christian, Protestant, heterosexual citizen are rounded up, "black-bagged," tortured (as were V and Evey), and exterminated. Although there are clear points of connection between the draconian anti-Catholic penal laws, which persisted for over two-hundred years in England (1559–1829), and the ideology of hatred, fear, and exclusion represented in *V for Vendetta*, there is a good deal of difference as well.

While many governments past and present, including the United States, have used ideological rhetoric to demonize "others" and justify violence against them, most of these governments have not been fascist. Tudor and Stuart England certainly could not be put into that category. Nonetheless, with its focus on media and collective activism, *V for Vendetta* highlights the power of propaganda to spread political ideas that can promote or destroy an individual's freedoms in any society. In several flashback sequences explaining the events leading up to the establishment of England's fascist government, there are obvious references to Hitler and his propaganda machine, as well as graphic depictions, mirroring Holocaust images, of mass graves filled with bodies of the "others" used for torturous medical testing. As Natalie Portman notes, it is an interesting coincidence that the film ended up being shot at Babelsberg Studio in Berlin, which was used by Josef Goebbels' infamous propaganda machine to produce nationalistic films such as Leni Riefenstahl's *Triumph of the Will* (1935) and anti-Semitic films like *Jud Süß* (dir. Veit Harlan, 1940). Portman describes the studio as "heavy with history...it gives so much weight to what we're doing."[20] The serendipity of the connections between the history of the studio and the themes of the film might lead us to suspect that anti-propaganda media, like this film, is still propaganda, just as a cold-blooded killer who takes joy in the destruction of people and property for personal and political reasons, as does V, is still a terrorist. Significantly, the Wachowski Brothers do not necessarily deny this notion throughout the film, particularly in their depictions of V's grotesquely violent, almost gleeful killing sprees and his torture of Evey, but the contrived (at best) triumphal ending of *V for Vendetta* does blunt this point.

In the final scene of *V for Vendetta*, Evey and Detective Finch, who finally understands the truth of V's situation and the government's culpability, stand gazing over the blazing inferno that simultaneously consumes Parliament and V's sacrificial body, which has been sent on a train full of explosives to the symbolic site. When Finch asks Evey who V was, she answers elegiacally, "He was Edmund Dantès [of *The Count of Monte Cristo*] and he was my father, and my mother, my brother, my friend. He was you and me. He was all of us." The speech, while attempting to inspire, feels contrived. As she finishes, the camera cuts to the sea of citizens wearing Guy Fawkes costumes as they finally doff their masks and, in wonderment, witness the Parliament building exploding in a series of fireworks celebrating their freedom from the fascist government that has oppressed them. As they reveal their faces, we recognize several "dissidents" the film has highlighted who have lost their lives under the tyrannical, malignant system: Evey's parents, the lesbian actor Valerie and her lover, Evey's homosexual boss. Though these individuals have sacrificed all for their nonconformity, the human spirit and drive for freedom has triumphed in the end. Soaring over the crowd is Tchaikovsky's *1812 Overture*, particularly resonant because written to commemorate the seventieth anniversary of Russia's victory over Napoleon's army. Russia was headed for a bloody revolution, of course, which would be followed by the ascendancy of a devastating totalitarian government. Nevertheless, the tone of the scene is unabashedly jubilant, and the spectacular display of victory (including a "V" spelled in the sky with fireworks) utterly overshadows the immediately previous scene in which the already dying V viciously slices up several armed soldiers who were simply following orders. The magnificent fireworks display effectively symbolizes hope while it trivializes and essentially erases V's cold-blooded, sometimes indiscriminate brutality and bloodlust. In the atmosphere of the swelling score, the unmasking of the crowd communicates the power of symbols and emphasizes the need to protect human rights for all. But is V's, or Fawkes', or Osama bin Laden's violent means the only or most effective way to achieve this? And should individuals choose political ideals over people and relationships, as do Evey's parents and V? These are important questions raised by *V for Vendetta*, and the film equivocates regarding the answers, perhaps purposely reflecting the complexity of the subject. I argue, however, that these thorny issues are regrettably obfuscated by the grand Hollywood finale. It is this sort of cinematic opportunism that prompted David Denby of *The New Yorker* to dub the film, "a dunderheaded pop fantasia that celebrates terrorism and destruction"[21] and Richard Porter of *Cineaste* to declare it a "joyously incoherent allegory."[22] While I sympathize with these views, I also acknowledge that in *V for Vendetta* the Wachowksi Brothers are attempting to ennoble the masses by praising the value of human freedom, art, and ideas. In the process, they endeavor to connect the struggles surrounding those issues today with those of the past, highlighting the transcendent qualities of human nature. It is clear that the propagandistic political posturing, activities, props, and costumes that appear throughout the history of Gunpowder Treason (a.k.a. Guy Fawkes) Day inspired Larry and Andy Wachowski to use this ever-changing, multivalent English event as the touchstone and primary metaphor in their politically charged spectacle of popular revolution. And, as always, Hollywood prevails.

Notes

1. Lucius Shepard, "Say You Want a Revolution?," *Fantasy and Science Fiction* 111 (2006): 121.
2. Alan Moore and David Lloyd, with Steve Whitaker and Siobhan Dodds, *V for Vendetta* (New York: Vertigo, 1990), 6.
3. Quoted in Moore and Lloyd, 272.
4. Quoted in Nicholas J. Xenakis, "T for Terrorist," *National Interest*, June 1, 2006, 134. http://web.ebscohost.com.
5. Moore and Lloyd, 245.
6. Antonia Fraser, *Faith and Treason: The Story of the Gunpowder Plot* (New York: Nan A. Talese/Doubleday, 1996), 90.
7. James Sharpe, *Remember, Remember: A Cultural History of Guy Fawkes Day* (Cambridge, MA: Harvard UP, 2005), 19–20.
8. Ibid., 19.
9. Ibid., 49, 10.
10. Fraser, 150.
11. Ibid., xv.
12. David Cressy, *Bonfires and Bells: National Memory and the Protestant Calendar in Elizabethan and Stuart England* (Berkeley: U of California P, 1989), 142.
13. Ibid., 179.
14. David Cressy, "The Fifth of November Remembered," in *Myths of the English*, ed. Roy Porter (Cambridge: Cambridge UP, 1992), 78–79.
15. Ibid., 79.
16. Ibid., 79.
17. Quoted in Cressy, "Fifth," 71.
18. *V for Vendetta*, DVD (2-Disc Limited Edition), directed by James McTeigue, screenplay by The Wachowski Brothers (2005; Burbank, CA: Warner Home Video, 2006).
19. Ibid.
20. "Designing the Near Future," special feature on *V for Vendetta* (see note 18).
21. David Denby, "Blowup," *The New Yorker*, March 20, 2006, 158.
22. Richard Porter, "Review of *V for Vendetta*," *Cineaste* 31 (2006): 54.

CHAPTER 6

Reading the Early Modern Witch: Horror Films of the 1960s and 1970s

Deborah Willis

In the first scene of Mario Bava's classic horror film *Black Sunday* (1960), the seventeenth-century Moldavian witch Asa faces execution by a group of hooded men. Though most of the film takes place centuries later, this scene from the early modern period is a necessary prelude to the film's main action. Flames fill the opening frames, and the camera pans slowly to reveal the terrified yet beautiful Asa bound to an upright wooden platform, near the dead body of a former lover. The Grand Inquisitor—also, as it happens, Asa's brother—pronounces sentence, condemning her for the many evil deeds she has committed "to satisfy her monstrous love." The instrument of her death is a metal "mask of Satan" with long sharp stakes inside, to be hammered on to her face by a hooded executioner. As the executioner approaches, she curses her brother and his house, threatening to live on in the blood of his sons and the sons of his sons: "You will never escape my hunger nor that of Satan."

This, I suggest, is the primal scene of films about the early modern witch. Though the witch takes many forms in contemporary popular culture, when designated specifically as an *early modern* figure, she is constructed as, above all, a victim of cruel and unusual punishment inflicted by male authority. The early modern witch cannot be imagined without also imagining the witch-hunter. Witch-hunting is, moreover, always symptomatic of the "old ways," the extreme forms of patriarchy and/or state and religious authority now considered to belong to an unenlightened, brutal past. Indeed, the very phrase "witch-hunt," in modern usage as well as in mass media, is used to label and critique practices that are widely (though not universally) viewed as unacceptable. At the same time, the woman accused of witchcraft remains in many films a troubling figure, associated with unacceptable desire, a monstrous love or hunger, that cannot be accommodated by either past or present-day norms. The witch must be punished not only for black magic but also for some type of sexual transgression, and the staging of her punishment tends to be eroticized by the camera, either overtly or covertly. In *Black Sunday*, for example, just before the phallic stakes of the mask of Satan are hammered into Asa's face, she is turned onto her back to look up in fear and trembling at the viewer. In close-up she is—briefly—made sexually available to the viewer's gaze. Her punishment is a spectacle of sadistic penetration, both murder and rape.

The torture and execution of witches in these films is the "undead" crime of the Renaissance, the past that won't stay buried. *Black Sunday* surely invites the viewer to see the Inquisition's enactment of "justice" as a crime, akin to a lynching or act of state terror. Yet as the film unfolds, victim becomes vigilante. Rapist father, one might say, arouses and invites retaliation from the magically destructive archaic mother, or what Barbara Creed has called the monstrous-feminine.[1] Whose crimes, then, really come first? In this film, revenge comes in so horrific a form that the audience must reassess its initial sympathy with Asa. When her grave is disturbed, releasing her to take vengeance on the descendents of her brother's family in the film's present, she clearly becomes the film's primary monster, embodying a transhistorical, diabolically inspired evil, raising the possibility that the Inquisition's seemingly barbaric procedures might be justified. At the end of the film, Asa is finally defeated and patriarchal normalcy is restored when her remains are burned. All that is needed is a more benevolent father-figure and an attractive suitor to channel the desires of Asa's double, her descendent Katia, into an acceptance of marriage and a traditionally compliant feminine role. She will not need to resort to diabolic power. Yet the sense of a brutal injustice done to Asa is not fully banished by the normative ending. The film's final frames suggest that her suitor will never be sure the woman he is kissing is Katia or Asa; Katia's soft, full, apparently yielding mouth might, if he fails to satisfy her, still turn into the hungry, all-consuming vampiric mouth of the witch. The rich visual elaboration of Asa's feminine monstrousness makes her a figure of continuing fascination, as the film goes further than most in opening up a space for female sexual and aggressive desires, however malevolent. At least on their surface, witch films released after 1960 often go further in their critique of patriarchal norms or political institutions, drawing inspiration from the countercultural challenges and emergent feminism of the late sixties and early seventies. Their conclusions are often more "modern," more intentionally open-ended. Yet, whatever the ending, the most compelling aspect of horror films about witches usually lies in the varying ways they identify problems—the underground of possibilities and unsettling disruptions associated with the return of the repressed.

There is, then, a tension that is not fully resolved in many horror films featuring the early modern witch, especially those released during the 1960s and 1970s. These films are, to one degree or another, doubly (and sometimes multiply) monstered. The monstrous punishments inflicted by the early modern witch-hunter, it seems, cannot be conjured up without raising the possibility of the early modern witch's monstrous sexuality and diabolic power. Similarly, the historical contingency of early modern witch-hunting in these films often cannot be fully disentangled from notions of a transhistorical (or even eternal) female evil. As such, these films can seem disturbingly close to the fantasies of the late medieval and early modern demonologists who promoted real witch hunts, developed concepts of the diabolic pact, the coven, and the witches' Sabbath, and presented witchcraft as a crime especially apt to be committed by women, due to their carnal appetites and sinful nature.[2] Some films use the burning of witches to produce a restoration of order, a quasi-happy ending, however qualified or ambivalent. Others feature scenes of undeniable "sexploitation." Arguably, a number of the films promote stereotypes of Satanic witchcraft that have done harm to Wiccans and other neo-pagan groups, reinforcing views taken seriously by the British tabloid press and even some in law enforcement officials.[3] For some critics, this will be cause enough to dismiss them as irredeemably reactionary.[4] Yet there is something about the stories told by demonologists and those of horror films that continue to excite the imagination and give pleasure. A part of us (of some of us at least) wants to believe in such things as the black mass, the diabolic witch, and the coven. The horror genre allows audiences to access and explore the nature of these pleasures without committing to the beliefs themselves in any literal sense. This chapter will examine some of these pleasures as well as consider some of the ways early modern histories are reproduced and reworked in these films. I offer a brief survey of witch films from the 1960s and 1970s and then discuss two representative films in more depth.

The period from 1960 to the mid-1970s can be thought of as something of a golden age for film witches.[5] In *Black Sunday*, the witch is still close to earlier monsters of classic horror, especially the vampire and the zombie. After 1960, the witch emerges as a distinct and important figure in her own right. The horror genre had found its first major female monster.[6] Not all of these films invoke an early modern past. The witch, after all, is not exclusively or even primarily an early modern figure, but appears in various forms in many traditions and time periods. The screen witch of the 1950s was just as apt to be linked to Africa, the Caribbean, or Salem as to early modern Europe. By the sixties, however, a number of horror films featured an early modern witch and/or a coven that traced its traditions back to the late medieval and early modern periods, including *Witchcraft* (1964), *The Witches* (1965), and *Rosemary's Baby* (1968). Others, such as *Witchfinder General* (1968) and *Cry of the Banshee* (1970), were set entirely in the sixteenth or seventeenth centuries. Still others, such as *Burn, Witch, Burn* (1962), *Season of the Witch* (1973), and *Suspiria* (1977) have what might be thought of as a "Renaissance unconscious"—that is, though they do not reference the Renaissance explicitly, they were influenced by (and, in turn, influenced) the witch films that directly engaged the early modern period. Most of these films are British, some come from other European countries, and a few are American.[7] They can be grouped according to the following key themes and devices:

1. **The "undead" witch**: This group evolves from what I have called the primal scene of the early modern witch film. A sixteenth- or seventeenth-century witch, made to suffer some cruel punishment in the past, takes vengeance in the present upon descendents of those who wronged her or others who resemble them. The early modern backstory may be presented at the beginning of the film or it may be revealed later on, as a way of explaining mysterious events happening in the film's present. Along with *Black Sunday*, this group includes *Witchcraft, Curse of the Crimson Altar* (1968); *Mark of the Witch* (1970); *Blood on Satan's Claw* (1971); and *The Terror* (1979). Many later films use variations on this device.

2. **The coven**: *The Witches, Rosemary's Baby, Cry of the Banshee, Season of the Witch*, and *Suspiria*, among others. The witch does not act alone but is part of a conspiratorial underground social organization that functions as a perverse yet alluring alternative to the traditional family, with affinities to the cell, the collective, the commune. Most film covens are groups that worship the devil, and are imagined in terms that resemble those of late medieval or early modern demonologists. But some are modeled more closely on the theories of Margaret Murray, who argued that those persecuted as witches in the early modern period were really members of a pagan cult—the "old religion"—who worshipped a fertility god, misunderstood by Christian authorities as Satan. In at least one film (*Season of the Witch*), the coven is based, relatively accurately, on a "British Traditional" Wiccan group. Film covens often provide an opportunity to explore some unusual sexual practices and queer desires: in *The Witches*, for example, the coven's high priestess, played

by Kay Walsh, is something of a "lesbian vampire," and the coven's orgiastic rituals include men fondling other men.

3. **Neighbors versus neighbors**: In *Burn, Witch, Burn*; *Witchcraft*; *The Witches*; *Rosemary's Baby*; and *Cry of the Banshee*, witches are the next-door neighbors, outwardly normal and friendly while concealing a malevolence within. The two families or groups in conflict may both use witchcraft (as in *Burn, Witch, Burn*); more often one family uses it against another who lacks access to supernatural power. The conflict between neighbors drives the plot, and the action generally takes place in communities where people live closely together and yet are isolated from the mainstream: a small university town (*Burn, Witch, Burn*), a remote English village (*The Witches*), a Manhattan apartment building (*Rosemary's Baby*).

4. **The witch-hunter as monster**: Although all films that reference the early modern witch represent both witches and witch-hunters as problematic figures, some films very clearly make the witch-hunter the primary monster. These films stress the abuses of power associated with witch-hunting: the use of torture to extract confessions, manufactured evidence in trials, gruesome public executions. *Witchfinder General*, loosely based on the life of the seventeenth-century witch-hunter Matthew Hopkins, is the most thoroughgoing and ominously compelling of these. Others are *Cry of the Banshee* and *Blood on Satan's Claw*.

5. **Mind-control and mental illness**: Though horror films typically give witches real supernatural powers, some contain their own form of skepticism, raising the possibility that witchcraft might really be some form of mind-control, hypnotic suggestion, or neurotic fantasy. *Burn, Witch, Burn* and *Rosemary's Baby* all arouse audience uncertainty about whether events are supernaturally caused or simply the paranoid or hysterical fantasies of neurotic women (e.g., what Rosemary's husband calls "the pre-partum crazies"). In *Witchcraft*, *The Witches*, and *Suspiria*, witch characters use mind-control techniques. Arguably, *Season of the Witch* offers the most inventively progressive variation on this theme: in this film, fully self-identifying as a witch allows the main character to resolve her neurotic crisis, bringing to an end a series of nightmares and visits to a psychiatrist.

In general, films released before 1968 were more likely to stress the diabolic nature of the female witch and to construct the coven in Satanic terms. By the later sixties and early seventies, covens are imagined more sympathetically and take on countercultural, Wiccan, or vaguely feminist traits. Paralleling this development, the films with the most emphatically monstrous witch-hunters all cluster in the years 1967–1972. By the time of *Suspiria* (1977), however, we are back to a powerfully sinister and Satanic all-female coven—as if to say decisively that the sixties are over. For a more in-depth look at these themes, let us consider two films, *Witchcraft* and *Cry of the Banshee*. The first, like *Black Sunday*, employs the device of an "undead" witch who comes from the past to take revenge on the descendents of her enemies. Set in contemporary England, it features a witch buried alive in 1630. The second film is set entirely in sixteenth-century England. Both films include covens, neighborly conflicts, and mind-control techniques, and construct the early modern past as a doubly monstered time when witches and witch-hunters committed crimes. Both reimagine the early modern past in light of 1960s concerns. Yet they also give very different spins to these features and can be used to illustrate two ends of the spectrum of witch films from the 1960s and 1970s. *Witchcraft*, though it contains some compelling class critique, is the more conservative of the two, ultimately linking the early modern to a tradition of Satanism in order to justify a quasi-colonial appropriation of land and status: the witch and her coven are the film's primary monsters. *Cry of the Banshee*, on the other hand, clearly makes the witch-hunters more monstrous than the witch, critiquing state and religious authority while inviting sympathy for a hedonistic, peace-loving, hippie-like coven. Nevertheless, the film is fascinated with the sadism of authority and the sexual objectification of women. Ideologically speaking, the films may not be as far apart as it first appears.

In *Witchcraft*, the seventeenth-century witch Vanessa Whitlock seeks revenge on the Lanier family, descendents of those responsible for her conviction and horrific death. Though it quickly becomes clear that Vanessa and her own descendents are guilty as charged—that is, they are indeed practitioners of black magic—the actions of the Laniers are also called into question. In the early modern backstory, the conviction of Vanessa enabled the Laniers to seize all of the Whitlock property, including the large part-Gothic, part-Tudor country home in which the Lanier descendents still live. (The Whitlock family, now reduced to an uncle and niece, live in a modest apartment.) Early on in the film, the youngest Lanier, Todd, explains the family history to his brother's wife, Tracy, an outsider. The Whitlocks—"Anglo-Saxon stock"—once owned all the land in the area, he tells her, while the Laniers were Normans and came later. During the witch hunts in the early 1600s, Laniers accused Whitlocks of witchcraft. "There have been cynics who felt their zeal was inspired more by greed than by righteousness," Todd comments. Whatever their motives, "they had Vanessa Whitlock killed and drove out her kinfolk. Then they took over." Since then the Whitlocks have made the destruction of the Laniers "the main item of business at their Sabbaths." That's the local folklore at any rate. Todd personally doesn't believe in witches, and laughs off the long-ago past, as if it has no bearing on the present. His is the voice of skepticism that the horror film always proves wrong.

Todd's remarks implicitly construct the Whitlocks as a colonized group, while the Laniers are colonizers who usurp their land and suppress their religious traditions. Moreover, the crime of the past is repeated in the present, as the affable Bill Lanier, head of a development company, again violates the Whitlocks' property rights. The film opens with a scene of a bulldozer, inexorably plowing its way through the Whitlock family's ancestral graveyard, breaking ground for a new subdivision. Morgan Whitlock, along with his niece Amy and a group of local people, try futilely to stop it. Though Lanier—who sees himself as a principled fellow—had hoped to prevent the desecration of the graveyard, his partner, Myles Forrester, refuses to wait. The "undead" witch Vanessa is released when her coffin is broken open. The camera lingers on the empty coffin as if it were a wound.

The film at first seems to use the early modern backstory to indict capitalist greed and unscrupulous development. And for much of the film's first half, the viewer is at least partly aligned with the perspective of Vanessa and the present-day Whitlock family. Eerily attractive with her corpse-like pallor, grey robes, long hair, arched eyebrows, and unblinking stare, Vanessa moves with grim determination, as if a specter of the Laniers' bad conscience. The aggrieved Morgan Whitlock also arouses some sympathy in the early scenes, a figure of righteous indignation as he confronts Bill Lanier about the graveyard. Even the devil-worshipping coven that Whitlock turns out to lead seems at first a rather pious group, not too different from the Catholic monks whose ceremonies they imitate, yet pervert. As one critic comments, "the Satanists in this film are actually moralists, punishing the corruption of the Laniers."[8] With sly wit the film invites the audience to take pleasure in seeing the Laniers' tea-drinking, cheerfully complacent world disrupted as Vanessa and Morgan Whitlock team up to exact their revenge. First to go is Lanier's partner, the voice of unrestrained greed and, not incidentally, a wearer of loud plaid suits. But Lanier's better taste and supposed scruples do not protect him or his family. Aunt Helen is killed, Granny injured in a fall, Bill and Todd narrowly escape driving into a deep rubbish pit, and Tracy nearly becomes the coven's sacrificial victim. "I should never have started this construction project," Lanier exclaims, as the casualties mount up.

At the same time, by confirming the Whitlocks are in fact devil-worshipping witches who murder the innocent as well as the guilty, the film undercuts its ostensibly progressive message. Vanessa's return from the past increasingly looks like the reemergence of a timeless evil, rather than a way of righting a historical wrong. The coven is completed by her return, the high priest is united with its high priestess, and they are literally part of an "underground": their ceremonies take place in a secret chamber beneath the Lanier house, accessible only through a tunnel from the Lanier family crypt. Though Vanessa sometimes uses witch-dolls to perform her magic, her scariest power is a form of mind-control: in some scenes she seems to bend her victims to her will merely through her unblinking stare. Similarly, Whitlock runs the coven in authoritarian fashion, and the members follow his directives with seemingly robotic precision. He is also a strict guardian of his niece Amy, trying to obstruct her romantic relationship with Todd, the youngest Lanier, and bullying her into remaining a loyal member of the coven. The camera that aligned us for a time with Vanessa now follows the gaze of the curious Tracy, wife of Bill Lanier, as she makes her way through long tunnels to the chamber, where she is shocked to discover the coven in the middle of a black mass, Amy among them. In place of a crucifix is a goat-skin and skeleton of a goat's head, arranged in a vaguely cross-like shape. But the climactic horror of the film is a scene offered by the camera only to the audience a little later: Tracy, newly outfitted in a long clingy gown, has been drugged and bound to a cross on the floor, awaiting sacrifice.

In the midst of this prim and proper film,[9] the suddenly eroticized view of Tracy is indeed a rather shocking spectacle: the next-door neighbors not only serve a different god and seek to reappropriate their property, they also want to do unspeakable things to their neighbor's wife. This is the hidden "truth" the film has been leading up to, the culmination of a series of images that repeats and yet surpasses the Laniers' initial "rape" of the land by the bulldozer and the open, violated coffin. The camera underscores the pre-ternaturally phallic threat of the Whitlocks by lingering on the many holes or openings that make the Laniers vulnerable to penetration: Aunt Helen's open bedroom window, the giant rubbish pit where she meets her death and where Bill and Todd almost die, the underground tunnels, the secret chamber, and finally the unprotected female body.

Arguably, the film does not completely erase the critique of the colonizer implied by the early modern backstory. Its final scene gives us a double perspective as the entire Whitlock coven and the Lanier family home burn up in a huge fire. Amy Whitlock has sacrificed herself in order to help save Tracy: not all Whitlocks are bad, and daughterly disobedience to a father-figure is validated. As Bill, Todd, and Tracy Lanier watch the fire, shock and horror register on their faces as they see their family home collapse. In their shock is also a form of recognition: they were not owners but merely occupiers of the house, and a rough justice has been done. Yet it's Granny who has the last word: "Born in evil, death in burning," she intones with satisfaction. For Granny, the only mistake in the past was to bury the witch alive instead of burn her. Laniers and Whitlocks both have to pay for their past and present sins, but one family pays far more than the other. Only the "good" girls survive, after having been taught a lesson about the dangers of self-assertion.

The film thus rewrites early modern witch-hunting and the notion of the coven in the light of Cold War anxieties and a traditional, early sixties view of gender norms. The authoritarian structure of the coven, its covert operations, and its leaders' tactics of mind control give the coven a subtext of loose associations with Cold War fears about a Manchurian Candidate-like communist menace.[10] At the same time, the early modern history of the Whitlock-Lanier feud and the reference to Norman appropriation of Anglo-Saxon lands could have a suggestive analogy to a contemporary history of colonial occupation and anticolonialist resistance, especially for a British audience.[11] The film gives expression to the guilty fears of an audience that has become more aware of its complicity in colonialism at home and abroad and of the contested nature of ownership, inviting a measure of identification with an (safely distanced, partly disguised) anticolonialist resistance. But, by its end, the film reassuringly rewrites that resistance as always already the demonic "other," the embodiment of an intrinsic evil predating and exceeding the wrongs perpetrated by the colonizers. Having at last destroyed all representatives of that evil, the colonialist can rest easy.

By contrast, *Cry of the Banshee* arouses far more sympathy for the witches than the witch-hunters. The film, set in a sixteenth-century English village, focuses on a conflict between the family of Lord Edward Whitman and a local coven, headed by a witch named Oona, a dignified matriarchal figure with thick long hair and pale blue robes, who calls her followers "my children." Her coven is first seen in the woods, dancing and chanting beside the ruins of a church, wearing flowers in their hair and flowing white toga-like robes and sheepskins. Their bodies sway sensually and rub against one another as they work up to what is most likely to be group sex. A young woman lies naked on a stone slab as Oona blesses her; a young man in a sheepskin gets ready to lie on top of her. Their activities suggest not only Greek fertility rites but also the love-ins of hippies or the countercultural gatherings at Woodstock and other outdoor rock concerts of the late sixties; a lot has changed in the six years since the film *Witchcraft* was made. This coven is not a Satanic cult, but a group following the "old religion"—a pagan nature-religion that uses magic for benign ends. As one captured witch explains, "Oona's not evil—Oona is good, Oona is peace, Oona heals, Oona is love."

Lord Edward, on the other hand, is almost a cartoon version of corrupt authority and rapacious witch-hunting. "They think me a monster in the village," he confesses, but defends the hunting of witches for "God and country" and to maintain authority: "I'm a hard magistrate, it's true. But authority is the main point of government and maintaining of authority is the main purpose of the law." The film makes it clear, however, that "authority" is merely a cover for abuses of power: he's a bully and a misogynist who likes to torture women and enjoy their sexual humiliation. Played by Vincent Price, Lord Edward looms over his court in sinister, domineering style and is dressed to resemble Henry VIII. In an early scene, he holds a feast where an alleged witch and her brother are brought in. Edward forces her to dance as entertainment for his guests, then she is passed around and groped by the males present, her bodice ripped open as Edward laughs. When her panpipe-playing brother is murdered for additional entertainment, she grabs a carving knife and tries to stab Edward, but is shot dead by one of Edward's henchmen. Not all of his guests enjoy this lurid and gruesome spectacle; Edward's daughter Maureen leaves in disgust, while his wife (Edward's third) is silenced when she tries to protest. (A traumatized beauty, eventually driven to despair by her husband's treatment, she later has an Ophelia-like mad scene in front of the court.) But Edward's son Sean and many in his court (including an attendant called "Bullyboy") share his abusive ways. Indeed, for Sean, witch-hunting is nothing more an excuse to rape and humiliate women.

The repressive violence unleashed by Lord Edward on villagers and especially on Oona's coven provokes retaliation and transforms the nature of the "old religion." Oona's emphasis on "peace and love" sets her followers up to be victims; many are brutally killed by Edward's men. She and her followers turn to "Lord Satan" for help. Via black magic (witch-dolls, conjuration, and graveyard artifacts) she curses Edward's entire family and proceeds to destroy them. Her agent of revenge is Roderick, a young man who is also the lover of Maureen, Edward's daughter. Oona's magic transforms Roderick into a "sidhe" (i.e., the banshee of the title), a werewolf-like figure with superhuman strength. Technically, he is the film's other monster. One by one he kills off members of Edward's family, even Maureen and her younger brother Harry, a university boy with liberal views. In the final scene, Lord Edward discovers their bodies, as Roderick drives him away in a black coach to his death.

Cry of the Banshee, then, in most ways reverses the emphasis of *Witchcraft*. The credits bring out the ostensibly progressive, if heavy-handed, parallels to the present, terming Lord Edward's family "the Establishment" and setting them apart from the "Witches" and "Villagers." The film all too obviously can be read as a critique of state power and patriarchal authority, and seems to be wholeheartedly on the side of Oona's coven, even when it turns to Satan-worshipping, a necessary tactic in the light of Edward's persecution. It is also on the side of Maureen and Harry when they question or resist their father's tyrannical authority. True, Oona's revenge goes too far when even these more sympathetic members of Edward's family must die, striking a note of dissonance. But when Oona herself is killed, she tells her "children" to "scatter to the hills and find back the ways of peace and love." The "old religion" will survive and learn from its mistakes.

Nevertheless, *Cry of the Banshee* ultimately sends a strongly mixed message. The "monster" Edward is the most vital, dynamic presence in the film, and the camera regularly adopts the point of view of Edward, his rapist son Sean, and Bullyboy, drawing the audience into the soft-core porn of many scenes. In one, Sean rapes his father's wife and she starts to enjoy it when he starts to perform oral sex. In several others, witches are interrogated and tortured while having their clothes ripped off and their breasts exposed, and several are killed after the men have had their way with them. The film offers some less offensive eroticism: Roderick and Maureen, for example, are equal partners in their lovemaking and Roderick's partly nude body briefly is presented to the female gaze. The coven's group sex scene is sensual, egalitarian, nonmonogamous, and occasionally bisexual. Yet it also seems rather silly—their rituals are made to seem too sweet, too "vanilla," and it is not until Edward's men burst on horseback and drag a few naked bodies through the mud that the scene really becomes a fraught, sexualized spectacle.

Thus, this film rewrites Renaissance witch-hunting in sharply ambivalent ways. Like *Witchcraft* and other films about early modern witches, it is doubly monstered and explores our imaginative engagements with both witches and witch-hunters. Yet here this tension is pushed to the point of outright contradiction. From one perspective, the audience is invited to side with the hippie-coven, its more egalitarian and polymorphous sensuality, and its matriarchal form of organization. Yet the visual impact of the film remains deeply aligned with phallocentric fantasy, inviting us to revel in the unrestrained voyeurism and sexualized violence of the patriarchal males. The return of the repressed here is the return of an identification with the sadistic father of the primal scene. For a feminist audience, the deaths of Sean, Bullyboy, and finally Edward himself cannot come too soon.

Of course, in 1970, the year that *Cry of the Banshee* was released, the women's movement was only beginning to emerge as a major force for change. It is not surprising, then, that this film—like others of the late sixties and early seventies—cannot resolve the tension between its pronounced antiauthoritarianism and its retrograde gender politics. Ambivalent about rejecting the sadistic father, filmmakers and audiences were not quite ready to set up shop with the victim-vigilante mother and her seemingly unappeasable desires. Hence the ongoing attraction of the double-edged potential in stories about early modern witches and witch-hunters. To varying degrees, horror films of the late sixties and early seventies use such stories to locate the monstrous in contemporary power relations and especially the patriarchal family, while exploring, through the idea of the devil-worshipping witch and her coven, a variety of alternative forms of social organization. Such alternatives, these films suggest, sometimes come with a monstrousness more grotesquely comic than truly dangerous or liberating.

Notes

1. *The Monstrous-Feminine: Film, Feminism, Psychoanalysis* (London and New York: Routledge, 1993). For Creed's discussion of this film, see 76–77.
2. Historians consider the idea of the demonic pact, the black Sabbath, and the coven to be the special contribution of late medieval and early modern European writers to witch beliefs. See, among others, Brian Levack, *The Witch-Hunt in Early Modern Europe*, 3rd ed. (Harlow, England: Pearson Longman, 2006), 51–61.
3. See Ronald Hutton, *Triumph of the Moon: A History of Modern Pagan Witchcraft* (Oxford: Oxford UP, 1999), 241–71 .
4. See, for example, Marion Gibson's discussion of American witch films in *Witchcraft Myths in American Culture* (New York: Routledge, 2007).
5. I do not mean that no witch films existed before 1960. However, the witch tended to belong to the realm of comedy—*I Married a Witch* (1942), *Bell, Book and Candle* (1958)—or children's films—*The Wizard of Oz* (1939), *Sleeping Beauty* (1959).
6. Cf. Creed, 73. For other studies of the witch in horror films, see Sharon Russell, "The Witch in Film: Myth and Reality," in *Planks of Reason: Essays on the Horror Film*, ed. Barry Keith Grant and Christopher Sharrett (Lanham, MD: Scarecrow Press, 2004), 63–71; and Leon Hunt, "Necromancy in the UK: Witchcraft and the Occult in British Horror," in *British Horror Cinema*, ed. Steve Chibnall and Julian Petley (London and New York: Routledge, 2002), 82–98.
7. American films are more likely to reference Salem than European witch-hunting. Though the term "early modern" could be stretched to include them, for reasons of space I do not discuss them here.
8. Nikolas Schreck, *The Satanic Screen: An Illustrated Guide To the Devil in Cinema* (London: Creation Books, 2001), 111.
9. British censorship severely limited sex and violence in films of this period. See Mark Kermode, "The British Censors and Horror Cinema," in *British Horror Cinema*, 10–22.
10. *The Manchurian Candidate* was released only two years earlier, in 1962. Note also that the novelist Dennis Wheatley, whose books about black magic and devil-worshipping covens were an inspiration for a number of horror films in this period, literally considered Communism to be linked to Satanism (*Triumph of the Moon*, 265).
11. If this sounds far-fetched, consider the opening scene of *The Witches*, released the following year: a British anthropologist in Africa is run out of her post in the jungle by an anticolonialist uprising led by voodoo-practicing witch-doctors, only to find a coven of witches in the small English village where she ends up. A local journalist (who turns out to be coven's high priestess) comments, "I think African voodoo and our old English tradition of witchcraft have a lot in common, don't you?"

CHAPTER 7

"Sportful Combat" Gets Medieval: The Representation of Historical Violence at Renaissance Fairs

Kevin J. Wetmore, Jr.

It's just someone's idea of the English middle ages crossed with Disneyland…It's all bollocks! You should spray 'em all with shit as they come through the gates. No lice. No nits. No rotting face cancers. When was the last time you saw someone with a bloody great tumor hanging off their face?
—Neil Gaiman, *The Sandman: The Wake*

The Living History Center (LHC) Renaissance Faire website describes the "Ren Faire" as "an amalgam of many things: it is partly a craft fair, it's partly historical re-enactment, it's partly performance art."[1] There are over two hundred Renaissance Faires in the United States alone and many more outside the United States in Europe and Australia, many of which embody the LHC definition. These three aspects are equally important: the Faire is a capitalistic venture in which one may buy and sell artifacts, clothing, food and other items; a "historical" recreation of Renaissance culture; and a theatrical event.

In this chapter, I briefly explore American Renaissance Faires as sites of contested historic "recreation" in the larger context of "representing" the Renaissance. I consider the representation of period violence, both in contemporary practice at Ren Faires and historic practice during the Renaissance.

Lastly, I examine how contemporary misrepresentation of medieval violence as Renaissance practice is actually an echo of the Elizabethan performance practice of representing historical combat nostalgically on stage and at public fairs; most Renaissance Faire combat is not renaissance but medieval in nature. Contemporary American Ren Faires are simultaneously imitative of the form and bases of actual fairs and completely uninterested in being faithful to the original. Instead, what is offered at most Faires is an idealized, romanticized conflation of popular culture and a fantasy of escapism that hinges simultaneously on acknowledgement of and freedom from historical accuracy. The jousting, period weapons, and sportive combat all celebrate a culture of chivalry that was already anachronistic by the Renaissance, and that the English themselves were already staging nostalgically by the reign of Elizabeth.

The Ren Faire is a site of contested meanings and values in which numerous histories and cultures are conflated in the name of historical authenticity. However, what is ultimately represented is the "Renaissance" as contemporary American culture, in which a variety of "Renaissances" are unified through representations of chivalry, combat, and period violence. As I shall note below, the contemporary Ren Faire owes as much to popular fantasy narratives (*Lord of the Rings*, *Pirates of the Caribbean*, and *World of Warcraft*, for example), Shakespeare, and American history as it does to any historical account of the Renaissance, as symbolized by the ever-present figure of the knight (or rogue) and his weapons. We might consider the Ren faire as part of the larger culture that Barbara Hodgdon refers to as "the Shakespeare trade," relying upon a forged Anglo-American identity, detached from historical context and reinvented as embodying the values of contemporary America (commerce, individuality, exploration, and the concept of the middle class as a new nobility).[2] Unlike the sites connected specifically to the Shakespeare trade in England, Canada, and the United States, the Ren Faire does not suffer an anxiety of authenticity since there is no claim to represent what actually existed on the geographic location of the Faire during the historic period of the Renaissance. In America the Ren Faire systematically detaches itself from historic context and roots itself in local and individual history rather than linking to a claimed authentic site of cultural heritage, by claiming a general idyllic past to which one can return by visiting the site.

In terms of Ren Faires as "historic re-enactment," let us begin by considering what, exactly, is meant by the "Renaissance" in Ren Faire. The term is used as a catchall that paradoxically limits and expands the definition of "Renaissance." In general, Faires limit the Renaissance to the popular (read: clichéd) image of early to late sixteenth-century England. Not d'Medici

Italy, *siglo de oro* Spain, or a France conflicted by religious wars but, instead, Elizabethan England. In the United States, Ren Faire performers affect a pop culture version of a British accent, parody English culture (offering turkey legs and mutton for sale, for example), perform English music, and frequently trade upon the name of Shakespeare. Costume, in many ways the heart of the Ren Faire, is often (though not always) based upon English fashion, not French, Spanish, or Italian. In fact, when the costume is from somewhere other than England, its entire purpose is to establish difference from the normative Englishness of American Ren Faires. In other words, individual performers will purposefully dress as Spaniards or Moors to distinguish themselves from the majority of Fairegoers or participants. Non-Englishness becomes a visible marker of difference precisely because of the dominance of English costume.

Some Faires, such as the Pennsylvania Renaissance Faire in Manheim, Pennsylvania, not only proclaim their English setting but are set in a specific year during the English Renaissance. In 2007, for example, the Faire, which runs on weekends from August through October, was set in 1601 and designed to highlight the nature of the queen's final years on the throne.[3] In previous years it has been set in 1570, 1558, and 1590, evoking a younger monarch and a different period of English history. Other Faires, however, define the period much more vaguely, suggesting only a kind of transhistorical English Renaissance. In short, American Ren Faires are more accurately English Renaissance Faires.

As mentioned earlier, many Faires enlarge our traditional definitions of the Renaissance by conflating it with other periods, times, and places, some of which have never existed outside of cinema, Disneyland, or a *Dungeons and Dragons* game. "Celtic" history, Viking history, pirates, and "Shakespeare" all are encompassed by some Faires. Medieval culture and technologies also overlap with the "Renaissance" at many Faires. Or, alternately, the Faire combines the Renaissance with current popular culture. The advent of the *Lord of the Rings* films (2001–2003) at the beginning of this decade resulted in many Faires featuring scenarios and characters from Middle Earth. The summer of 2007 featured numerous "Jack Sparrow"s (from Disney's *Pirates of the Caribbean* [2003]) and a renewed interest in pirates in general. Thus, it is quite possible to encounter both Queen Elizabeth I and a Johnny Depp look-alike in the same Renaissance "historic recreation," as "history" is not as important as the commerce aspect of the Faire, and Captain Jack Sparrow can claim as much legitimacy in shaping the experience of "English history" as popular versions of Elizabeth I, linked as they are through mass media.

What Douglas Lanier says of Shakespeare in popular culture is, I believe, equally valid about the contemporary Ren Faire: both offer a fantasy of historical presence, bridging the gap between modern America and an imagined and romanticized past, "a symbolic alternative to—and thus potentially a critique of—the alienation and fragmentation characteristic of postmodern life."[4] Over and above the critique such fairs potentially offer, Ren Faires are popular because of the opportunities they offer for escapism and role playing. For example, the geeky kid in high school becomes Lord Simon of Blackpool; the retail clerk by weekday becomes Sir Gawain or Lady Marwyn for the weekend Faire. One might note a much higher percentage of aristocracy and peerage at Ren Faires as opposed to actual Renaissance England. Very few choose to be peasants, unless the peasant is played comically.

The actual construction of the Renaissance at a Faire is shaped by media expectations for and popular representations of the Renaissance far more than by the actual history. Linked to such a construction is the idea that everyone in the Renaissance carried a sword and fought duels and followed a code of chivalry. Renaissance culture is a culture of violence, as represented at Faires. In short, the Ren Faire tends to romanticize the Renaissance, as the quotation from Neil Gaiman's graphic novel in the epigraph demonstrates, with a focus on the weapons and their use. I know of no Renaissance Faire with an "experience the black plague" event. I know plenty where you can witness and even experience Renaissance combat. One may buy period weapons or pay for the experience of firing a real crossbow or watching knights joust. While the Ren Faire tends toward a lack of historical realism, the aspect of Renaissance culture that forms a locus for the Faire is the depiction of period combat. Ironically, as will be argued below, realism is sacrificed even in the violence, but a pretense of accuracy is made in terms of combat.

As the definition that began this essay suggests, Ren Faires are first and foremost craft fairs—in other words, a capitalist exercise. Although some Ren Faires, such as the Alabama Renaissance Faire, are free of charge to attendees, most require admission fees—from $18 at the Arizona Renaissance Faire, to $25 at the Renaissance Pleasure Faire in Irwindale, California, to as much as $50 at *12th Night in San Diego*, an actual Renaissance-style Twelfth Night celebration held annually each January; the average admission fee is between ten and twelve dollars.[5] At the Faires, one of the largest draws is the number of merchandise booths. One may purchase "period" clothing, food, weapons, crafts, jewelry, books, and numerous other Renaissance, medieval, and fantasy-related items. One might note that in its listing of "Faires and Festivals," *Renaissance Magazine*, the bimonthly publication dedicated to Faire culture, lists the number of sales booths at each Faire before the attendance numbers, weapons policies, and information regarding camping accommodations.

Ren Faires are actually on very solid historical recreation ground by making a key focus the purchase of Renaissance-related goods. As Evelyn Welch writes in her study of fairs during the Renaissance, "fairs were supposed to be special events, times outside of the banality of the everyday," in which citizens could spectate at shows of skill, artistry, and danger, as well as purchase goods not available every day.[6] Likewise, Marina Belozerskaya notes that markets and fairs were places of cultural display and international commerce. They "provided opportunities for producers, traders, and customers from all over Europe to sell and purchase goods that could not be obtained at home."[7] Change the word "Europe" to "California," "Texas," "Pennsylvania," or "Iowa," and Belozerskaya is describing the contemporary American Ren Faire as well. So in the sense that Ren Faires recreate the mercantile basis of the historic Renaissance fair, they *are* historically accurate.

As noted above, spectacle is also essential to both historic and contemporary fairs. Central in the contemporary Ren Faire experience is the recreation of period violence: matches with living chessmen, jousts, comic combat, duels of honor, and performances of violence and brawls are offered up as "historical re-enactments" of "life back then." Paradoxically, while much of the staged violence at Ren Faires is not historically accurate, the practice of conflating centuries of martial practice both to entertain and to present history live to an audience finds strong precedence in the English Renaissance.

Such anachronistic violence is crucial to the marketing of a fantasy Renaissance to the general American public. One might well ask why period violence has such an important place in the recreation of the Renaissance when religion, nationalism, and other markers of the Renaissance are so visibly absent. I wish to argue that the symbolically central display and use of premodern weapons is the most visible marker of the creation of a historic past. Whereas fancy dress, the presence of horses, and the sale of strange food are emblematic of many experiences, including contemporary ones, the appearance of a sword hanging at one's side is the embodiment of a specific vanished past. In the popular imagination, broadswords and rapiers are markers of the Renaissance in the same manner that a samurai sword is a synecdoche for Tokugawa Japan or a gladius is a synecdoche for the gladiators of Rome. The Renaissance sword stands for chivalry. The sword is also a marker of swashbuckling, combat, and adventure. Swords, in a word, are "cool" because they hinge upon fantasies of a less restrained time, one in which the suppression of natural instincts has not been fully enforced. The sword is nostalgia and wish fulfillment combined in a single piece of material culture. From the lightsaber of the *Star Wars* films to the swords of films such as *Blade, Highlander,* or *Hellboy II,* in which contemporary characters eschew firearms in favor of blades, the sword requires skill and elegance, and shows itself more effective than the gun. The sword can become a physical form of contact with the past. To hold and use a sword at a Faire is to connect nostalgically with what we perceive as the best of the period, rather than physically experiencing, say, the as-real but fundamentally negative health experiences of the Renaissance. We might enjoy seeing others, either through historical display or character performance, experience plague and lice, but we ourselves have no wish to experience these things in the same manner that we wish for a direct experience of using a sword.

There are two variations of combat at Ren Fairs. The first is "sport" or "contest" combat, involving individuals or teams of trained combatants who engage primarily in jousting—horse mounted combat in which riders race toward each other at a high rate of speed and attempt to unhorse one another with lances. The riders wear armor and their lances are much safer than historical lances since they are made of lighter woods. In some cases, unhorsed riders may continue with the combat via swords or other hand weapons with dull blades.[8]

This type of combat usually occurs within a highly trained, legally incorporated company of performers, who are organized hierarchically with a king, knights defined according to rank, and squires. For example, Noble Cause Productions, which performs at the Colorado Renaissance Company, is ruled (and run) by Bryan Beard, who goes by the stage name "Sir William, Lord of Whitehall." He oversees training, arranges the schedule of performances and matches, and also competes with his own men at the joust. The horses are specially trained for jousting, and there always exists the possibility of injury. Within the companies, the performers genuinely compete with one another during jousts. There are rules that must be followed, and the code of chivalry is often invoked as a guide of behavior.[9]

Jousting as sportive combat is so linked with Ren Faires that the primary image in many Ren Faire adverts is the jouster, or the armor-clad, horse-riding knight with lance in hand racing toward his opponent. The significance of the joust as a central part of the Ren Faire cannot be overstated, and yet the irony is that jousting is by and large a medieval practice. The primary sportive combat at Ren Faires does not actually originate in the Renaissance, but instead in an earlier period. The deeper irony, however, is that by conflating the Renaissance with the Middle Ages in terms of spectacle, the performers are echoing, however inadvertently, the Renaissance practice of representing medieval combat for entertainment.

In *Brawl Ridiculous: Swordfighting in Shakespeare's Plays*, Charles Edelman identifies the tradition of representing violence on the English Renaissance stage as "Elizabethan neo-medievalism."[10] The battles and violence of the stages of the English Renaissance were, for the most part, not depictions of contemporary combat practice, but rather a historical presentation of medieval war. While Elizabethan actors wore and used rapiers in their everyday life (indeed, Ben Jonson and Kit Marlowe got in trouble for publicly dueling with theirs, and Richard Tarleton, in addition to being a celebrated clown, was a celebrated "Master of Defence"), most of Shakespeare's plays feature combat with broadswords and shields—medieval combat, in other words. Medieval swords are much wider and thicker than Renaissance swords. The English longsword and the bastard sword (so called because it was not quite a one-handed sword and not quite a two-handed sword and thus designed to be used as both but was not particularly effective as either) were used in the fourteenth, fifteenth, and early sixteenth centuries. By Shakespeare's time, however, the Italian rapier had been naturalized for everyday wear and use. This transition is documented in one of Shakespeare's only two plays about contemporary fighting: *Romeo and Juliet*.[11] In this play, members of the younger generation—Romeo, Mercutio, Tybalt, and Paris—fight with rapiers and use the terminology of contemporary dueling schools, while the older generation, represented by Capulet, calls for "my long sword, ho!" (1.1.73).

The representation of medieval battle was both historical recreation and epic staging *reductio ad absurdum*. Philip Sydney writes of the experience of watching combat in history plays in their original Elizabethan context in *Defence of Poesie* (c. 1583), observing, "…while in the meanetime two armies flie in, represented with four swords & bucklers, and then what hard hart will not receive it for a pitched field…"[12] On the Renaissance stage, historical combat conflated several centuries of martial practice, was represented by a reduced and emblematic number of combatants, and offered anachronistic violence as popular spectacle. In other words, the English Renaissance theatre was the original Society for Creative Anachronism—historical violence presented in the history plays for the pleasure of a paying audience. Ren Faires do virtually the same thing: they present recreations of historical violence for entertainment and for "history," conflating many periods into one as popular spectacle and narrative.

The second type of staged violence at Ren Faires, street dueling, is much closer to representative, or quotidian, Renaissance combat. These are staged shows (or staged encounters in the "streets") in which performers fight one another as part of a larger story. This type of combat is not sportful, it is, in fact, most often choreographed. This type of combat also usually involves Renaissance weapons, such as rapier and dagger or quarterstaff. This type of staged violence most often takes the form of staged shows involving Renaissance characters, such as traveling brawlers "Dirk and Guido

The Swordsmen," best known for "Stupid Sword Tricks," or Colorado Renaissance Faire's "Puke and Snot" who stage comic fights using rapier and dagger, or "Shattuck," a performance collective who stage a variety of fights and scenes between a variety of multicultural Renaissance characters at the Iowa Renaissance Faire. Unlike the jousters, who embrace medieval culture as a form of sport and competition, the performers of stage dueling use much faster weapons in choreographed fights. One does not know who will win a joust. All the performers already know who will win a duel, as the scenario and choreography are mapped out prior to the performance.

There is a third type of anachronistic violence at Ren Faires, which is a combination of the first two, best represented by the "Living Chess Match." Two performers sit on opposite sides of a giant chess board, and the chessmen are enacted by other performers. The players call out their "moves," and the performers representing the pieces then "fight," with the captured piece eventually losing the combat. Although the fights are less random and sportive than the joust, they are also more random and less choreographed than the stage shows. One piece does not simply replace another when taken on the giant chess board; the actual taking of a piece is a fight between the two performers. "Knights" carry swords, "bishops" have maces, "pawns" often carry staves, and thus the combative aspects of both chess and medieval/Renaissance battle is reinforced. This practice of a chess game played with living pieces also comes from the Renaissance and has been represented in one form on stage in Middleton's *A Game at Chess* (1624), in which the chessmen and the game form an allegory for the continuing intrigues between England (the white pieces, so the white king is James I) and Spain (the black pieces, so that Philip IV is the black king) over the proposed marriage between the English Prince Charles and the Spanish Princess Maria, which never came to pass.

Given these variations on combat at Ren Faires, we might note that even the staged fights with period-accurate weapons are not entirely accurate. Missing from the Ren Faire is the gun, which was already a regular part of Renaissance martial culture. By 1327, *pots de fer* that used an early form of gunpowder to fire bolts were in use in the Hundred Years War. The English were using small guns by the Battle of Crecy in 1346, Henry V used canon and artillery at the siege of Harfleur in 1414 (and depicted on stage by Shakespeare, albeit without firearms), and James II of Scotland died in a firearms accident in 1460.[13] Francis Bacon, writing in 1620, places gunpowder alongside the printing press and the compass as the three inventions that "changed the appearance and state of the whole world" in history.[14] If one is to be historically accurate about Renaissance combat, firearms were a part of combat and violence on a regular basis. Bert S. Hall notes that, by mid-sixteenth century, firearms spelt "the end of knighthood" as a partial presence in society and on the battlefield.[15] Wheel-lock pistols, harquebus, and cannon were part of the everyday reality of combat in Renaissance Europe, and Hall even argues that "a contest between swords and pistols was an unequal one,"[16] so much so that the sword was less an instrument of battle than an instrument of skill and personal combat by the Renaissance.

Even by the late Middle Ages, firearms were not only a presence but a key part of battle. I cite but a single example from many in Shakespeare: guns at the battle of Shrewsbury in *Henry IV, Part 1*. Falstaff tells Hal that the soldiers he has raised are "food for powder" (4.2.64–65), a reference to the fact that they are cannon fodder, whose purpose is to draw gunfire to protect the real combatants. Later, during the battle, Falstaff offers Hal his pistol when asked for his sword, although the "pistol" in Falstaff's case turns out to be a bottle of sack (5.3.50–52). The fact that Falstaff has both pistol and sword, and that Hal is willing to accept the latter demonstrates the accepted presence of firearms in both the Middle Ages at Shrewsbury and the later Elizabethan English knowledge and acceptance of that fact.

In fact, Shakespeare embodies this tension between "old school" combat with swords and the "new school" of firearms in the character of Ancient Pistol from *Henry IV, Part 2* and *Henry V*, who, by his very name and title draw attention to this opposition. When first introduced in *Henry IV, Part 2* he is identified repeatedly by his rank of "Ancient" (2.4.69, 109, 110), indicating military service, yet also indicating something old. He continually brandishes his sword, which he has named "Hiren" (2.4.159), and his bombast echoes (and in some cases parodies) plays about traditional warriors, such as *Tamburlaine* and Peele's *The Battle of Alcazar*. He sees and presents himself as a classical or medieval warrior/hero, but Falstaff continually jokes about his name ("No more, Pistol, I would not have you go off here. Discharge yourself of our company, Pistol" (2.4.136–37)), reminding the audience that he is no such thing. "Ancient Pistol" is a firearm that pretends to be a sword, thus dramatizing the tension between medieval combat and the transforming technologies of Renaissance warfare.

Renaissance drama thus romanticized medieval combat. As Greg Colón Semenza observes, "the decline of chivalry" was "directly linked to the development of guns."[17] New technologies created new strategies and tactics, thus transforming combat (or at least its perception) from individual feats of bravery by aristocrats to collective infantry using weaponry that required less training and easily overcame both armor and the physical skills of any opponent.[18] Firearms, while the great equalizer, also radically transformed warfare, making it, in Semenza's words, "less heroic" by the late sixteenth century.[19] Thus, in the plays of Shakespeare, such as the one cited above, the medieval practice of individual combat with swords was already being romanticized on stage, reflecting a reality that had not existed in real combat for decades.

Most Ren Faires do not include the historical reality of period firearms. The Ren Faire thus also romanticizes firearms out of the Renaissance, and even out of the Middle Ages, unless they are in the hands of pirates or "Jack Sparrow," celebrating a culture of chivalry that was already anachronistic by the Renaissance. Although jousting remained a form of popular entertainment during the Renaissance, it is primarily a medieval form, and was, in its Renaissance incarnation, a form of Elizabethan neo-medievalism, celebrating and romanticizing history, just as the Ren Faire does today. In the English Renaissance, jousting, fairs, and staging the Middle Ages were a form of identity, a form of escapism, and a celebration of the beginning of the empire. As John M. Ganim notes in *Medievalism and Orientalism*, as soon as the middle ages were over, they began to be romanticized and fantasized: "It is that foreign land in which we are always at home."[20] Medieval England becomes the mirror in which the Renaissance English saw themselves. Medieval/Renaissance England becomes the mirror by which "Progressive America" both "links medieval ideals with lost civic virtue" and escapes through a fantasy of history "filtered though the lenses of Tolkien, Disney...and even Las Vegas."[21] This absence of firearms transforms the Renaissance into part fantasy world, part neo-medieval anachronism, romanticizing and conflating several centuries of English history, popular culture, and an American sense of heroism and individual achievement. Or as one Fairegoer put it, "No guns in Middle Earth, man." And the "Middle Earth" he was referencing was a combination of Tolkien's books, Peter Jackson's films, and the epiphenomena surrounding the trilogy.

In this sense, at least, the contemporary Ren Faire is very much like the actual English Renaissance entertainments it references in that it offers anachronistic violence as spectacle. And like the entertainment it references, it is actually the medieval period that is most often represented in the guise of "sportful combat"—especially in the form of jousting. When rapiers are drawn, however, the combat moves from medieval to Renaissance, and also becomes much more choreographed. At heart, the Ren Faire, like the Renaissance fair, is a commercial enterprise that, in the words of Lanier, offers "the interplay between 'authentic' artifacts, reconstructed nostalgia, and projection of the present onto the past."[22] The authenticity of the artifacts and the practices is questionable at best, but the attendees do not mind, as they are there to escape and enjoy, not have a history lesson. The projection of the present on the past includes an erasure of the ugly and negative aspects of Renaissance culture, as noted in the epigraph above. Plague, tumors, virulent nationalism, lack of sanitation, public torture, and religious conflict are erased and nullified, replaced with romanticized combat, a sanitation staff, complimentary parking, and good food—a Renaissance that is "just like now," just without electricity and with funny accents.

Even the Faires that are historically inclined, or linked to Shakespeare festivals, are no longer concerned with representing the Renaissance accurately. The bottom line is, of course, the bottom line. Faires that used to be operated by the not-for-profit Living History Center, for example, were bought out in 1995 by for-profit Renaissance Entertainment Corporation, which grossed $10.5 million that year alone, $625,000 of which was profit.[23] The shift reveals that Ren Faires are now truly like Renaissance fairs, filling coffers while offering the commoners nostalgic recreations of things that never were. In doing so, they offer an opportunity to contact and experience the past, but a safe, Hollywood-inspired, fantasy past.

The Faire is a critique of postmodern life, but a safe critique that allows us to maintain all of the safe, convenient, and technological aspects of contemporary America. One can have one's Renaissance cake and eat it in the modern era, too. The experience, relying as it does on anachronistic and ahistorical combat practices, reimagines contemporary America as fantasy Renaissance, privileging the middle class as a new nobility and conflating chivalry, commerce, and entertainment. In doing so, it does not recreate a historically accurate Renaissance experience, but, ironically, the practice of not doing so is itself a Renaissance one.

Notes

1. "Renaissance Faire Overview," *Renaissance Faire Homepage*, posted May 1999. Accessed January 9, 2007. http://www.renfaire.com/General/faire.html. See also the list provided by *Renaissance Magazine* at http://www.renaissancemagazine. com/fairelist.htm., which includes 226 faires at the time of writing.
2. Barbara Hodgdon, *The Shakespeare Trade: Performances and Appropriations* (Philadelphia: U of Pennsylvania P, 1998), xi.
3. See http://www.parenaissancefaire.com/. Accessed March 6, 2007.
4. Douglas Lanier, *Shakespeare and Modern Popular Culture* (Oxford: Oxford UP, 2002), 145.
5. Admission costs taken from http://www.renaissancemagazine.com/fairelist.htm. Accessed March 6, 2007.
6. Evelyn S. Welsh, *Shopping in the Renaissance: Consumer Cultures in Italy, 1400–1600* (New Haven: Yale UP, 2005), 167.
7. Marina Belozerskaya, *Rethinking the Renaissance: Burgundian Arts across Europe* (Cambridge: Cambridge UP, 2002), 230.
8. This type of combat is documented in the DVD documentary *American Jouster*.

9. Information on jousting and Noble Cause Productions is taken primarily from *American Jouster*. DVD. Dir. Richard P. Alvarez. Pierrot Films. 2005.

10. Charles Edelman, *Brawl Ridiculous: Swordfighting in Shakespeare's Plays* (Manchester: Manchester UP, 1992), 38.

11. The other is *Hamlet*, which, though it is set in Denmark during the middle ages, demonstrates contemporary dueling culture in the final act. See Edelman, 173.

12. Philip Sidney, *The Defense of Poesy* (Boston: Ginn and Company, 1890), 48.

13. Ewart Oakeshott, *A Knight and His Weapons*, 2nd edition (Chester Springs, PA: Dufour, 1964 [1997]), 96, 97, 99, 101.

14. Francis Bacon, *Francis Bacon: A Selection of His Writings* (Toronto: Macmillan, 1965), 373–74.

15. Bert S. Hall, *Weapons and Warfare in Renaissance Europe* (Baltimore: Johns Hopkins UP, 1997), 190.

16. Ibid., 196.

17. Gregory M. Colón Semenza, *Sport, Politics and Literature in the English Renaissance* (Newark: U of Delaware P, 2003), 72. See also Henry J. Webb, *Elizabethan Military Science: The Books and Practice* (Madison: U of Wisconsin P, 1965), and J.R. Hale, *War and Society in Renaissance Europe, 1450–1620* (New York: St. Martin's Press, 1985) for further information on the transformative effect of firearms on the culture of chivalry and medieval and Renaissance warfare.

18. See Semenza, 41–42.

19. Ibid., 72.

20. John M. Ganim, *Medievalism and Orientalism* (New York: Palgrave, 2005), 104.

21. Ibid., 9, 5.

22. Lanier, 46.

23. Todd White, "All's Fair: Renaissance a Crowd-Pleaser," *Variety* (October 9, 1995), 80.

PART III

Renaissance Sounds

The First Adaptation of Shakespeare and the Recovery of the "Renaissance" Voice: Sam Taylor's *The Taming of the Shrew*

Deborah Cartmell

There's remarkably little critical attention given to the coming of sound in the first mainstream Shakespeare "talkie," Sam Taylor's *The Taming of the Shrew* (1929). While clearly chosen as a star vehicle for the most famous couple of the silent period, Mary Pickford and Douglas Fairbanks, as a play ultimately concerned with the silencing of a woman, it can be regarded as both a peculiar and appropriate choice for the first mainstream film to give Shakespeare back (some of) his words. This chapter contextualizes the film within debates about sound versus silent cinema, a debate in which cries for fidelity from publicists and journalists become "louder" than ever before; in this sense, the representation of Shakespeare and the Renaissance is in the spoken words. The fetishization of the period through its language becomes the unique selling point of the film in its publicity materials, a feature that bestows upon this adaptation, and its successors, its popularity, or, in other words, a low rather than high cultural status.

Film criticism and popular journalism were very much at odds in their attitudes to adaptations. In this brief period from the end of the 1920s to the beginning of the 1930s, sound, on the whole, was regarded as the enemy of film. Talking adaptations, especially talking Shakespeare films, were ineligible as "art," regarded by cineastes and literary scholars as intellectually undemanding, blatantly popularizing the Shakespearean narrative. However, for the popular press, sound didn't just enhance an adaptation, it constituted one. The pressbook for *The Taming of the Shrew* makes it clear that sound enables theatrical and literary works to be adapted *for the first time*, revealing a seemingly uncontested view that an adaptation cannot be an adaptation without the words that it is based on.

A reasonable assumption today is that the coming of sound, the bringing "back" of Shakespeare's words, would have been welcome to Shakespeare critics and film reviewers, but, on the whole, it was greeted in the late 1920s early 1930s with fear and loathing. Concerns that film was being thrown back to its theatrical origins and that the talking film would be a much inferior version of both film and theater were highly prevalent. One of the sound film's more famous opponents was Aldous Huxley, who outspokenly attacked the talkies in his journalism as well as in his novel *Brave New World* (1932). While inviting comparisons with Shakespeare's *Tempest* in its title, Huxley's novel savages film adaptation of Shakespeare through "the feelies" (a thinly veiled version of the recently introduced "talkies"); *Othello* becomes debased and unrecognizable as *Three Weeks in a Helicopter*, "AN ALL-SUPER-SINGING, SYNTHETIC-TALKING, COLOURED, STEREOSCOPIC FEELY. WITH SYNCHRONIZED SCENT-ORGAN ACCOMPANIMENT."[1] As the only mainstream Shakespeare talkie available at the time in which Huxley was writing, it's possible that it is Taylor's *Shrew* that's being satirized here. The repulsively seductive and debasing experience caused by this adaptation echoes Aldous Huxley's disgust, followed by self-loathing upon experiencing *The Jazz Singer* ("I felt ashamed of myself for listening to such things, for even being a member of the species to which such things are addressed").[2] In spite of his initial repugnance to "the talkies," Huxley eventually warmed to the art of screenwriting, even settling down in Hollywood and adapting, with some pride, the likes of Jane Austen.[3]

It's hard to imagine why someone would feel so offended by the advent of the sound film, but Huxley wasn't alone in his initial abhorrence of the talkies. The use of sound, words in particular, made an adaptation more "literary" or "theatrical" and therefore less "filmic." Hard-line opponents of sound were largely those who campaigned for cinema to be regarded as art, and were concerned that sound would both throw film back to a dependence on theater and would be used for commercial rather than artistic reasons. In 1929, cultural commentator Gilbert Seldes (*An Hour with the Movies and the Talkies*) distinguished between "movies" and "talkies," the latter often "a chaos distasteful to the orderly mind."[4] In the same year, in "The Art of Sound," René Clair complained that:

> Although the talkies are still in their first, experimental stage, they have already, surprisingly enough, produced stereotyped patterns. We have barely "heard" about two dozen of these films, and yet we already feel that the sound effects are hackneyed and that it is high time to find new ones. Jazz, stirring songs, the ticking of a clock, a cuckoo singing the hours, dance-hall applause, a motorcar engine, or breaking crockery— all these are no doubt very nice, but become somewhat tiresome after we have heard them a dozen times in a dozen different films.[5]

In 1931, film critic Paul Rotha in *Celluloid: The Film Today* divided films into two categories, one good, one bad: "Cinematography to-day seems to be distinguished by parallel courses of development. On the one hand, there is the cinema proper, compounded from the elements of the medium, discovered and built up by the Russians up till the beginning of the dialogue era; whilst on the other, there is the vast output of ordinary narrative talking films of sensational interest that occupies the capitalist studio organizations of Western Europe and America."[6] The talking narrative film was not allowed entrance into "cinema proper" and was regarded in this transitional period as "impure cinema" in its double reliance on literature and theater. Expanding on his essay in the inaugural issue of F.R. Leavis' *Scrutiny*, William Hunter identified the sound film as addictively infantilizing while mourning the loss of "the efficacy of words." The film, in particular the talkie, was effectively banned from any serious literary journal, having no part to play in the Leavisite "great tradition."[7] Hunter's attack on the narrative talking film, significantly, in the first volume of *Scrutiny*, perhaps reveals a latent anxiety among literary scholars that there may be something like "Adaptation Studies" looming on the horizon, something that clearly needs to be nipped in the bud.

Not all literary critics saw the talkie as parasitic and patronizing. In 1936, Renaissance scholar Allardyce Nicoll optimistically saw film not just as the new Literature but as "the new Shakespeare," and in sound saw new possibilities for cinema. Nicoll went so far to pronounce, astonishingly given so much hostility to adaptations in this period, that Shakespeare can be more "Shakespearean" in the cinema than on the stage:

> Critics have complained that in the film nothing is left to the imagination, but we must remember that in the Shakespearean verse is a quality which, because of changed conditions, we may find difficulty

in appreciating. Its strangeness to us demands that an attempt be made to render it more intelligible and directly appealing. Such an attempt, through the means of expression granted to the cinema, may merely be supplying something which will bring us nearer to the conditions of the original spectators for whom Shakespeare wrote.[8]

For Nicoll, cinema, especially, the "talkie," potentially offers a window into the past, in the uncertain age of modernity, a vehicle for a return to an "authentic" version of the Renaissance. At the time, Nicoll, as an academic, was in a minority in his defense of the talking picture, indeed of the Shakespeare adaptation. The bringing of words to Shakespeare films occurred within a climate in which both adaptations and talkies were met with scorn from literary and film critics alike. This was impure cinema: too popular, too commercial, and too dependent upon literature and theatrical traditions to be of any value as "art."

Huxley is not alone in identifying Shakespeare "talkies" as implicitly the most despicable of all film adaptations. As Neil Forsyth has recently argued, so too did art historian Erwin Panofsky in the much discussed essay, "Style and Medium in the Moving Pictures" (revised version published in 1947). Panofsky, like Nicoll, singled out the Reinhardt-Dieterle film of *A Midsummer Night's Dream* (1935), condemned as "the most unfortunate film ever produced" as falling victim to the pitfalls of the "talkies" in its overreliance on theatrical rather than filmic traditions.[9] His argument seems to be that the more poetic a character is, the worse the film: "It is certainly terrible when a soft-boiled he-man, after the suicide of his mistress, casts a twelve-foot glance upon her photograph and says something less-than-coexpressible to the effect that he will never forget her. But when he recites, instead, a piece of poetry as sublimely more-than-coexpressible as Romeo's monologue at the bier of Juliet, it is still worse."[10] Rather than provide film with artistic kudos, the use of Shakespeare's language (and by implication, that of other canonical writers) is seen not to uplift (as has often been argued), but to devalue cinema. Curiously, there's little, if no mention of an earlier film in academic debates on the talkie adaptation. Sam Taylor's *Taming of the Shrew* (1929) is the first feature-length Shakespeare "talkie"[11] and as such deserves a very special place within the canon of Shakespeare on screen.

Although receiving some critical attention in recent years, the film has been overshadowed by the Reinhardt-Dieterle film of 1935, and it has not been read in relation to its use of sound, a peculiarity given the context in which it was produced. The film was immediately notorious due to its infamous credit line, "by William Shakespeare with additional dialogue by Samuel Taylor," and, possibly, for this reason, largely overlooked in

Shakespeare on film scholarship. Roger Manvell, in *Shakespeare & the Film* (1971), devotes only two and a half pages to it, citing anecdotal evidence of the film's designer, Laurence Irving's (son of the famous Henry Irving) attempts to persuade Taylor not to make himself a laughingstock by adopting the credit.[12] While the film is still best known for its credit line, there is no evidence that it was ever used and close scrutiny of the film reveals only a few "additional" lines.[13] Samuel Crowl gives it short shrift in his recent survey of Shakespeare on screen preferring like those before him to concentrate on the 1935 *Midsummer Night's Dream*.[14] The little work that has been done on Taylor's film focuses unsurprisingly on gender. Russell Jackson has argued that Mary Pickford's wink to Bianca at the end of her lecture on wifely obedience brings Katherine into the twentieth century, making Petruchio the one who is duped.[15] Barbara Hodgdon, on the other hand, sees Katherine's momentary triumph allayed by the alleged cruel treatment of her by her costar (her husband, Douglas Fairbanks) while on set and in the final moments when Petruchio "stops her mouth" (to paraphrase from *Much Ado*) with a final forced kiss.[16] Diana E. Henderson is somewhere in the middle in her reading; Katherine becomes "the sneaky servant rather than the Stepford wife of patriarchy."[17] Taylor uses leading actors Mary Pickford and Douglas Fairbanks in the title roles for the first time together. Undeniably a star vehicle, the film can be seen to voyeuristically expose and exploit their well-known relationship (which, unknown to the audience, was troubled at the time of shooting). The actors' success in the silent period (Pickford was exceedingly well known as "America's sweetheart" while Fairbanks' fame was based on his death-defying athleticism and masculinity) is referenced throughout the film. Fairbanks runs everywhere at amazing pace, demonstrates superhuman strength and agility in restraining Katherine, and picks up and hurls his servants as if they're made of feathers. Pickford is continually shown in quintessentially Pickford-esqe poses, especially in close-up, her famous purse-mouth and quivering eyes looking pleadingly at the camera.

Released simultaneously as a talkie and a silent film,[18] this is a very pared down version of Shakespeare's play, cutting out the induction, replacing Lucentio with Hortensio as Bianca's wooer, excising a number of characters including Lucentio's servant, Tranio, Lucentio's father, Vincentio, and the widow whom Hortensio marries. In the film, the central pair find that their love of brandishing whips is a point they have in common; upon meeting Petruchio for the first time, Katherine gazes at Petruchio's exceptionally long and heavy whip and instantaneously hides her much smaller weapon behind her back,[19] or as the pressbook stresses: "Her whip, which had lashed the back of many a suitor, looked small and puny when compared to his blacksnake."[20] The whips, I suggest, are visual correlatives to the whiplike tongues of the central pair. It's worth remembering that the shrew in the sixteenth century was regarded as having an overactive tongue and punishment sometimes involved the physical removal of the offending woman's organ. The play, on one level, is a battle of tongues, with undeniably phallic associations:

> *Petruchio*: Who knows not where a wasp does wear his sting? In his tail.
> *Katherine*: In his tongue.
> *Petruchio*: Whose tongue?
> *Katherine*: Yours, if you talk of tales, and so farewell.
> *Petruchio*: What, with my tongue in your tail? Nay, come again, Good Kate. I am a gentleman.[21]

As Ann Thompson has observed in the Cambridge edition of *The Taming of the Shrew*, David Garrick's 1754 adaptation, which prevailed until the mid-nineteenth century (and upon which this film is based), included a line indicating that Petruchio "shook his Whip in Token of his Love" and a whip was later added as a property by John Kemble in his 1788 production. According to Thompson, the whip became a standard property for future stage performances,[22] but the Taylor film extends its significance by including the property in virtually every frame of the movie. Katherine carries hers around as if it's a handbag. Easily recalled as "the film with the whips," these seemingly gratuitous strips of leather are the dominant image of the film, and while the whips can be explained as signifiers of the central characters' sadomasochistic sexuality, their use can be explained literally as a means of achieving discipline and silence: a whip, of course, is a word used to refer to both a person who ensures discipline (a Congressional or Parliamentary whip) and a call issued to stamp out deviance in the interests of harmony. It seems a peculiar accident, if it is an accident, that the first mainstream Shakespeare "talkie" is an adaptation of a play concerned not with the celebration of words but with the suppression of words, and that it makes this theme blatantly apparent through the extensive use of the whips.

But the film's pressbook repeatedly emphasizes that this is a talkie. While contemporary "so-called serious" writers on film condemn sound movies as popular, formulaic, and infantilizing, the writers of the very detailed pressbook continually stress the uplifting quality of sound. Numerous articles in the pressbook, while overly keen to praise, inadvertently allude to anxieties about the film's reception in its capacity as an "all-talking" adaptation of Shakespeare. Indeed, the publicity materials covertly address the anticipated criticisms of the likes of Huxley and Panofsky. The book arms itself against purist objections to the production of a talking Shakespeare film by directly and audaciously addressing the question of fidelity. In brief, the message of the pressbook is that sound allows for the first time fidelity on screen to an author's work and, by extension, to the period in which it was produced. Perhaps the most striking notion to emerge from the pressbook is its perception of *The Taming of the Shrew* not just as the first mainstream talking adaptation of Shakespeare but *the first* adaptation of Shakespeare (obliterating all silent predecessors). The pressbook reiterates in its summaries that this is the first film adaptation of the play: "in this screen story of the Bard's immortal comedy, brought to the screen for *the first* time in the history of motion pictures"[23] or "the glorious comedy which has come *finally* to motion pictures after four centuries of success on the legitimate stage."[24] Notwithstanding what the "legitimate stage" is meant to signify, it could be argued that the publicity writers failed to do their research or refused to acknowledge earlier versions (1908, 1911, 1923, the first directed by D.W. Griffith). But it is more likely that these adaptations were disqualified as adaptations due to their lack of words. Mary Pickford herself echoes the repeated assertion, "Shakespeare brought to the screen for the first time,"[25] in an interview by Julian Arthur:

> Also there is another reason why we wanted to be the first to bring Shakespeare to the screen. It somehow seems an advance toward a higher standard in talkie dialogue, and there is something really worthwhile and constructive in this idea. The great mass of people who are unfamiliar with Shakespeare will be introduced to him in a manner that will make his work attractive. We have spared no pains to preserve authenticity in every detail and we have lost none of the spirit of the play in the transcription.[26]

Pickford (or someone pretending to be Pickford) claims that Taylor, Fairbanks, and herself are "the first to bring Shakespeare to the screen," implying again that what went before wasn't Shakespeare at all. Embedded in the pressbook is an assumption that an adaptation isn't an adaptation unless the words in the adapted text are spoken.

Pickford's reported speech contains a number of well-known arguments for the justification of filming Shakespeare: to uplift the value of film, to bring culture to the masses, and to somehow capture "the spirit" of "the original." Clearly the film's producers anticipated the latter point would be contentious and the pressbook has a number of articles reassuring us of the film's authenticity. Beginning with the catchline, "The big three—Mary, Doug and Bill,"[27] the pressbook features an imaginary interview, with "the big three" illustrated with them seated in chairs, discussing the movie. Fairbanks opens with the introduction, "Mary, this is Bill Shakespeare. He wrote our last picture"[28] and goes on, with the help of Mary, to convince Shakespeare that if he were alive in 1929, he would be writing for the movies and that this film of his play is "better the way we have shortened it."[29] In "Adapting Shakespeare to the Talking Picture Screen," Arthur J. Zellner declares that "orthodox worshippers of Shakespeare who clothe his every word with an aura of sanctity should not take offense,"[30] and goes onto question the authorship of the play and point out some examples of successful theatrical truncated versions, such as Garrick's (whose eighteenth-century production, *Catherine and Petruchio*, is claimed as inspiration for the film). Critic James Agate writing in *The London Pavilion* (November 11, 1929) introduces the film to cinema audiences, confidently averring that "it is safe to say that if the cinema had been known in Shakespeare's day, there is nothing in the present picture which Shakespeare would have disowned."[31]

The pressbook mixes pseudo scholarship with tabloid-style journalism, clearly in anticipation of attacks from Shakespearean "purists," the likes of Aldous Huxley, who will not abide Shakespeare's words being spoken on film. As mentioned earlier, the dominant theme of the pressbook is the film's fidelity to Shakespeare, a subject quite clearly instigated by the use of sound in this production. Repeatedly, we are told that all the words are Shakespeare's:

> . . . not one bit of the glorious Shakespearean dialogue has been sacrificed when in keeping with the fast moving comedy, director Sam Taylor has re-told the story with the deftness so characteristic of his work . . .[32]

> Every line of dialogue used in the picture stands as written by the Bard himself.[33]

> . . . every bit of dialogue spoken in the film was taken from the original Shakespeare and every bit of atmosphere, from the characters to the sets, is in keeping with the customs of the fifteenth century.[34]

These repeated assertions of pure authenticity seem to have been swallowed by contemporary viewers.[35] A review in *The Film Spectator* notes the problem of convincing an audience that this is actually Shakespeare,[36] and the reviewer of *Picture-Play Magazine* sees the film as "a pioneering effort to bring Shakespeare to the talking screen."[37]

Without doubt, the sound, by today's standards, is dreadful, with Pickford and Fairbanks shouting out all their lines with little trace of emotion. Pickford claimed to be disappointed with her own performance, retiring from acting shortly after the film; rather than presenting Katherine as an equal to Petruchio in strength and wit, she felt that she played the part like a "spitting kitten."[38] Most critics have claimed that Fairbanks steals the show, with Pickford looking uncomfortable and out of place throughout.[39]

Strikingly, however, all the emotion is conveyed in the nonspeaking sections, as Taylor's film oscillates between the talkie and silent modes, very much a film aware of its transitional and dual status. Given the talkie was seen as a purely commercial enterprise and despised by those advocates of pure cinema and literary critics who saw the coming of sound as a further invasion and violation of their artistic territory, the contrasting styles, the talkie and the silent, are indeed pertinent. It's worth noting that the film is framed by much talking while the middle section of the film is dominated by silence that "upstages" the very theatrical opening and close. The shouting of the central actors is in sharp contrast to the superiority of their silent performances.

Significantly the first mainstream Shakespeare talkie is a play about the "successful" suppression of the dangerous female tongue, as mentioned, blatantly visualized by the whips in this production. But it is a success that is not altogether unqualified, given that Katherine finds a voice (albeit one that is music to the ears of a patriarchal society) at the end of the play. The film, on one level, exploits the fame of the central couple while, on another, self-consciously juxtaposes the visual with the verbal, the silent film with the talkie. Surprisingly, aesthetically, silence wins over words in the final impression of the film as Katherine's spectating is far more eloquent than Petruchio's verbal declarations. Take the scene in which Petruchio sends Katherine to bed and returns to eat the rejected food. As Henderson notes, Katherine "remains the one who sees more than her husband, creating a silent connection between her perspective and the filmmaker's own."[40]

Katherine, after miraculously undergoing a makeover from a mudsoaked and bedraggled wreck to a perfectly groomed starlet complete with diaphanous white peignoir, opens the bedroom door and gazes down at Petruchio who is at the table with his dog, Troilus. At this point of the film, Katherine has been transformed from bad to good girl, symbolized in the change of costume from black riding suit (worn at the outset of the film) to virginal white. Positioned at the top of the staircase, she literally and metaphorically looks down at Petruchio. Unable to speak, she is given a voice in her enforced silence. The eavesdropping Katherine speaks visually throughout the sequence, gradually moving from the shock of the spectacle to plotting revenge (in anticipation of the finale, concluding with a knowing wink to the camera). Petruchio, oblivious to the fact he's being watched and overheard, brags to the dog (which has physically and symbolically taken Katherine's place at the table). The juxtaposition of the two characters, one silent, one carelessly and unnecessarily wordy, reflects the film's transitional status between silent cinema and talkie. Clearly the more eloquent of the two is Katherine and in the debate between what Gilbert Seldes refers to as "the talkies" and "the movies," the talkie is shown to be vastly inferior: stupid, infantile and lacking in subtlety due to its unnecessary wordiness. Against the grain of the pressbook, the film seems to be at pains to reinforce the old adage that a picture speaks louder than words or that the central pair, especially Pickford, are making a final and fruitless plea for the survival of silent cinema in anticipation that the new talkie will end both careers. Retrospectively, Pickford lamented in her autobiography: "The making of that film was my finish. My confidence was completely shattered, and I was never again at ease before the camera or microphone."[41]

This is Shakespeare with and without words: Katherine is "silenced" (as Pickford writes in her autobiography, she was asked to adopt Pickfordian characteristics in her portrayal of Kate)[42] and while Petruchio's words are victorious, sound is vastly overshadowed by silence. The film, it seems to me, champions silence, not words, and the end product is in direct opposition to the publicity surrounding it. (Significantly, Sam Taylor himself makes no contribution to the pressbook and its valorization of words.) Claims that this is the first ever Shakespeare film and declarations about its fidelity to Shakespeare in its preservation of the words are contradicted in the film by the primacy of the visual over the verbal, or the silent film over the talking adaptation. Indeed the film itself, contrary to the message of the pressbook, seems to fight against its status as an adaptation. One reviewer, betraying the contemporary elitist hostility to adaptations, offered some advice for selling the film: "It might be best to suppress the name of the author."[43]

In "Adaptation the Genre," Thomas Leitch has attempted to draw boundaries around the field of adaptations by identifying four features of an adaptation qua adaptation. The traits he identifies that encourage a film to be watched as an adaptation are all, in some way, concerned with period authenticity:

1. a period setting and an emphasis on costume
2. period music that functions to fetishize history
3. an obsession with authors, books, and written words (I would also include "art work"—sets that prominently feature paintings, sculptures, period furniture)
4. the use of intertitles

The authors of the pressbook would insist on a fifth requirement: spoken words. *The Taming of the Shrew*'s pressbook reveals that the coming of sound enabled the birth of adaptation, and while the promoters of the film do their utmost to proclaim the film as an adaptation, indeed the first Shakespeare adaptation ever, the film itself does the opposite, demonstrating the superior eloquence of silence.

Sound is the basis for claims of fidelity (and acknowledgement of lack of originality) resulting in adaptation's exclusion from the accolade of "art." While, obviously, the talkie was eventually accepted by serious writers on film, sound continued to stigmatize adaptations. While the pressbook of *The Taming of the Shrew* repeatedly marvels at Shakespeare's words on screen, the image of the whips suggest throughout that this is a film that fiercely asks its characters to "shut up."

There is no doubt that hostility to screen adaptations is still felt today. John Patterson's recent rant in *The Guardian* echoes the sentiments of an outraged Aldous Huxley at the beginning of the sound age:

> I think a 10-year, worldwide moratorium on adapting novels into movies would be an excellent tonic for both the novel and the movie. Novelists would soon rediscover, once deprived of those tasty movie-rights deals, that building a novel on a screenplay base is no path to originality or formal advancement, and perhaps pursue different routes to their shrinking audience. Meanwhile, film-makers—especially the literate ones, the ones who really need their English Lit thought-patterns beaten out of them—might delve more deeply into the possibilities unique to film once they realise, finally, that cinema is not a branch of literature, and that the opposite is now true.[44]

Patterson argues that this inexplicable will to adapt is killing both literature and film.

Sam Taylor's *Taming of the Shrew* is remarkable in enacting the debate between sound and silence (to adapt or not to adapt?) in this transitional phase of film history. The film's pressbook boldly claims that the coming of sound reinvented what constitutes an adaptation: fidelity to the words of the author and authenticity to the period in which the text was produced. Claims that the film recreated the "real Shakespeare" and the "real Renaissance" branded the adaptation as popular entertainment. This unachievable but persistent proposition resulted in the exclusion of film adaptations of literary and dramatic texts from a place in the history of art as well as from a place within literary and film studies for most of the twentieth century.

Notes

1. Aldous Huxley, *Brave New World* (London: Vintage Press, 2004), 145.
2. "Silence is Golden," in Harry M. Geduld, *Authors on Film* (Bloomington and London: Indiana UP, 1972), 73.
3. See Virginia M. Clark, *Aldous Huxley and Film* (New Jersey and London: The Scarecrow Press, 1984).
4. Gilbert Seldes, *An Hour with the Movies and the Talkies* (London: J.P. Lippincott Company, 1929), 8.
5. René Clair, "The Art of Sound," http://lavender.fortunecity.com/hawkslane/575/art-of-sound.htm (April 1, 2008).
6. Paul Rotha, *Celluloid: The Film Today* (London, New York, Chicago, Boston and Toronto: Longmans, Green and Co., 1931).
7. William Hunter, *Scrutiny of Cinema* (London: Wishart & Co., 1932).
8. Allardyce Nicoll, *Theatre and Film* (London, Bombay, and Sidney: George G. Harrap & Company Ltd., 1936), 181.
9. Erwin Panofsky, "Style and Medium in the Moving Pictures," in *Film Theory and Film Criticism: Introductory Essays*, 1974, 4th ed., ed. Gerald Mast, Marshall Cohen, and Leo Braudy (Oxford: Oxford UP, 1992), 233–48; 238. See Neil Forsyth, "Shakespeare and the Talkies," in *The Seeming and the Seen*, ed. Beverly Maeder, Jürg Schwyter, Ilona Sigrist, and Boris Vejdovsky (Bern, Berlin, Bruxelles, Frankfurt, New York, Oxford, Wien: Peter Lang, 2006), 79–102.
10. Panofsky, "Style and Medium," 238. Olivier's *Henry V* is seen as the exception, largely because of what it leaves out and what it adds to the play.
11. As Kenneth Rothwell points out, the first "talkie" of a Shakespeare play was a ten-minute trial scene from *The Merchant of Venice* in 1927, made by De Forest Phonfilms. *A History of Shakespeare on Screen: A Century of Film and Television* (Cambridge: Cambridge UP, 1999), 29.
12. Roger Manvell, *Shakespeare & the Film* (London: J.M. Dent & Sons Ltd, 1971), 24–25.
13. In a letter to *PMLA* (Vol. 108: 1, January 1993, 152–53), Thomas A. Pendleton notes that the print of the Film in the Museum of Modern Art (Fairbanks's copy) contains no tagline and the film contains very little additional dialogue. Additions include "O Petruchio, beloved" (after Katherine hurls a stool at Petruchio's head), her howl passing for "I do" at the wedding, and lines lifted from Garrick's adaptation of the play. At the end of the wooing scene and after arriving at Petruchio's estate, Katherine states: "Look to your seat, Petruchio, or I throw you / Cath'rine shall tame this haggard; or if she fails / Shall tie her tongue up and pare down her nails" (as quoted in the letter above).
14. Samuel Crowl, *Shakespeare and Film: A Norton Critical Guide* (New York and London: Norton, 2008).
15. Jackson, "Shakespeare's Comedies on Film," *Shakespeare and the Moving Image*, ed. Anthony Davies and Stanley Wells (Cambridge: Cambridge UP, 1994), 99–120, 112.
16. Barbara Hodgdon, "Katherina Bound," *The Shakespeare Trade: Performances & Appropriations* (Philadelphia: U of Pennsylvania P, 1998), 1–38, 15.

17. Diana E. Henderson, "A Shrew for the Times, Revisited," in *Shakespeare The Movie II: Popularizing the Plays on Film, TV, Video and DVD*, ed. Richard Burt and Lynda E. Boose (New York and London: Routledge, 2004), 120–39, 125.

18. Robert F. Willson, Jr., *Shakespeare in Hollywood, 1929–1956* (Madison, Teaneck: Fairleigh Dickinson UP, 2000), 19–20.

19. Maria Jones has pointed out some confusion over the whips in the film. Jackson argues that Katherine throws Petruchio's whip into the fire, thereby disarming him, while Hodgdon sees Katherine as throwing her own whip into the fire in an act of capitulation. Maria Jones, " 'His' or 'Hers?' The Whips in Sam Taylor's *The Taming of the Shrew*," *Shakespeare Bulletin* 18 (2000): 36–37.

20. *The Taming of the Shrew* Pressbook, 1929, 10

21. *The Taming of the Shrew*, ed. Brian Morris (1981 rpt. London: Thomson, 2006), 2.1.213–17.

22. Introduction to *The Taming of the Shrew*, ed. Ann Thompson (Cambridge: Cambridge UP, 1984), 19.

23. Pressbook, 9. My italics.

24. Ibid., 10. My italics.

25. Ibid., 10.

26. Ibid., 15.

27. Ibid., 4.

28. Ibid., 5

29. Ibid., 5

30. Ibid., 16. He loses some credibility when he refers to "the stilted phrases of the 15th century" (16).

31. James Agate, *London Pavilion*, November 11, 1929, no.768.

32. Pressbook, 10.

33. Ibid., 10.

34. Ibid., 10. Of course, Shakespeare's play would have been set in the sixteenth century—this is typical of the "scholarship" of the pressbook.

35. See note 14.

36. "Mary and Doug Manage to Liven Up Shakespeare," *The Film Spectator* 8.8 (September 21, 1929), 6.

37. "*The Taming of the Shrew*," *Picture-Play Magazine* 32.1 (March 1, 1930), 65.

38. Willson Jr., *Shakespeare in Hollywood*, 26.

39. See Barbara Hodgdon, *The Shakespeare Trade*; and Diana E. Henderson, "A Shrew for the Times."

40. Henderson, "A Shrew for the Times," 125.

41. Qtd. in Henderson, "A Shrew for the Times,"124.

42. As Russell Jackson and Diana E. Henderson note, Pickford claims in her autobiography, *Sunshine and Shadow* (1956), that she was told to rely on her silent tricks rather than attempt something more dramatic: Jackson, "Shakespeare's Comedies," 120; and Henderson, "A Shrew for the Times," 124.

43. "*The Taming of the Shrew*," *The Bioscope* 81.1207 (November 20, 1929), 31.

44. John Patterson, *The Guardian*, Saturday, March 15, 2008.

CHAPTER 9

God Save the Queene: Sex Pistols, Shakespeare, and Punk [Anti-]History

Greg Colón Semenza

Even thirty years later, one discerns from footage of Johnny Rotten what made the Sex Pistols so terrifying to the British establishment: in jam-packed clubs overwhelmed by the seeming chaos of human bodies in motion, under a storm of "gobs" and flying beer bottles, over the sounds of breaking glass, piercing screams, and Steve Jones' (guitarist) intimidating "wall of sound," the twenty-year-old Rotten channels a genuine rage, a barely restrained violence all the more menacing because of the unmistakable intelligence in his eyes. The infamous characteristics are all there: the dramatic hunchbacked postures, the writhing upper body, the angry sneer, and the unblinking, open-eyed *Clockwork Orange* stare (see figure 9.1). One knows that all of the violence in the room is being orchestrated and, at the same time, held in check by Rotten himself: if he sneezes, one feels, there just might be a riot.

Yet John Lydon has repeated throughout his post-Pistols career that "I've never seen anything solved by violence,"[1] which reveals what few conservatives seem to have realized during the heyday of the punk movement: that Johnny Rotten was largely Lydon's manufactured creation—a stage persona. What no one knew was that Lydon had fashioned Rotten from Shakespeare's Richard III, mainly, though not exclusively, as Laurence Olivier had performed the character in 1955: "If I could caricature myself,

Figure 9.1   Johnny Rotten Channels Richard III (from Dir. Temple *The Filth and the Fury*).

the closest I've seen to it would be Laurence Olivier's *Richard III*. That's so funny. I can see bits of me in there.... Beneath his hunched deformity, Shakespeare's Richard was wicked and psychotic, mixed with a fatally cruel sense of humor" (see figure 9.2).[2]

In Julien Temple's 2000 documentary on the band *The Filth and the Fury*, Lydon confesses that the "persona of, say, Richard III helped when I joined the Sex Pistols" and explains why the character appealed to him in such a powerful way: "Deformed, hilarious, grotesque—and the Hunchback of Notre Dame is in there, and just bizarre characters that somehow or other, through all of their deformities, managed to achieve something."[3] Lydon focuses interestingly on the "achievement" of an individual who rises to power in spite of physical deformities. To Lydon, whose spine was permanently curved as a result of childhood meningitis, Richard III represents an alienated individual—as opposed to the monster or animal whose physical and moral differences are said in the play to set him off from the rest of humanity.[4] The importance of Richard III for the Sex Pistols and for the punk movement, however, goes far beyond the lead singer's mere identification with a Shakespeare character. As I hope to show, the Sex Pistols' numerous confrontations with Richard constitute merely one aspect of punk's engagement of English popular "history" and suggest much about cultural uses and abuses of the Renaissance and its icons.

Figure 9.2 Olivier as Richard (from Dir. Olivier *Richard III*).

Punk, History, Negation

As an amalgamation of working-class youth protest and avant-garde politics and rhetoric, British punk embraced from the moment of its origin in mid-seventies London the sort of cultural and class contradictions that enabled it to affect a large audience quickly. On the one hand, there was the consider-able anger, alienation, and cynicism of poor working-class youths like Lydon and Steve Jones, who, like all nonaffluent Britons, would have been con-fronted daily by the contradictions of a jingoistic national media machine, the elitism of an anachronistic education system, and the hypocrisy of a world that appeared literally to be collapsing down upon them. In Derek Jarman's *Jubilee* (1977), which many commentators regard as the first punk film, London is depicted literally as a wasteland—a bombed-out urban des-ert of abandoned factories with fires burning on every street corner.[5] This is the same apocalyptic London that The Clash sing about in "London's Burning," their 1977 lament of the hopelessness and ennui that has beset a generation of British youth.[6] Punk imaginings of the city's decline were not entirely exaggerative. As Jon Savage reminds us, "By July 1975, England was in recession. The unemployment figures for that month were the worst since the Second World War....This didn't seem like a temporary crisis but the acutest angle of long, slow decline."[7] In the summer of 1976, just as the Sex Pistols were about to begin their meteoric rise, England also was suffering from its worst heat wave since 1940, an event that exacerbated the general sense of claustrophobia and contributed to the end-of-days rhetoric being spewed by politicians and both the tabloid and mainstream press.

Punk both appropriated and resisted this rhetoric. Neil Nehring argues that in addition to constituting a genuine social protest movement, "punk was a parody of public representations of political emergency, of a generation in crisis."[8] Ironically, though predictably, conservatives would succeed in countering anger toward a sick British society by representing punks as the cause—rather than the symptom—of the UK's decline. Peter Wicke claims that the appearance of an angry youth mob unified under an anarchist banner provided "the crisis with a cultural symbol which pushed this society's pathological nature to monstrous heights."[9] Each time punk pushed the boundaries, the boundaries were redrawn more severely, and more open displays of state/media aggression seemingly vindicated the anarchist tendencies of punks. Dylan Clark calls early punk a form of "simulated 'anarchy:' the performance of an unruly mob," and says that "So long as it could convince or alarm straight people, it achieved that enactment."[10] Certainly the Sex Pistols' success as performers had to do with "their articulating and enacting most conspicuously the collision with authority, and the rhetoric of anarchy."[11]

The rhetoric of anarchy was part of what Lydon claims to have discovered in *Richard III* as a small boy. And it was something he developed further once he began to socialize with the mix of eccentric working-class and art school personalities associated with Malcolm McLaren and Vivienne Westwood's "Sex" shop, a boutique on the King's Road specializing in slashed T-shirts, slogan-wear, and fetish gear. Early in 1974, McLaren had taken over the management of a declining American rock group, the New York Dolls, having found himself attracted to the rebellious clothing styles of bands associated with the CBGB's music scene in lower Manhattan. After the Dolls' breakup in early 1975, McLaren set himself the goal of managing a London band that could bring the energy of New York protopunk to the King's Road, in part so that he could promote his boutique's image of rebellion and anarchy. After a few managerial decisions that included the sacking of the original bass player, McLaren's band consisted by 1975 of three working-class youths: Steve Jones (guitar), Paul Cook (drums), and the newly recruited Glen Matlock (bass), who was also the most knowledgeable musician of the bunch and the only one who could write music (Matlock would be replaced in 1977 by Sid Vicious). Feeling that the band lacked a spectacular enough lead vocalist, McLaren stumbled upon Lydon, the eccentric working-class son of Irish immigrants from north London, whose appearance fit the image of the band McLaren envisioned. Lydon had never sung before, which was ideal, and when McLaren asked him to sing over Alice Cooper's "Eighteen" on the juke box in the back of the boutique, he claims he was so nervous that he latched onto the first "fictional" character he could think up, which happened to be Richard III. As McLaren recalls, he sang the song "like the Hunchback of Notre Dame."[12] In addition to being so original-looking, Lydon's intelligence was obvious, and he could write lyrics. Johnny Rotten was born.

During his art school days, McLaren had been profoundly affected by the 1968 Paris riots, whose proponents' anarchism had tapped rather deeply the anger and rebelliousness in his personality. From an aesthetic point of view, McLaren was fascinated by the Situationist International-inspired artistic apparatus undergirding the movement—especially the posters and graffiti that packaged so efficiently the ideological imperatives of the protesters. Based in large part on Guy Debord's numbered aphorisms in *The Society of the Spectacle* (1962), the political art and rhetoric of the Situationists and *les Enragés* alike were notable for their popular accessibility: "Their cryptic phrases were the perfect medium for this meditated revolt—novel, easily packageable and paradoxical. Phrases like 'Demand the impossible' or 'Imagination is Seizing Power' inverted conventional logic: they made complex ideas suddenly seem very simple."[13] In school at this time with McLaren was Jamie Reid, whose ransom-note-style lettering (especially on Sex Pistols concert flyers, T-shirts, etc.) and iconoclastic record designs would become emblematic of a punk style directly influenced by Situationist ideals and French countercultural propaganda. Punk would succeed by marrying bottom-up (working-class or low-culture) rage and expression, and an artistic and stylistic apparatus associated with the avant-garde.

As Greil Marcus has argued, the shared methodology of protest for the post-Situationists and punks in the UK was negation, which Marcus associates with cultural anarchism and distinguishes from nihilism: "Nihilism means to close the world around its own self-consuming impulse; negation is the act that would make it self-evident to everyone that the world is not as it seems.[14] Neil Nehring traces negation's ironic dialectic from Hegel, "who understood negation as a critique of conformist common sense": "negation is in fact the genuinely creative passion, a democratic urge feared and condemned by those in power, who correctly see in it the seeds of the destruction of privilege."[15] Without question, and especially with the advantage of hindsight, punk's *modus operandi* was to call into question many of the most basic values of British society:

Damning God and the state, work and leisure, home and family, sex and play, the audience and itself, the music briefly made it possible to experience all those things as if they were not natural facts but ideological constructs.... What had been good—love, money, and health—was now bad; what had been bad—hate, mediocrity, and disease—was now good.[16]

This would explain, of course, the establishment's brutal response to the Sex Pistols and also the reason that a critic like Marcus can argue with such certainty and persuasiveness that "Johnny Rotten was perhaps the only truly terrifying singer rock 'n' roll has known."[17]

In attempting to negate the values bequeathed on the present by the past, punk managed to rewrite a great deal of English history for its own political and artistic purposes. Punk's simultaneous focus on the lies of the past and the figurative and perhaps literal absence of any future for its youth suggested mainly the futility of the past—the uselessness of high cultural canons, of heroes, of taste; in the minds of individuals like McLaren and Lydon in the context of 1970s London, Shakespeare and Handel and Churchill had only led England to the brink of doom, and so why should anyone worship them? Freed from the suffocating burdens of an *a priori* position of inferiority or the conservative and mind-numbing strictures of fidelity-based models of adaptation and appropriation, historically informed punks could make history useful by rejecting History and its heroes.

Marcus' *Lipstick Traces* contextualizes punk negation in a history stretching back to the medieval period—arguing essentially for punk as a transhistorical phenomenon. Though he ignores Rotten's appropriation of Shakespeare, Marcus analyzes connections between the Sex Pistols and the Lollards, seventeenth-century Ranters like Abiezer Coppe, and numerous avant-garde groups such as the Dadaists. Nehring's considerable expansion of Marcus' work, *Flowers in the Dustbin*, seeks to theorize British music subcultures in relation to the literary works that they appropriate, manipulate, and put to practical use. Considering, for example, mod appropriations of Burgess' *A Clockwork Orange* or punk uses of Graham Greene's *Brighton Rock*, he shows that "The astute use of literature in youth subcultures undermined cultural authorities along distinctively avant-garde lines...contradicting elitist value judgments on popular cultural activity."[18] In what follows, I consider the ways in which the Sex Pistols used *Richard III* to negate British cultural authorities and especially official versions of British history.

Rotten and Richard III

"I've got news for you. Dogs bark at *me*."

—John Lydon, 2000

When Lydon was seven, he entered the hospital for almost an entire year after contracting spinal meningitis, an event he has described as "the first step that put me on the road to Rotten."[19] The illness caused him to slip in and out of a coma for more than six months and resulted in disabilities crucial to Lydon's stage image: "They would draw fluid out of my spine, which was bloody painful. I'll always remember that because it's curved my spine. I've developed a bit of a hunchback."[20] He goes on to explain the origin of his legendary stare ("I have to look hard at things to focus in and see what they are"), which, in many ways, would come to symbolize the psychotic rage defining punk.[21] Lydon also suffered significant memory loss, what he describes as a complete "brain wipe."[22] Meningitis accounts for both the physical characteristics and self-perception of otherness that triggered Lydon's strong identification with Richard III.

The Olivier film made one year before his birth introduced him to the character, and it left a significant impression:

> I loved the way Laurence Olivier played Richard III . . . as so utterly vile, it was great. As I said before, Johnny Rotten definitely has tinges of Richard III in him. I saw it a long time before I conceived Rotten. No redeeming qualities. Hunchback, nasty, evil, conniving, selfish. The worst of everything to excess. Olivier made Richard III riveting in his excessive disgust. Having seen it aeons ago, I took influences from Olivier's performance. I had never seen a pop singer present himself quite that way.[23]

The emphasis here is tellingly on Olivier's "performance" of the character, even if some of the features that appeal to Lydon refer back rather directly to the play itself. One should be careful not to mistake Lydon's specific enthusiasm for the Olivier film as a sign of his unfamiliarity with Shakespeare more generally. He has discussed Shakespeare on numerous occasions, conveying overall a sense of ambivalence. Lydon seems to admire the actual plays— talking at times about how difficult he originally found the language to be until he came to understand how iambic pentameter works ("Once I got into the poetic beat of it, I began to understand the gist of Shakespeare")[24] and at other times about Shakespeare's creation of rounded and morally complex characters: "Reading Shakespeare, I found his characters vivid."[25] In another passage, Lydon shares that "At Kingsway College (where he worked on his A levels), they explained to me that it would lose its point and purpose to modernize. . . . It's the same logic as to why you can't live out a seventies punk rock environment today in the nineties. It's not valid now, and it doesn't connect with anything around it. You had to get into the dream of it—a vision complete unto itself."[26]

But in keeping with punk aesthetic principles, Lydon's belief that a text is a product of its historical moment says nothing about the sanctity of the text. To Lydon, the "academic" notion that one should not modernize Shakespeare is just one of many educational abuses of Shakespeare: "I wouldn't listen to the rubbish the English teacher was spouting about Shakespeare. I knew he was talking rubbish, and I proved it a few years later when I finally did get to take my exams."[27] He elaborates in *The Filth and the Fury*: "We were doing Shakespeare. A teacher would give me a hard time and he wouldn't tell me what I wanted to know. I'd ask outright questions, and you're not supposed to do that. You're just supposed to accept it: Shakespeare's great, you're not." For Lydon, then, Shakespeare is a writer whose characters are complex and "vivid," whose language is complex, and whose institutional role is oppressive. But Lydon keeps asking questions, at times going so far as to get his Kingsway teachers drunk so he could learn the "ins and outs of…Shakespeare."[28]

Throughout his early life, Lydon was stockpiling scraps and bits of information about Shakespeare that could be put to use later. The punk montage aesthetic defines fairly directly how Lydon approaches historical artifacts, whether literary classics or classic rock. For example, before gaining confidence as a songwriter, Lydon covered "classics," but fidelity was the furthest thing from his mind: "If I like other people's songs, I put a twist on them.… 'Substitute' [by the Who] I liked, but I didn't like certain phrases so I'd twist them about. [In sarcastic voice] 'Oh no, you can't do that. It's a classic.' FUCK OFF."[29] The music that Lydon created with the Sex Pistols, and later with Public Image Ltd., in many ways supports Dick Hebdige's argument that "subcultural styles do indeed qualify as art but as art in (and out of) particular contexts; not as timeless objects, judged by the immutable criteria of traditional aesthetics, but as 'appropriations,' 'thefts,' subversive transformations, as movement."[30]

Like McLaren, Lydon is an enigmatic figure, and It isn't always easy to know how much of what he says is tainted by egotism, playfulness, willful revisionism, or the distorting power of time on memory. One thing is certain, though: his relationship with Shakespeare is crucial to his self-image and the public image of intelligence he wishes to cultivate. Without question, Lydon's appropriation of Richard III is wonderfully complex: for one, his attitude toward Shakespeare and the Renaissance period reveals a sense of both the potential subversiveness and conservativism inherent in the "texts" he adapts. On the former point, Lydon not only finds Richard attractive and seductive, but implies that Shakespeare must surely have done so too. Lydon understands the gap, that is, between what Shakespeare wrote and the "rubbish" his teachers tell him about Shakespeare's writing, and he insists on finding out the truth about him. In his complaints about the manner in which Shakespeare is used to intimidate schoolboys—about the uses of Shakespeare as a socializing tool, that is—Lydon teases out further a belief that regardless of what Shakespeare's art might actually be about, conservative appropriation, distortion, and downright lies have suppressed its true power. In such a way, Lydon's comments about the uses and abuses of Shakespeare unwittingly anticipate 1980s debates between literary scholars who read plays like *Richard III* as radical tragedy, and others who see them as apologies for state power and oppression. Second, Lydon's appropriation raises interesting questions about the degree to which one can really appropriate "history," due to the fact that his indirect adaptation of the character is mediated by a hypertext: Olivier's twentieth-century film. Punk "thefts" of historical events and figures are in a sense authorized by what they reveal about the intrinsic relationship between source and adapted text. In this case, Lydon's engagement of Shakespeare through Olivier merely echoes Shakespeare's own pop-cultural engagement of the medieval villain through Hall, Holinshed, and Tudor propaganda—calling attention to Shakespeare's own punk-ness. If Lydon's retrospective insistence on the usefulness of *Richard III* poses Shakespeare as cultural capital, his appropriation of the character through the cinematic hypertext, with little regard for Shakespeare's high cultural status, suggests the radical potential of Shakespeare in the age of mechanical reproduction.

The Filth and the Fury

As we have seen, punk's uses of English artifacts and/or historical events and personages are complex because punk stylizes itself predominantly as a form of negation. Punk doesn't regard history or historical artifacts as sacred. For Lydon, there is little difference between a Kinks song and a Shakespeare play—both are there to be cut up, painted over, stuck through with safety pins, and put to whatever uses can be found for them. As Temple notes, Johnny Rotten's very presence constitutes an act of literary/cinematic appropriation: "He had this illness that gave him a kind of hunchback and when you saw him at the microphone it certainly wasn't Elvis Presley, it was . . . the things that came from further back. . . . and, you know, I think he was always aware of Richard III and there's a strange dialogue between his body language and that Olivier performance." Temple's riveting tribute to the Sex Pistols, *The Filth and the Fury*, seeks to tell the band's story through contemporaneous visual and sound artifacts, what Temple calls a "scattershot use of archive" that imitates the styles that influenced and eventually defined punk: concert footage, newspaper clippings, home video, music videos, and so on, all edited in a furious punk style.

Despite the film's reliance on archival footage, one should approach Temple's documentary cautiously. In 1980, Pistols fan and friend, Temple, directed *The Great Rock'n'Roll Swindle*, a McLaren-driven project claiming that practically all of the band's activities were little more than publicity stunts, designed to make a buck and point a middle finger at the shallowness of the mainstream media industry; the film suggested unabashedly that McLaren had micro-managed it all himself (a suggestion few take seriously today). Lydon had refused to participate in that earlier project, but he and other band members jumped at the opportunity to retell their story when Temple offered in 2000 to re-document the Sex Pistols' rise and fall. *The Filth and Fury* claims, then, to properly rehistoricize events that Temple's earlier documentary had deliberately mis-contextualized. If the earlier film is McLaren's mythmaking history of early British punk, *The Filth and Fury* is the band's revisionist one.

Shakespeare's pervasiveness in *The Filth and the Fury* seems systematically intended to reinforce Lydon's creative control over the Sex Pistols' image and music. The film features approximately twenty clips and sound bites from Olivier's *Richard III*, a clip from Olivier's *Hamlet* (1948), multiple references to Shakespeare in band interviews, and a director's commentary that repeatedly invokes the Renaissance poet-playwright and his period. Temple structures his film heavily upon clips from the Olivier film, which he weaves in at thematically appropriate moments. For example, to demonstrate the degree of animosity with which the establishment responded to the Sex Pistols, Temple follows Lydon's statement that "God Save the Queen" had "alienated the entire country" with Richard III's command, "Chop off his head." As the government and media begin their crackdown on the Pistols, the film cuts to the scene in Olivier's film in which Hastings is decapitated and then lingers on the bloody axe blade. In another section, Anne spits on Richard, prompting him to ask "Why dost thou spit at me?"[31] Temple explains on the commentary track that because of the fad of "gobbing" at early punk concerts, "It was great to find Claire Bloom spitting on Richard's face." Other uses of Shakespeare films are more arbitrarily playful: for example, during a segment focused on the sacking of the original guitar player, Wally Nightingale, Olivier's Hamlet studies a skull that he holds just inches from his face, saying "Alas, poor... " before the name "Wally" is sloppily dubbed over "Yorick." When Temple explains that "I like the sense of co-opting other things and using them in completely different ways: *Richard III*, um, seemed very irreverent... take whatever you need and use it in a way that it works," he reveals the degree to which the montage style of the film is itself a sort of homage to Rotten's irreverent appropriation of Shakespeare.

But the film's evocation of Renaissance is not limited to Shakespeare alone. Temple's film at once echoes and declares historically valid the arguments of numerous punk historians, especially Marcus, who have contextualized punk negation within a British tradition of dissent dating back to Shakespeare's age and beyond. From the opening credit roll, Temple alludes directly to the Elizabethan age so famously imagined by Olivier's film, panning the camera down over a parchment scroll with illuminated images of the Tower of London and royal family trees, which repeats almost verbatim the words appearing on the same scroll at the beginning of *Richard III*: "HERE BEGINS ONE OF THE MOST FAMOUS, AND AT THE SAME TIME, THE MOST INFAMOUS OF THE LEGENDS ATTACHED TO THE CROWN OF ENGLAND." The "N" in "CROWN" has a huge graffitied, red X through it, however, and a "D" has been written directly above the X (see figure 9.3).

Though the word "CROWD" is intended both to introduce a term relevant to rock culture and to shift the focus of the title away from the royals and onto the people (the mob)—suggesting again the idea of punk as a bottom-up art form—the focus of the appropriation remains squarely on the word "CROWN," since, above all else, the Sex Pistols will be forever remembered for their "infamous" attack on Elizabeth II during the 1977 Queen's Silver Jubilee. The very imposition of the X, in fact, may allude to the most iconographic of images associated with the Sex Pistols, the imposed ransom-style letters over Elizabeth's face on the sleeve of the vinyl single, "God Save the Queen." The link between Richard III and Rotten,

Figure 9.3 Opening Captions from Temple's *The Filth and The Fury.*

in other words, is established as early as the opening credits through the suggestion that the scandal around "God Save the Queen" constitutes one of the most famous, and at the same time infamous, legends attached to the crown of England, at least since the time when the crown of England mattered.

By linking such obviously disparate events in British royal history as the Wars of the Roses and the Sex Pistols scandal, Temple's film parallels Marcus' work in claiming that the Pistols should be understood within a larger tradition of British popular protest: "There's always been this Lord of Misrule figure in English culture and the Sex Pistols tap into that hugely. . . . in Elizabethan Roaring Boys. . . . There are many models of it." According to Temple, punk was systematically fashioned by its earliest practitioners as deriving from this revolutionary tradition: "This was something we were very interested in at the time, and people like Greil Marcus have expanded that idea in interesting ways . . . comparing them to the Ranters and the Diggers and English revolution and so on. They always seemed quite Chaucerian to me."[32] One sees from Rotten's appropriation of Richard III, from Elvis Costello songs about Cromwell and Clash songs about Rimbaud, from Derek Jarman's *Jubilee*, from Temple's comparison of the Sex Pistols revolution to the Gordon Riots in his earlier film, *The Great Rock 'n' Roll Swindle* (1980), that punk sought simultaneously to desacralize English history by manipulating it and rendering it a useful tool, and to build its very ethos on an authoritative, if decidedly radical, British tradition linking Chaucer, medieval heresy and revolution, Shakespeare, seventeenth-century separatism and radical Protestantism, the English civil war, and so on. Taking the cue from Johnny Rotten himself, who mocked the authorized version of English history as a tool of national propaganda and sought to turn it onto its head ("oh, God save his-story"), punk sought change through negation. If fascism operates through the erasure and/or fabrication of history, then punk—like the dissenting and avant-garde traditions it celebrates—operates through the exposure of authorized history as nothing more than lies.

God Save the Queene

Temple's focus on the Rotten/Richard III relationship suggests that *Richard III*'s influence on Lydon extended beyond style and into his politics and rhetorical strategies of negation. Of course, there is the fact that the Sex Pistols were, like Shakespeare's Richard III, self-fashioned villains whose anarchism grew directly out of anger, alienation, and disability. The group presents such outsider status as allowing one a greater ability to see the world for what it is—a position in which one can pierce the ideology of state and achieve what Althusser would call a "knowledge effect." In an essay discussing the opposing forces of "Anarchy and Order" in *Richard III*, Ronald Berman focuses on how the villain's position "outside of the normal course of human development" contributes to "The emancipation of Richard's morality"— meaning that his outsider status explains the development of his relativism and ironism.[33] As we have seen, Lydon's beliefs about such official institutions as God, state, family, and history all seem to correspond fairly neatly with Richard's own. Furthermore, because Lydon sees himself as free from the ideology of state- and religion-sponsored moralities, he determines to prove himself a villain, hating the idle pleasures of the ruling elites and wreaking havoc on their institutions.

Lydon claims that "the first line I ever wrote" was "I am an antichrist," citing the opening of the Sex Pistols first single "Anarchy in the U.K.," whose second line is the half-rhyming "I am an anarchist." Upon the release of that song in November of 1976, Lydon introduced himself as a cultural force of negation through the "I am" of the omnipotent, omniscient, and omnipresent creator God of the Western religious tradition (Exodus 3:14); in doing so, he echoed, in turn, not only Richard's famous performative announcement that "I am determinèd to prove a villain," but also the character's echo of Exodus in Act 5 where he despairingly concedes his own guilt: "Richard loves Richard: that is, I am I" (5.3.184). In his famous soliloquy in *3Henry VI*, just seconds after murdering the king, Richard shares with the audience for the first time those "plots" he mentions having laid in the opening of *Richard III*: describing his physical deformities, which he views as the heavens' curse upon his person, Richard famously declares, "I am myself alone," a statement one might read as either despair or an assertion of complete autonomy (5.6.83). The earlier play is also a part of the Sex Pistols' appropriation. In *The Filth and the Fury*, Temple splices in Olivier's imposition onto *Richard III*'s opening soliloquy those lines from *3Henry VI* in which Richard laments his body as being "like to a chaos" (3.2.161), and Temple repeats the line in voice-over at least three more times as a sort of verbal metaphor for the seeming anarchy caused by the Sex Pistols.

Lydon describes his political beliefs in terms akin to anarchism: "There's no master conspiracy in anything, not even governments. Everything is just some kind of vaguely organized chaos. Chaos was my philosophy."[34] He speaks regularly about the importance of freeing one's mind from the bonds of oppressive institutions, coming close on several occasions to just saying "I am myself alone": "I'm not a revolutionary, a socialist, or any of that. That's not what I'm about at all. An absolute sense of individuality is my politics."[35] Berman has said about Richard III that "The rejection of old beliefs and a new faith in the self will be the basis of his success."[36] Certainly, the same might be said about Lydon, whose repeated assertions of autonomy from controlling influences ("I don't have any heroes") and tradition ("Don't accept the old order. Get rid of it")[37] were governing ideals of punk.

Although Lydon reads *Richard III* like a critic, his reading is not bound by the orthodox strictures, or the ideology, of the Shakespeare industry— especially the one in place in the mid 1970s—and this results in a far more interesting appropriation than the sort we typically find in mainstream cinema, the popular stage, the classroom, or even traditional scholarship. As we have seen, punk sought to call into question the lies that history tells, and Lydon might be called its most influential spokesperson: "I loved history because I don't believe any of it.... Any kind of history you read is basically the winning side telling you the others were bad."[38] Though the quote conveys a common enough belief about history, the conclusion is provocative because of the well-known Tudor whitewashing of Richard III's actual reign. Lydon's view of Shakespeare encompasses both a profound sense of his plays' radical potential and disgust over what Shakespeare represents in British culture. His belief in the subjectivist and highly political processes that determine how history is taught and understood accommodates well the sorts of issues raised by Shakespeare's English history plays. Perhaps more than any other play besides *Henry V, Richard III* raises important questions about the degree to which Shakespeare was either a sly critic of or a propagandist for the providentialist Tudor myth.

Berman argues what I would refer to as the traditional line, which is that the sort of anarchism promoted by Richard could never "have elicited the respect of the Elizabethans," and so Richard must be punished and, à la Tillyard, the "natural" order of things must be restored.[39] Although scholars have debated for half a century now whether the history plays reinforce or challenge Tudor history, a majority of commentators since the seventeenth century have agreed with Phyllis Rackin's assessment that "In the providential world of *Richard III*, Richmond's victory will be clearly marked as the will of God, not only by the judgments of the other characters but also by the prophecies, curses, and prophetic dreams that give direct and unambiguous directions for its interpretation."[40] The classic expression of how such a fact impacts the audience's relationship with the titular character is outlined in a 1970s article by William E. Sheriff that seeks to understand why Richard stops being funny after Act 3, arguing that the murder of the princes forces a break between Richard and his audience, that "the man changes," and his descent into tyranny makes further identification practically impossible.[41]

Such a claim assumes many things about the play but the most problematic point, of course, is that we *should* stop identifying with Richard after the third act—that we should buy into the play's ostensible argument that anarchists such as Richard must be punished, and many recent critics have challenged this idea. It seems worth pointing out, though, that prior to the advent of punk, only a handful of scholars led by A.P. Rossiter had challenged it. In his important essay, "Angel with Horns," Rossiter contended that in spite of the obviousness of the play's providential telos and the inability of an audience to escape the fact that Richard is punished according to a scheme of divine justice, "The paradox is sharpened by . . . the repulsiveness, humanely speaking, of the justice. God's will it may be, but it sickens us."[42] Interestingly, Rossiter's argument hinges on the elucidation of two of the play's characteristics, which parallels Lydon's own thinking: first, the realization of the interplay between fiction and history, both in actuality and in Shakespeare's history plays: "To think that we are seeing anything like sober history in this play is derisible naïvety";[43] second, that the play offers us in the character of Richard III a "huge, triumphant stage personality" who essentially serves to negate the hypocritical goodness or morality of the characters he destroys: "[Richard] inhabits a world where everyone deserves everything he can do to them."[44] Though it is possible that Lydon read Rossiter's essay at some point, or was taught by someone who had read it, I would suggest the greater likelihood that both his working class background and punk aesthetic allowed him to see that whereas the providential view of history championed by conservatives seeks to "oppose change and justify hereditary privilege, the Machiavellian view, by contrast, validates change, mobility, and individual initiative," all of which are early punk buzzwords and ideals.[45]

Certainly, Lydon's songs continued to pay tribute to the seductive, anarchic energy unleashed by figures such as Richard III and to reject the providential view of English history, nowhere more profoundly than in the controversial punk anthem "God Save the Queen." What would come to be known as the Sex Pistols' Jubilee protest is a scathing attack on the British monarchy and the ideology sustaining it. As Nehring comments, "The song is widely considered the most effective political effort in the history of British rock music, for managing to be both ideologically scabrous and a meteoric number-one hit" (actually the song never officially hit number one because it was banned by the BBC and IBA).[46] Over roughly three and a half minutes, Rotten slides smoothly from a sarcastic voice of consent ("God save the queen"; "Oh God save history"; Oh Lord God have mercy / All crimes are paid") to one of harsh critique ("God save the queen / She ain't no human being") to one of apocalyptic sermonizing, especially in the introductions to the "no future" refrains:

> There is no future
> In England's dreaming
> Don't be told what you want
> Don't be told what you need
> There's no future, no future
> No future for you.

But the song's most powerful turn occurs when Rotten's warnings to the oppressed British people are redirected to the establishment itself: "When there's no future / How can there be sin / We're the flowers in your dustbin / We're the poison in your human machine." Here the social justification of sin hinges on two factors, the hypocrisy of the forces upholding the moral consensus (the "human machine") and the absence of any hope for the oppressed. Insisting even today that the "Royal family makes Britain seem preposterous and prehistoric,"[47] Lydon says, "You don't write a song like 'God Save the Queen' because you hate the English race. You write it because you love them and you're fed up with them being mistreated."

How can there be sin when there's no future? Mark Robson posits connections between promises (contracts of various sorts) and "the realms of subjectivity, law, reason, morality, and temporality" as governing the basic structure and themes of *Richard III*, reminding the reader that all social contracts hinge on the seeming inevitability of futurity: "promising may be seen as a fundamental aspect of an understanding of the nature of political subjectivity. In Plato, the unspoken agreement to become a citizen provides the subject with both benefits and obligations, and this citizenship renders one subject to law, even unto death.... Hobbes also recognizes the futural logic of the promise, suggesting that contractual promises must be characterized as deferred gifts."[48] In 1970s Britain as in late fifteenth-century England, the gifts the state was to give its citizens must have seemed endlessly deferred. In the minds of working-class and impoverished citizens, Elizabeth II seemed to be no more in "the giving vein" than Richard III, and the mandatory celebration of the Silver Jubilee must have seemed like something of a cruel joke. The identification here, though, should not be between the audience and Buckingham, whose promised gifts are deferred in the scene alluded to above. In ways, Rotten's identification always remains with Richard himself, whose non-future can be viewed as the source of a country's "sins."

Derek Jarman clearly understood the power of Lydon's implicit appropriations because in *Jubilee*, which was released only months after "God Save the Queen," the antiheroine Amyl Nitrate (played by the punk icon and Sex Pistols groupie Jordan) pens the following preface to her alternative history of England: "History still fascinates me. . . . You can weave facts any way you like. Good guys can swap places with bad guys. You might think Richard III of England was bad, but you'd bc wrong." If accepted—or official—history can be described the way Lydon characterizes it, as lies told by the winning side, then what happens when the winning side is exposed as a fascist regime or, as the question is phrased by Rotten, what happens when it is revealed that "our figurehead / Is not what she seems"?

Jarman believed that one answer was chaos, and he seems to have made *Jubilee* in response to punk manifestos like "God Save the Queen." Unfortunately, neither Marcus nor Nehring acknowledge the film, which is perhaps the first avant-garde commentary on punk treatments of British history and the unlikely blueprint for the liberal academic arguments scholars would make about punk years later. Set in an anarchic 1978 London that has just witnessed Queen Elizabeth II's murder by a random mugger, the film focuses on a group of punks who pillage and murder their way through London's streets. They do so, however, under the surveillance of Elizabeth I who—thanks to the assistance of John Dee and a conjured angel called "Ariel" (Jarman's next film would be *The Tempest* [1979])—has been granted the ability to travel in time from Elizabethan England to the present day in order to view "the shadow of this time [1578]." Jenny Runacre doubles as Elizabeth I and Bod (or Bodicea, which in Jarman's notes translates as "Queen of a new age"), the leader of the anarchist group, suggesting that the graceful Virgin Queen has been replaced by a dissolute postmodern lowlife. Though the film shares punk's view that England's future is devastatingly bleak, it presents the working-class youths who are history's victims in a highly ambiguous fashion, critiquing especially their destructiveness and shallowness.

In the film's final scene, after several of Bod's followers have been killed off and the rest join an aging Adolph Hitler living in fascist Dorset, John Dee and Elizabeth peer over the white cliffs of Tilly Whim, waxing nostalgic about the golden days of their youth; Ariel's voice-over laments the "howling Chaos" and "black rain that falls without ceasing" in the "north," and ends by describing hopefully the "departure" of Dee and Elizabeth who begin walking away from the camera on the coastal path and into an infinite distance as the screen fades to black. The voice-over continues: "and now, Elizabeth and Dee go along the same great highway, and the air about them seems somewhat dark, like evening or twilight, and as they walked, the Phoenix spoke and cried with a loud voice, 'Come Away.'"

On the surface, Jarman answers punk indictments of British history by lamenting the decline of Britain since the Renaissance, the golden age of Elizabeth and Shakespeare. The wings of the Phoenix have spread over the east, and that beckoning voice promises at least the potential of rebirth through the flames. A Virgin Queen will be reborn, as Dee prophecies in the opening scene, and England will be granted new life through her. But even as the film pines for a more civilized and peaceful age, it also renders conspicuous the naiveté of its own nostalgic thrust. Early in the film, one of the anarchists, Mad, relates her version of the punk mantra against heroes: "The world is no longer interested in heroes.... We know too much about them, don't we?" So Jarman undermines his depiction of the Renaissance as another Eden, and of Elizabeth as a savior, not only by doubling Runacre's role as Gloriana and Bod, but by exposing through Elizabeth's own nostalgic impulses the falseness of the Elizabethan myth. Just before walking into the darkness, she asks, "Oh, John Dee, do you remember those days? The whispered secrets at Oxford, like the sweet sea breeze?" At precisely the same moment that the film audience is made to long for a return to the golden days of Elizabeth's reign, she reveals her own longing for a simpler time before becoming England's Queen. The film's exposure of nostalgia as a psychological response to immediate crisis reminds the audience that this Elizabeth I is anything but historical. This is an audience, after all, no longer naive enough to believe in heroes, and no longer ignorant enough to romanticize Elizabethan politics. And so the English Renaissance looms as indecipherable potentiality in *Jubilee*: a mythical golden age whose "memory" lights the darkness; a terrifying spotlight on the inevitability of the police state we occupy.

Conclusion

The Sex Pistols collapsed in January of 1978. The whole thing lasted barely two years. By the time it was over, punk's central moment as a radical subcultural movement was arguably over as well.[49] Though its influence on music, fashion, and cultural theory continues to be felt to this day, its true power as a force of negation was stifled not by popular apathy or shifting consent but, literally, by the state's repressive apparatus and the public's general complicity with the state. The combination of the banning and removal from record stores of *Never Mind the Bollocks*, the tying up of the group in drawn-out legal proceedings over "obscenity" charges, local law enforcement's inability or unwillingness to protect the group from actual physical violence, and bans on them playing live throughout Great Britain all proved too much.

As if seeking to conclude the Richard III/Rotten relationship, Temple has pointed out the ways in which even the fall of the Sex Pistols mirrors the fall of Richard III:

> there's a great metaphor really for the whole Machiavellian ascent of Richard III to the throne, you know, executing his relatives...to get there and...the whole thing turns to dust before his eyes....and, in a sense, the Sex Pistols' ascent to the charts, the pop charts where they had to get rid of Rod Stewart and execute the Bay City Rollers or whatever they had to do to get to #1—the throne—which was then abolished in their honor and the whole thing kind of crumbled as well.

Although Lydon claims that to this day he occasionally assumes the role of Richard III,[50] Temple places the punctuation on a systematic appropriation that began with Lydon's disability at age seven and ended with the band's breakup and, more symbolically, the drug overdose-death of Sid Vicious a year later. The queen, of course, was still very much alive. And worse, so was Rod Stewart.

And while Shakespeare is, of course, still kicking, the idea of the Renaissance that he is used and abused to represent seems quite a bit closer to death after punk. Powerful music, like all powerful performance art, is an enigma, in part because it defies history so forcefully, even when it is most historically referential and so much a part of its own time. Marcus centered his history of pop negation on the Sex Pistols because, even twenty years after their demise, "Rotten's first moments in 'Anarchy in the U.K.'...remain as powerful as anything I know.... Nothing like it had been heard in rock 'n' roll before, and nothing like it has been heard since."[51] Although the Sex Pistols broke up in 1978, it would be too much to say that their peculiar art of negation was simply contained; certainly, for an entire generation of British youth (and for later generations who would continue to discover their music), many of the basic institutions the band took on, especially the monarchy, would no longer have the same ideological or symbolic power.

Nor should we diminish the intelligence or systematic intentionality of this particular mass cultural phenomenon. In telling their peculiar story about Shakespeare and the age in which he lived, the punks seem to have noticed much the same things as materialist critics, who over the past thirty years have theorized the socializing functions of the authorized version of Renaissance history and culture and debated the complexity of Shakespeare's role in perpetuating its lies. In much of this work, there often is an attempt to separate what the plays say and what they have been made to say to later generations. Richard Helgerson, for example, who feels that

Shakespeare's histories mainly "celebrated…the power and mystery of the crown," is also careful to emphasize the gap between reality and representation: "Shakespeare has stood, as he still stands today, for Royal Britain, for a particularly anachronistic state formation based at least symbolically on the monarch and an aristocratic governing class,"[52] and that, in spite of the histories' subversive potential, "neither it nor their festive power of inversion have in fact often made themselves felt in any historically disruptive way."[53]

The Sex Pistols' festive power of inversion certainly made itself felt in a historically disruptive way, and one major component of the band's various techniques of negation was Lydon's systematic appropriation of a major Shakespeare character. The Sex Pistols succeeded in unleashing the subversive potential of Shakespeare's writings precisely by negating what he has come to stand for in royal Britain. In answer to Shakespeare's punishment of Richard, and to the twentieth-century fashion of holding up Richard as the embodiment of fascist tendencies, Rotten pointed out, in a time when it was less fashionable to say so, that it isn't so much Richard who threatens fascism as it is the monarchy itself—the existence of the royal family, the English class system, and the culture that supports such "prehistoric" institutions and their rituals. English history is shown to be oppressive, elitist, and a pack of lies.

If we agree with those scholars who see Shakespeare as an apologist for the Tudor regime, we might say that the sham of *Richard III* is the sham of most conservative views of history: the idea that a natural, benevolent order has been restored, that the virtuous have been returned to power and the wicked punished, that God has righted the devil's wrongs—or, as Rotten would sing, that "All crimes are paid." In punk terms, such a Shakespeare would be a sellout. If, on the other hand, we agree with those scholars who see in *Richard III* the relentless mockery of royal power and systematic exposure of historical mythmaking, then Shakespeare starts to look an awful lot like a punk. When Rotten screams "God save the Queen / Her fascist regime," and declares accusingly that "It made you a moron," he might be said to be adapting Shakespeare's own version of that historically mobile anthem "God Save the Queene." Even after punk, such a Shakespeare might be worth heroizing, and if he's not, all we'll have to do is cut him up and transform him into something else.

Notes

1. John Lydon, *Rotten: No Irish, No Blacks, No Dogs* (New York: Picador, 1994), 20.
2. Lydon, 17.

3. *The Filth and the Fury*, dir. Julien Temple, perf. Paul Cook, Steven Jones, John Lydon, Glen Matlock, and Sid Vicious, Fine Line Features, 2000.

4. For an excellent recent account of the play's animal imagery, see Greta Olson, "Richard III's Animalistic Criminal Body," *Philological Quarterly* 82 (2003): 301–24.

5. *Jubilee*, dir. Derek Jarman, perf. Adam Ant, Jordan, Jenny Runacre, and Toyah Wilcox, Megalovision, 1977.

6. The Clash, "London's Burning," *The Clash*, CBS Records, 1977.

7. Jon Savage, *England's Dreaming: Anarchy, Sex Pistols, Punk Rock, and Beyond* (New York: St. Martins, 1991), 108.

8. Neil Nehring, *Flowers in the Dustbin: Culture, Anarchy, and Postwar England* (Ann Arbor, MI: U of Michigan P, 1993), 284–85. Dick Hebdige argued in 1979 that "the punks were not only directly *responding* to increasing joblessness, changing moral standards, the rediscovery of poverty, the Depression, etc., they were *dramatizing* what had come to be called 'Britain's decline.' " See *Subculture: The Meaning of Style* (London: Methuen, 1979), 87.

9. Pete Wicke, *Rock Music: Culture, Aesthetics and Sociology* (New York: Cambridge UP, 1990), 141.

10. Dylan Clark, "The Death and Life of Punk, the Last Subculture," in *The Post-Subcultures Reader*, ed. David Muggleton and Rupert Weinzierl (Oxford: Berg, 2003), 223–36, 233.

11. Nehring, 285. David Simonelli has pointed out that punk "anarchy" was a vague catchall term, "Anarchy, Pop and Violence: Punk Rock Subculture and the Rhetoric of Class: 1976–78," *Contemporary British History* 16 (2002): 121–44, 124.

12. *Filth and the Fury*.

13. Savage, 28.

14. Greil Marcus, *Lipstick Traces: A Secret History of the Twentieth Century* (Cambridge, MA: Harvard UP, 1989), 9.

15. Nehring, 2, 6.

16. Marcus, 6, 67.

17. Ibid., 11.

18. Nehring, 28.

19. Lydon, 16.

20. Ibid., 17.

21. Ibid.

22. See *The Filth and the Fury*, and Lydon, 16–18.

23. Lydon, 154.

24. Ibid., 63.

25. Ibid., 62–63.

26. Ibid.

27. Ibid., 22. Lydon discusses the place of Shakespeare a bit more fully during an interview in which he mocks rather hilariously the British examination

system: see Fred and Judy Vermorel, *The Sex Pistols: The Inside Story* (London: Universal, 1978), 131–34.

28. Lydon, 62.
29. *Filth and the Fury.*
30. Hebdige, 129.
31. See *Richard III*, 1.2.144.
32. "Director's Commentary," *Filth and the Fury.*
33. Ronald Berman, "Anarchy and Order in *Richard III* and *King John*," *Shakespeare Survey* 20 (1967): 51–60, 51.
34. Lydon, 3.
35. Ibid., 309.
36. Berman, 52.
37. *Filth and the Fury.*
38. Lydon, 16.
39. Berman, 54. See E.M.W. Tillyard's seminal *Shakespeare's History Plays* (New York: Macmillan, 1946).
40. Phyllis Rackin, *Stages of History: Shakespeare's English Chronicles* (Ithaca, NY: Cornell UP, 1990), 51.
41. William E. Sheriff, "The Grotesque Comedy of *Richard III*," *Studies in the Literary Imagination* 5 (1972): 51–64, 51.
42. A.P. Rossiter, "'Angel with Horns:' the Unity of *Richard III*," in *Critical Essays on Shakespeare's "Richard III*," ed. Hugh Macrae Richmond (New York: G.K. Hall and Co., 1999), 129–45, 143.
43. Rossiter, 143.
44. Ibid., 130, 140.
45. Rackin, 43.
46. Nehring, 297.
47. Lydon, 313.
48. Mark Robson, "Shakespeare's Words of the Future: Promising *Richard III*," *Textual Practice* 19 (2005): 13–30, 18.
49. I cannot do justice here to the immense debate in culture studies regarding the post-70s theorization of subcultures, but two excellent opposing surveys are the new introduction to the second edition of Hall and Jefferson's *Resistance Through Rituals* (vii–xxxii); and the introduction to Muggleton and Weinzierl's *The Post-Subcultures Reader* (3–23).
50. "Occasionally I think of Richard III when I do interviews with journalists I don't like. I'm very sharp and give one-word answers. I bounce off people's characters. I do that a lot" (Lydon, 154).
51. Marcus, 1.
52. Richard Helgerson, *Forms of Nationhood: The Elizabethan Writing of England* (Chicago: U of Chicago P, 1992), 241, 244.
53. Helgerson, 244.

PART IV

Renaissance Cinema

Jacques Rivette and Film Adaptation as "Dérive-ation": *Pericles* in *Paris Belongs to Us* and *The Revenger's Tragedy* in *Noiroit*

Richard Burt

The crisis in historicity now dictates a return…to the question of temporal organization in general in the postmodern force field, and indeed, to the problem of the form that time, temporality, and the syntagmatic will be able to take in a culture increasingly dominated by space and spatial logic. If, indeed, the subject has lost its capacity actively to extend its pro-tensions and re-tensions across the temporal manifold and to organize its past and futures into coherent experience, it becomes difficult enough to see how the cultural productions of such a subject could result in anything but "heaps of fragments" and in a practice of the randomly heterogeneous and fragmentary and the aleatory.

—Fredric Jameson, *Postmodernism or, The Cultural Logic of Late Capitalism*[1]

One of the basic Situationist practices is the *dérive,* a technique of rapid passage through varied ambiences. Dérives involve playful-constructive behavior and awareness of psychogeographical effects, and are thus quite different from the classic notions of journey or stroll. In a dérive one or more persons during a certain period drop their relations, their work and leisure activities, and all their other usual motives for movement and action, and let themselves be drawn by the attractions of the terrain and the encounters they find there. Chance is a less important factor in this activity than one might think: from a dérive point of view, cities have psycho-geographical contours, with constant currents, fixed points and vortexes that strongly discourage entry into or exit from certain zones.

—Guy Debord, "Theory of the Dérive"[2]

Missing Out: Spectre 1

Let me begin, for heuristic purposes, by repeating a critical move long gone out of fashion and exhausted, namely, the new historicist anecdote. In 1862 Paris, Doctor Guillaume Duchenne de Boulogne published a book entitled *The Mechanisms of Facial Expressions*, the first study to use photographs in the service of scientific experiments, more precisely, to use photographs to demonstrate how electric shocks to the face could show how muscles controlled facial expressions.[3] The acknowledged precursor of neurologist Jean-Martin Charcot, whose photographs of hysterical patients are far better known, Duchenne divided his book on the "orthography" of the face into two parts, the first entitled "scientific" and the second, "aesthetic."[4] In the latter part, Duchenne, "inspired by the tragedy of *Macbeth*," included three photos (Plates 81–83) of a young woman posing as Lady Macbeth along with an explanatory commentary.[5] All three photos turn on Lady Macbeth's character as defined both by her having been a mother and by her Oedipal desire to have Macbeth murder Duncan.[6]

In his book *The Invention of Hysteria: Charcot, Photography, and the Iconography of the Salpêtrière*, Georges Didi-Huberman links the theatrical posing of Charcot's patients in the Salpêtrière hospital to a serial practice that he calls repetition, rehearsal, and staging.[7] According to Didi-Huberman, Charcot coerces his patients into posing for photos as documentary evidence, even though he repeatedly rehearsed his patients to appear hysterical. The doctor's mastery of repetition deprived the bodies of his patients of resistance.[8] The "psychic theatricality of the Salpêtrière" displaced a "dazzling temporality of repetition (anticipating Freud's *Wiederholzungwang* [repetition compulsion])" with a "regulated temporality . . . of their hypnotic rehearsal [repetition] (in the sense of theatrical performances)."[9] Hence "a *perverse relation*" is initiated in Charcot's iconography between doctor and patients involving a double take by the doctor who always looks twice, seeing and photographing, in order to "suspend time and keep the madwoman mad."[10] Women hysterics eventually managed to turn the tables by "playing too much," and, in a "*battle to the death*," created a "rupture of the fiction" that turned "theater into disaster" such that Charcot's experiments came to an end.[11]

The three photos of Lady Macbeth in Duchenne's book depart from Didi-Huberman's Freudian model of repetition as doubling in that they constitute the only triple series in Duchenne's entire book (the plates total one hundred). Moreover, the series is narrated as a sequence by Duchenne, where each plate is meant to make the woman posed as Lady Macbeth look more cruel and less beautiful. About the second plate 82, based on Lady Macbeth's "Come you spirits that tend on mortal thought" soliloquy in Act 1, scene 5, Duchene writes "I tried more strongly to mark the forehead of Lady Macbeth with the seal of cruelty.... [Plate 83, where] the muscle of aggression (*m. Procerus*, P, Plate 1)...has been maximally contracted, is a striking proof of this. Who would recognize the young person in this figure whose face is transfigured, in such a stunning way by divine or human love?"[12] Yet the sequence as narrative progression gets derailed as Duchenne makes up a scene for the third photo: "I imagine Lady Macbeth to myself, coming down on Duncan, dagger in hand, with the ferocious air that I have photographed in Plate 83.... I have imagined that Lady Macbeth, recognizing a resemblance between Duncan and her father, lost her courage to strike and collapsed onto a seat. (This scene is not in Shakespeare.)"[13] In Duchenne's photos, we have something like the Freudian uncanny, as the boundaries between science and artifice, authentic text and appropriated text blur. But the blurring exceeds Freud's repetition compulsion in that it arises from a triple serial repetition and supplement (a scene not in Shakespeare) rather than a doubling.

Re-Situating, Re-Directing

I begin with this out-of-fashion gesture not to return to new historicism but to put into question its somewhat dogmatic definition, after its death, as the surprising juxtaposition of a canonical literary text and an anecdote of an exceptional event culled from the archives.[14] I turn now from Duchenne and Charcot to two films by French New Wave filmmaker Jacques Rivette, *Paris Belongs to Us* (1960) and *Noiroit* (1976), in order to consider the ways in which his interest in serial repetition challenges definitions of new historicism in so far as these definitions rely on chronological narratives of its birth and death, its lifespan moving from energetic fullness to exhausted emptiness.[15] *Paris Belongs to Us*, which involves a parallel plot about a theatrical production of Shakespeare's *Pericles*, and *Noiroit*, which adapts Thomas Middleton's *Revenger's Tragedy*, both evince Rivette's preoccupation with theater, especially the ways in which various kinds of repetition may blur distinctions between scripted and improvised performance, rehearsal, and production.[16]

Rivette's exclusive anti-psychological interest in acting as exteriorizing gesture, the repetitions of scenes that produce narrative incoherence, and the centrality of women actors in his films, all invite us to rethink the dominant way of defining film adaptation in terms of textual fidelity or the lack thereof and instead as "dérive-ation," an admittedly extravagant bilingual word complete with typographical hippogriff I coin by playing on a word coined by Rivette's contemporary, Situationist Guy Debord: namely, the "dérive." Debord defined the dérive as a social practice of passively flowing through a city that is not entirely up to chance but subject to contours routing the traffic of a city's inhabitants.[17] Despite Rivette's relative obscurity in comparison to New Wave directors Jean-Luc Godard, Francois Truffaut, and Eric Rohmer, close attention to Rivette's *Paris Belongs to Us* and *Noiroit* reward our attention by showing both his indebtedness to and departure from Debord's dérive. Like Frederic Jameson's later account of postmodern space as a threat to history and temporality, Debord's account of the dérive positions the city's regulation of its spatial organization as a threat to the free temporal flow of its citizens. *Paris Belongs to Us*, in particular, breaks down Debord's opposition between going with the flow and going in directions regulated by the state as the film "dérives" and, if I may coin still another term, "dé-rive-iates," because something or someone goes missing, gets missed, or gets misread, and deviates from the literary text it also derives from. Dériv(e-i)ation (de)rails the film's narrative toward both total, paranoid meaningfulness, on the one hand, and fragments of discursive babel, on the other.[18] Unlike Debord's spatial model of urban psycho-geography, Rivette's dérive-ative film practice involves, by definition, stills in motion, and hence seriality, with editing intervening to produce narrative kinds of temporal repetitions, returns, detours, and so on. Perhaps the most experimental of all of Rivette's films, *Noiroit* pushes past the ending of *Paris Belongs to Us*, which leaves open the possibility of continuing with the production of *Pericles*, and into a tightly structured narrative incoherence that takes a double form: on the one hand, *Noiroit* announces itself as an adaptation of *The Revenger's Tragedy* (at the end of the opening title sequence with Cyril Tourneur credited as its author); on the other hand, the last title card places the film's events on a small island, thereby announcing that Noiroit adapts *The Revenger's Tragedy* by adopting the form of a pirate film like Jacques Tourneur's *Anne of the Indies* (1951), about a cross-dressing woman captain. Repetitions of lines of dialogue from *The Revenger's Tragedy*, gestures, and shots, especially in the film's last twenty minutes, produce a noticeably incoherent narrative that I will call, largely because women are the dominant and even mythic characters, hystericized.[19] Rivette's film acts out what Jameson calls a crisis of historicity by showing that a tension between sequence and seriality within cinema (as motion pictures) rather than space and psycho-geography poses the deepest threat to the narrative coherence on which historicism depends: repetition does not lead to full exposure and revelation but to dérivation as "re-veil-ation."[20]

North by North Westerly, or the Big What-zit, Again?

As do many of Rivette's films, *Paris Belongs to Us* has a double plot, one involving the murder of a Spanish leftist named Juan and another about a production of *Pericles*.[21] Characters from both plots cross over into the other and turn on the retrieval of a stolen tape of guitar music Juan made just before he died. The overlap between the two plots forces the question of the meaning of their relation: is there a conspiracy or only coincidences? Was Juan murdered (by the CIA), as his sister believes? Or did he commit suicide? Is the film a political thriller and ghost story? Precisely because these questions and others are left unanswered, Rivette's *Paris Belongs to Us* was received by some on the left when first released as a right-wing film (both too invested in the notion of artistic genius and obscurantist).[22] More recently, Rivette's film has been praised precisely for being elusive and enigmatic. The reviewer in the BFI DVD edition writes, for example, that the film "is memorably eerie. And today it looks fresher than ever in its anticipation of seventies paranoid cinema. Films such as *The Parallax View, Night Moves*, and *The Conversation*."[23] This double take on the value of the film's elusiveness misses how radically it hesitates between what I take to be paranoid meaningfulness and meaninglessness, and its indebtedness rests on its tendency to drift rather than plot.[24] Reviewers of Rivette's films nearly always provide plot summaries that are notable for what they leave out: in summaries of *Paris Belongs to Us*, for example, *Pericles* tends to be brushed aside, and they leave out entirely formal sequences in the film that stand out as recollections through fragments, including the screening of the Tower of Babel sequence from Fritz Lang's *Metropolis* (1929); the montage of photos of the fashion model, Bridget; and the last ten shots of the film. (Plot summaries of *Noroit* typically leave out *The Revenger's Tragedy* entirely.)

To be sure, *Paris Belongs to Us* alludes to film noir, particularly Robert Aldrich's 1955 *Kiss Me Deadly*, famous for its complex plot.[25] Yet the resistance to Rivette from the Left arises in part from what Rivette does with the film noir genre, putting the "Vague," if I may make a translingual pun, squarely into la Nouvelle Vague (New Wave). Situationists (Guy Debord) also used film noir while attacking New Wave directors for being pop revolutionaries.[26] The Situationists remade maps as collages in order to open up different kinds of urban drifts and mobility. One collage Debord made with Asger Jorn is entitled "The Naked City," after a 1948 film noir of the same title set in New York and directed by Jules Dassin, himself a victim of McCarthyism who made his last films in London and Paris. An image pasted on Debord and Jorn's "Naked City" collage entitled "Life Continues to be Free and Easy" looks like a quasi-parodic map and battle plans, with large arrows pointing in different directions and citizens drawn out of scale as nineteenth-century French soldiers.[27] In contrast to Situationist efforts to map space relatively clearly, characters in *Paris Belongs to Us* refer to an invisible war between parties that may or may not be killing characters in the film, letting us think that Gérard Lenz (Giani Eposito), the director of the failed *Pericles* production, has been killed (he hasn't), while the leftists kill Pierre (François Maistre), the brother of the film's heroine, Anne Goupil (Betty Schneider), a Parisian literature student. (The ex-patriot American Terry Yordan [Françoise Prévost], Gérard's ex-lover, turns out to be something of a nourish femme fatale.)

The leftist attack on Rivette may have been sparked not only by the formal deviation of his film from those of other New Wave directors but by Rivette's refusing to play traffic cop, refusing to imagine utopian city dwelling (and cinema viewing) as inhibited solely by the state. Rivette's refusal to make his film either cohere or not, to put a stop to redirection and misdirection, to end or dead end his narrative, indirectly calls attention to an unacknowledged contradiction within Debord's dérive.[28] Situationists do not want to free traffic so much as they want to redirect it, that is, take over the role of the state in order to struggle against it. Rivette's interest in adapting literature in a dériv-ative manner anticipates Jacques Derrida's practice of deconstruction, especially his account of Romeo and Juliet missing each other in *Romeo and Juliet*, and "destinerrance," or error being always already inscribed in any writing relayed to a destination.[29] By traveling through indeterminate networks and "zones of translation," Rivette's film adaptation practice of "dérivation" puts into question both the politics of (re)direction and the spectrality of politics.[30]

It Won't Play

We can best appreciate the extent to which Rivette puts the coherence of *Paris Belongs to Us* at risk by turning to its account of *Pericles* as possibly fake Shakespeare and of its rehearsal in repetitious and fragmented form. After Anne, who is later cast as Marina, responds to a question posed by Jean-Marc (Jean-Claude Brialy), a fellow student and friend, as they lunch at Église Saint-Sulpice, about what she thinks of *Pericles* by saying she thinks it is "very good," Jean-Marc counters, "Oh, some very good scenes, but not all of a piece. It wasn't Shakespeare's work" (see figure 10.1A).

When, on the Pont des Arts, just west of Ile de la Cité, Gérard, the director of *Pericles*, asks Anne to take the part of Marina since the actress who was to play the role has left the production to do a film instead, a conversation about the coherence of *Pericles* ensues (see figure 10.1B):

Gérard: What's your opinion of *Pericles*?
Anne: It's rather disconnected, but that doesn't matter?
Gérard: Why?
Anne: Because it's on another level. Is that the right answer?
Gérard: Full marks. Everyone says I'm crazy, even Terry, but the reason I want to stage it is that it's "unplayable." It's shreds and patches [in English subtitles], yet it all hangs together. Pericles may traverse kingdoms, the heroine dispersed, [*sic*] yet they can't escape it. They're all reunited in Act 5. I want to show that. Do you think I'm crazy?
Anne: We must make people try and understand that. It shows a chaotic but not absurd world. Rather like our own, flying off in all directions, but with a purpose.

Figures 10.1A–10.1D   Shakespeare in Rivette's *Paris Belongs to Us*.

This conversation about *Pericles* might stand as an emblem for the film, not only because it is "chaotic, but not absurd," and "shreds and patches" that "hang together," but because the coherence is supplied by the supplement in the form of a quotation, at least in translation, from *Hamlet* (a King of "shreds and patches").[31]

The paradoxically unplayable production *Pericles* is further evinced by variations in the rehearsal of the same scene. The cast never rehearses in the same location twice but (re)stages two scenes with Marina. Anne first delivers Marina's line "Is the wind westerly that blows?" from Act 4, scene 4, in an indoor rehearsal, and later delivers it a second time in an open air rehearsal at an amphitheater on the Left Bank of the Seine river[32] (see figures 10.1C–10.1D).

After the production of the play collapses, an actor from the production quotes the same line near the end of the film, to which I shall return shortly.

The film's fragmented representation of *Pericles* is also notable in the narrative structure of the film. On the one hand, there is a linear narrative: after seeming to get off the ground when Gérard successfully books his production of *Pericles* for the Théâtre du Châtelet, the production finally breaks down when the producer fires Gérard. Yet there is a loop in the narrative as well: the production of *Pericles* is in crisis from the very beginning. Jean-Pierre mentions it to Anne because he wants to withdraw from a production of the play to do a TV commercial instead, and she is cast because the previously cast actress leaves for similar reasons. The repetitions of cast members departing and of the same lines of dialogue do add a kind of coherence to the narrative. Film and television do not in themselves pose threats to Gérard's production, however. In answer to Anne's question "What can we do to show it clearly?" in her interview on the Pont de Neuf, Gérard responds that he wants Juan's tape: "I'm counting on the music. He hadn't time, to make the music for it. One night, at Terry's, he made a tape, improvising on a guitar. Just what I needed for *Pericles*. But I don't have it." At the Théâtre du Châtelet rehearsal, Gérard uses a sound recording of seagulls crying.

Parallel to the fragmented production of *Pericles*, a cinematic fragmentation occurs when Gérard, a cineaste as well as theater director, screens part of the Tower of Babel sequence from Fritz Lang's *Metropolis* (1927), credited in the opening title sequence as an "extract," at an upscale party in his apartment. The Babel sequence is screened as a film within a film in Lang's *Metropolis*: in a catacomb of the Underground City, the "good" Maria (Brigitte Helm) screens a sermon on the need for cooperation between labor and management to the factory workers (mutually assured destruction will result in the absence of cooperation). The screening in Gérard's apartment begins with the title "Babel" followed by just four shots from the sequence that alternate with three shots of the guests watching Lang's film. In addition to abbreviating the Babel sequence, Rivette fragments *Metropolis* in other ways: Gérard does not mention either the film's title or its director; moreover, Lang's framing of the Babel sequence as a film within his film is missing; and, finally, the film on the reel unexpectedly breaks, and Gérard does not attempt to splice it. Theater, film, tape-recording of music, and even photographs all refract similar kinds of tensions between fragments from which something is missing (actors from *Pericles*, the frame of the Babel sequence, the tape itself).[33] More pointedly, the title of the "extract," "Babel," invites us to think of intellectual conversation in 1957 Paris, in which all the characters, according to Gérard, are exiles, as a babel of miscommunications and misunderstandings. Shakespeare's play figures into this babel: all lines from *Pericles* are recited in French while all other citations are spoken in English.[34]

Although *Paris Belongs to Us* follows the conventions of film noir in that all plot questions are resolved by the end of the film (Terry gives Gérard the tape and tells Anne she had her brother killed; Gérard turns up alive; and Juan turns up dead), it calls into question the coherence of its linear narrative through sound and editing, both of which blur the presumed boundary between interior memory and exterior media recording.[35] During the open-air rehearsal by the Seine, Juan's tape becomes an antidote to memory loss. When Anne forgets her lines, Terry suggests they play Juan's tape at that point in the performance to help her remember them, even though Terry secretly has the tape in her possession and continues to withhold it. At other moments, the ontological status of sound is ambiguous. When first played at a party, Juan's guitar music appears to be coming from a record. After a few minutes, however, we see him playing it live at this party. The belatedly clear distinction made in this scene between live and recorded music is called into question near the end of the film when Terry plays the tape: the music on the tape is almost exactly the same as the music played live at the party.

De-Situationist Place

By attending closely to the subtle editing of the final sequence (ten shots) of *Paris Belongs to Us*, we may best grasp how Rivette's formal repetitions, or dérive-atives, deconstruct a distinction between interior memory and exterior recording page. This sequence, I suggest, is Rivette's dérive-ative cinematic adaptation of *Pericles*. The editing style of this sequence drifts between the continuity editing used in the rest of the film and the Eisensteinian montage sequence of the photos of the Danish fashion model.[36]

Anne does not say whether she will join the remaining actors to mount a production of *Pericles* (see figure 10.2), but the more striking aspect of the ending of the film is the way the actor's quotation from the play calls up the following shot of the Pont Neuf (figure 10.2).

Partly because the shot does not follow (within the logic of continuity editing) and partly because the sound track becomes extra-diegetic (church bells are heard, just like when she and Gérard talked on the bridge from the Pont des Arts), the shot of the Pont Neuf recalls the interview Anne had with Gérard (figure 10.1).[37] The surprising and brief return to Paris creates a brief montage of sound, image, and memory composed of three shots that both "belongs to us" and belongs to no one. The final sequence of *Paris Belongs to Us* gives, in fragmentary and allegorical form, a dérive-vative film adaptation of *Pericles*: the unsituated, because out of sequence, Pont Neuf shot, stilled through montage editing, may serve as a figure of "dérive-vative" film adaptation as a remainder, a stranded yet unmoored image that breaks with a continuous series through montage into shreds and patches rather than flows smoothly into a coherent series, and the sound of the bells similarly arrives belatedly as an estranging supplement, a recalling of what now misses and has been lost. Anne sits on a grounded, upside down boat with nowhere to go, much like the swans that take off from a pond and quickly land on the same pond. Similarly, the soundtrack continues to be inconsistent in surprising ways: if the repeated sound of the church bells recalls the missing tape of Juan's guitar Gérard discussed with Anne, and if the sounds of the birds flying across the pond recall the recorded bird sounds heard during Gérard's last rehearsal serve to unify the narrative, the startling lack of sound made by the rock one of the actors throws in the pond splits that unity apart. A sense of belonging occurs in *Paris Belongs to Us* only retrospectively and in exile, when one belongs nowhere.

From the Nouvelle Vague to the Nouvelle Blague

The tension between seriality and sequence in narrative cinema already evident in *Paris Belongs to Us* (1960) is more strikingly pronounced in Rivette's *Noiroit* (1976). *Noroit* powerfully shows that what Jameson calls a crisis of historicity is an enduring crisis of historicism per se rather than a symptom of a particular historical moment of postmodernism: the kind of coherent experience Jameson opposes to heaps of fragments as the condition of historicity is for Rivette a false opposition. Cinematic seriality makes narrative sequence possible, even without editing, but the repetitions of shots, gestures, scenes, and dialogue that take serial form through editing divert

Figure 10.2   Final Sequence of Rivette's *Paris Belongs to Us*.

and derail narrative sequence. Because narrative is always both linear and looping, for Rivette, it will always be (in)coherent, equally open both to an unhappy ending as in *Paris Belongs to Us*, and to a happy ending, as in *Celine and Julie Go Boating*.[38] The arbitrariness of Rivette's endings is heightened by the form of a serious and playful joke, or "blague" in French: at the (un)happy and uncertain end of *Noroit*, the main characters stab each other with daggers at the same time, then each take turns laughing even though mortally wounded, and fall over dead at the same time.

Rivette planned *Noroit* as one of a projected four-part series. The film's opening title, "Noroit (une vengeance)," is preceded by a title marking it as the third of a tetralogy "Series of Parallel Lives: 3."[39] Rivette made only two of the planned four films (*Duelle* was the other, also made in 1976), leaving *Noroit* part of a broken series, part of a missing sequence. *Noroit* places itself in an incomplete series of parallels most clearly through its double plot consisting of *The Revenger's Tragedy* and a pirate film. The main characters in the film, Morag (Geraldine Chaplin) and Giulia (Bernadette Lafont), loosely resemble Vindice and the Duke in *The Revenger's Tragedy*. The film begins with an establishing shot of Morag hunched over her dead brother on a Brittany beach in the early dawn and vowing vengeance on the killers who live in a nearby castle. Morag follows her account of her desire to revenge her brother's death by quoting the following lines of Vindice (subtitled in French):

> Impudence,
> Thou goddess of the palace, mistress of mistresses,
> To whom the costly-perfumed people pray,
> Strike thou my forehead dauntless marble,
> Mine eyes steady sapphires; turn my visage,
> And if I needs must glow, let me blush inward,
>
> (Act I, scene 3, 5–10)

Morag is a double character from the start, part pirate and part Vindice, just as her enemy Giulia is both a Queen and a pirate captain and her subjects both courtiers and pirates, some with names (shown on the film's opening and end credits) from *The Revenger's Tragedy* and others from pirate films. Near the beginning of the film, Morag meets her friend and accomplice Erika (Kika Markham) outside Giulia's castle and, much like Vindice, disguises herself as a pirate killer in order to infiltrate Giulia's court so Morag may take her revenge. Yet the parallels in the film extend well beyond the two revenge plots. As Hélène Frappart astutely notes in the DVD commentary she wrote for *Noroit*, the film draws both visible and invisible combats and compacts between Morag and Giulia, the brunette and the blonde, and the moon and the sun; and *Noroit*; and earthlings and extraterrestrials. I would argue that these combats are fought by marginal characters as well as main characters, and are typically fought over a third person, sometimes a man, but usually a third woman. For example, the pirate women Elisa (Elizabeth Lafont) and Regine (Babette Lamy) fight over a pirate named Jacob (Humbert Balsan).[40]

Close attention to the precise ways in which Rivette adapts and cites *The Revenger's Tragedy* in *Noroit* will enable us to grasp how the engine d(é)rives Rivette's film toward incoherence by constantly remixing opposed symbols and characters, both within and across the two plots, in ways that deprive the plot of meaning. For example, Morag, a brunette, forces Regine, a blonde, to kiss the corpse of Morag's dead brother, and then makes her watch her girlfriend making love with a man. This scene "derives" from the similar scene in *The Revenger's Tragedy* in which Vindice dupes the Duke into kissing the poisoned lips of Vindice's dead girlfriend and then forces him to watch his wife and stepson having sex: whereas the scene is later performed for Giulia and her court as a kind of Hamletian Mousetrap, here this scene is adapted and integrated into the pirate plot (see figure 10.3).[41]

Figure 10.3 *The Revenger's Tragedy* in Rivette's *Noiroit*.

When Morag and Erika later stage the same scene from *The Revenger's Tragedy* before Giulia and her pirates, Morag plays the Duke and wears a blonde wig (figure 10.3).[42] Morag's change of roles from Vindice to Duke and from brunette to blonde have no significance, however, in terms of the film's narrative; They are rather just two of the manifold ways in which the narrative proceeds, more or less coherently, by alternating a version of the same scene played as "real" and as rehearsed or acted. After the performance of *The Revenger's Tragedy* scene, Giulia leaps up to kiss Erika on the mouth, knowing that Erika's lips are not really poisoned, and Giulia then proceeds to grab Romain (Anne Bedou), one of Morag's courtiers/pirates, take out a dagger, and slit her throat (the stage blood looks quite fake).

The pirate plot and *The Revenger's Tragedy* are not simply parallel, but mix in with each other and repeat, constructing and deconstructing a distinction between "real" action and "pretend" acting.[43] Consider two ways in which the scene from *The Revenger's Tragedy* performed by Morag and Erika has elements that are repeated in a manner resembling a scratched vinyl record that skips or even gets stuck: before Morag kills the blonde by having her kiss the corpse, Morag and Erika rehearse the Vindice and Duke scene spontaneously, repeating each other's lines while walking in the same circle around what turns out to be a corpse, on the beach (see figure 10.3). Each character repeats only two lines, in slightly truncated form: "I have not fashioned this only for show / And useless property…E'en in its own revenge." Both characters play the same role. Similarly, near the end of the film, we return to the open establishing shot of Morag on the beach (figure 10.3), repeating only the first two lines from *The Revenger's Tragedy* at the beginning of the film: "I have not fashioned this only for show / And useless property." Erika (Kika Markham) appears on the beach and squats down to talk to Morag, repeating the same lines spoken by Morag, each time louder, until she walks off. Morag then gets up and runs her down and kills her by stabbing her with a dagger.

No Joke: Out of Here

While many New Wave films include jokes, usually very good ones, they do so quite openly. In Jean-Luc Godard's *A Woman is a Woman* (1962), for example, a magazine cover in a news shop attributes Jules Verne's *20,000 Leagues Under the Sea* to Walt Disney (the magazine is a tie-in with the Disney film adaptation), and a sign on the street says in Franglais "Buyez Coca-Cola." The humor of Rivette's "Nouvelle Blague" cinema is more subtle because it is often difficult to tell in a film like *Noroit* how serious or playful or seriously playful or playfully serious Rivette means for us to take his film. As a final example of what I take to be a tension between seriality and sequence in *Noroit*, I turn to the repetition of Giulia's explosive laughter at the end of the scene of the Duke's death and her equally explosive laughter at the end of the film after she and Morag simultaneously stab each with daggers that Giulia, sporting streaks of newly red tinted hair, has provided them when challenging Morag to a duel to the death. When in the last third of the film a number of characters die, the cinematic takes become noticeably shorter, and, for the first time, parts of scenes shot in either high contrast, grainy black-and-white film, or with an orange filter are inserted into the otherwise all-color film. Moreover, no sound is used with the black-and-white footage (as it were, the film had temporarily assumed silent form). Each killing is performed differently, magically in two cases, through mime in another, realistically in another. Through some magic power, Giulia electrocutes Jacob after he discovers the pirate treasure in a cave. In a later scene, Giulia similarly electrocutes Regine just after Morag gives Regine a necklace, and Regine falls back dead in slow motion. Shot in an orange filter, Morag duels with Jacob in mime, circling each other as if they had daggers; after Morag seems to slit his throat (shot in black-and-white footage), he also falls down in slow motion, as if dead. In the final duel, Giulia and Julia seem to kill each other with daggers.

The final duel scene has a sequential logic to it. After eliminating their enemies, Morag and Giulia arrive at a showdown (see figure 10.3). Each death sequence loops back to the previous one by briefly inserting both orange filtered and black-and-white footage. Adding to the seriality of the scene is the way they circle each other as characters have done in so many earlier scenes. Adding to its sequentiality, however, Morag is shot in medium close up in black-and-white after they stab each other, looking as if she is just realizing that she has really been mortally wounded. The film then cuts back, in color, to Giulia and Morag, both hunched over before falling to their knees, each facing the other and occupying the same position in each half of the shot, as if they were mirror images. When Giulia laughs wildly before falling to her knees, she implies that she and Morag are, of course, just actresses acting, the daggers being just stage props. Yet when Morag and Giulia collapse on the grass as they die, the film ends not because the characters are back in character, as if the actress playing Giulia had temporarily fallen out of character when laughing during their fight, but because Morag and Giulia are out of characters. What I earlier described as Rivette's tightly structured film editing makes *Noroit*'s varied kinds of repetitions more intelligible as a looping pattern even as the editing makes intelligible the film's resistance to historicism through a serious/absurd, dérive-ative (in)coherence in its narrative structure.

Notes

1. Fredric Jameson, *Postmodernism or, The Cultural Logic of Late Capitalism* (Durham, NC: Duke UP, 1991), 25.
2. Guy Debord, "Theory of the Dérive," *Internationale Situationiste.* 2 (Paris, December 1958), in *Situationist International Anthology*, ed. Ken Knabb (Revised and Expanded Edition, 2006). This article is available online at: http://www.bopsecrets.org/SI/2.derive.htm. Psycho-geography is defined by the Situationists as "the study of the specific effects of the geographical environment, consciously organized or not, on the emotions and behavior of individuals." See Deron Albright, "Tales of the City: Applying Situationist Social Practice to the Analysis of the Urban Drama," *Criticism* 45 (2003): 89–108. Debord's most influential work remains *The Society of the Spectacle*, trans. Donald Nicholson-Smith (Cambridge, MA: MIT Press, 1994), in which he regards everyday life in modernized and mediatized countries as having become a total cinema event. See also a special issue of *October* (Winter 1997) devoted to the work of the Situationist International.
3. For an engraving of the apparatus Duchenne used for his experiments, as well as photos of an actual apparatus, see http://chem.ch.huji.ac.il/history/duchenne.html.
4. G.B. Duchenne de Boulogne, *The Mechanisms of Human Facial Expression*, ed. and trans. R. Andrew Cuthbertson (Cambridge: Cambridge UP, 1990), 3.
5. Ibid., 120.
6. To explain the meaning of the first photo, Duchenne quotes from the exchange between Lady and Macbeth Act 2, scene 2 in which she pressures Macbeth to murder Duncan, italicizing the line "Had he not resembled / My father as he slept, I had done't."
7. Georges Didi-Huberman, *The Invention of Hysteria: Charcot and the Photographic Iconography of the Salpêtrière*, trans. Alisa Hartz (Cambridge, MA: MIT, 2004), 175–257. Didi-Huberman twice cites lines from Lady Macbeth's mad scene (2004, 232). Tom Gunning links Duchenne's interest in photographs of facial mobility to an interest shared by some early motion pictures: "In Your Face: Physiognomy, Photography, and the Gnostic Mission of Early Film," *Modernism/Modernity* 4 (1997): 1–29; and Robert A. Sobieszek discusses what I take to be the most Oedipal of Duchenne's Lady Macbeth photographs (plate 81) in a chapter on Duchenne from *Ghost in the Shell: Photography and the Human Soul, 1850–2000* (Los Angeles: LACMA, 1999), 36–79, 71–73. For a broader consideration of the role of instantaneous photography in the development of the cinema, see Tom Gunning, "'Animated Pictures': Tales of Cinema's Forgotten Future," *Michigan Quarterly Review* 34 (Fall 1995): 465–85.
8. Ibid., 232–33.
9. Ibid., 244.
10. Ibid., 247.
11. Ibid., 252, 253, 257.
12. Duchenne, "The Mechanisms," 120, 121.

13. Ibid., 122.
14. See Stephen Greenblatt and Catherine Gallagher, *Practicing New Historicism* (Chicago: U of Chicago P, 2000), especially where they define what new historicism was (20–48).
15. There is as yet no systematic critical account of Shakespeare in French New Wave cinema. For useful discussions of Shakespeare in a few Jean-Luc Godard films, see Timothy Murray, *Drama Trauma: Specters of Race and Sexuality in Performance, Video, and Art* (London: Routledge, 1997), 86–87; Thomas Cartelli and Katherine Rowe, *New Wave Shakespeare on Screen* (Cambridge: Polity, 2007), 46–48; and Timothy Murray, *Digital Baroque: New Media Art and Cinematic Folds* (U of Minnesota P, 2008), 85–110.
16. "Noiroit" means "North Northwesterly." Rivette stages similar kinds of productions of plays from the early *Paris Belongs to Us* (1960), *Out 1* (1971), recut the same year as the much shorter *Out 1: Spectre, Love on the Ground* (1984), through *Gang of Four* (1988) and the more recent *Va Savoir* (2001). Each of these films contains a plot with characters producing a play. *Gang of Four* begins with a young woman reading a play in a Paris bar, losing it, and performing the play on stage with another young woman. Only after a few minutes does the camera pan to the right to show us that these women are students rehearsing for a class. *Celine and Julie Go Boating* (1974) is also very much concerned with theater, this time in the form of a music hall act, and with the relation between acting and reading. The film begins with Julie (Dominique Labrourier) sitting in a park reading a book about magic and following Celine (Juliet Berto) to give her back a scarf Celine unknowingly dropped. It ends in an inverted loop with Julie sitting in the same park and picking up the book Julie was reading in the beginning. Although a book frames by bookending, as it were, the film's narrative, a text does not determine the film: the dialogue was not scripted, but improvised.
17. Most of Rivette's films are available on DVD. The British Film Institute has released handsome DVD editions of *Paris Belongs to Us, Love on the Ground*, and *Celine and Julie Go Boating. Noiroit* is available in French, along with *Duelle* (1976) in a French two disc DVD edition. Each film is accompanied by an excellent critical supplement written by Hélène Frappart, also in French only.
18. On the paranoiac as the one who sees everything as meaningful, as opposed to the psychoanalytic as the one who allows that sometimes a cigar may just be a cigar, see the postscript to Sigmund Freud's "Psycho-Analytic Notes on an Autobiographical Account of a Case of Paranoia (Dementia Paranoides)," *The Standard Edition of the Complete Psychological Works of Sigmund Freud, Volume XII (1911–1913)*, ed and trans., James Strachey (London: Hogarth Press), 78–79.
19. Jacques Tourneur's *Anne of the Indies* is available on a French DVD edition, with the original English and a brief introduction to the film in French only.
20. Had I world and time, I would end this essay with a discussion, entitled "Being John Webster," of Mike Figgis's *Hotel* (2001), an explicitly experimental film about the making of a film adaptation of John Webster's *The Duchess of Malfi* in Venice while the cast and crew stay at a hotel run by cannibals. Something

of a black comedy, *Hotel* both adapts and satirizes film adaptation as vampirization, cannibalization, and sexual perversion. In a rather virtuoso manner, Figgis makes a show of using various kinds of film stock, split screens (two, three, and four shots running at the same time), widescreens, and full frame digital video with infrared lighting, overexposed and underexposed lighting, and time lapse photography in an effort to limit the ways he repeats himself to only a few shots. Unlike Rivette, Figgis provides narrative coherence, albeit of a neurotic sort, by dividing the film in two parts, the first part involving rehearsals with a director who wants to make a Dogme film rather than a Merchant Ivory film of Webster's play (the satire is underlined by the casting of Julian Sands, who appeared as George Emerson in James Ivory's *A Room with a View* (1985), as a cannibal tour guide) and the second half involving the actual filming by a rival director who is interested in making a more (porno)graphic film. John Malkovich appears in a cameo as well, after having appeared recently before as F.W. Murnau in *Shadow of the Vampire* (dir. E. Elias Merhige, 2000), another film about the making of a film.

21. *L'Amour fou* (1969) focuses on the production of Racine's *Andromache* and is formally split: a crew filming the rehearsals is shot in handheld 16 mm, and the rest of the film is shot in 35 mm. In *Out 1*, two different theater groups rehearse two of Aeschylus' tragedies, *Seven Against Thebes* and *Prometheus Bound*. In *Love on the Ground*, actors rehearse a play written by a playwright character in the film. And in *Gang of Four*, students rehearse a play that includes "double" in its title, namely, Pierre de Marivaux's *La double inconstance* (*Double Infidelity*).
22. See notes to the BFI DVD edition of *Paris Belongs to Us*, released in 2006.
23. Ibid.
24. For a useful account of Rivette's obscurity in relation to Francois Truffaut, Jean-Luc Godard, and Eric Rohmer, see Hamish Ford, "*Paris Belongs to Us*" http://archive.sensesofcinema.com/contents/cteq/07/43/paris-nous-appartient.html.
25. The sports car driven by Terry Yordan in *Paris Belongs to Us* closely resembles the one driven by Mike Hammer (Ralph Meeker) in *Kiss Me Deadly*, and Philip Kaufman's (Derek Crohem) constant references to "they" resemble the constant references to "the big what's it" in Aldrich's film.
26. See, for example, "Cinema After Alain Resnais," *Internationale Situationniste* 3 (December 1959), Trans. Reuben Keehan http://www.cddc.vt.edu/sionline/si/resnais.html.
27. For excellent reproductions, see Debord and Jorn's "Life Continues to be Free and Easy"; "Naked City"; and the "Guide Traide de Paris," 1951; Simon Sadler, *The Situationist City* (Cambridge, MA: MIT Press, 1998), 82–83.
28. Rivette is more akin to the "philosopher cop" (Benoit Regent) in Rivette's *Gang of Four*, who tends to speak in paradoxes and such as "planned coincidences."
29. For Jacques Derrida's reading of the balcony scene in *Romeo and Juliet*, see "Aphorism Countertime," in Derrida's *Acts of Literature*, ed. Derek Attridge (London: Routledge, 1992), 414–34; see also Derrida's comments on that article in an interview with Derek Attridge in the same book, 62–69. For a useful

entryway into Derrida's notion of "destinerrance," see J. Hillis Miller, "Derrida's Destinerrance," *MLN* 121 (2006): 893–910, who defines it as a "spatio-temporal figure" naming "a fatal possibility of erring by not reaching a predefined temporal goal in terms of wandering away from a predefined spatial goal."

30. Emily Apter, *The Translation Zone: A New Comparative Literature* (Princeton: Princeton UP, 2006). For Rivette, what Apter calls the " 'cartography' of global literature" (148) proves difficult to outline in part because translation extends to adaptation and recording and involves sound as much as it does text. Notably, Rivette uses panoramic shots of Paris in *Paris Belongs to Us*.

31. On subtitling, see Atom Egoyan and Ian Balfour, eds., *Subtitles: On the Foreignness of Film* (Cambridge, MA: MIT Press, 2004); and Mark Betz, *Beyond the Subtitle: Remapping European Art Cinema* (Minneapolis, MN: U of Minnesota P, 2009).

32. Rehearsals of scenes from *Pericles* in the film also include Gower's prologue and the brothel scene 4.1.1–56.

33. Similarly, the montage sequence of the Danish fashion model is preceded by a shot of a photo of the missing Juan so brief as to be nearly invisible. *Metropolis* is a perfect choice for a film about the city in that its politics, pro-fascist or antifascist, have long been subject to debate, in part because the film's screenwriter, Thea von Harbou, remained in Germany and joined the Nazi party while Lang claims, without any corroborating evidence, that he left Germany because Hitler admired *Metropolis* and wanted Lang to work for the Reich. On the trickiness of this famous anecdote about why Lang left Berlin, see Tom Gunning, *The Films of Fritz Lang: Allegories of Vision and Modernity* (London: BFI, 2000), 9–10. Lang plays himself in Jean-Luc Godard's *Contempt* (1963). Terry Yordan alludes to Hitler's defeat ("we thought it was over").

34. In the film's first shot, Anne reads aloud in English Ariel's song, "Full fathom five thy father" (Act I, scene 2), from a copy of *The Tempest*. Later in the film, one of the actors in the *Pericles* production recites "Tomorrow, and tomorrow, and tomorrow" in English as he says goodbye to Gérard. Gérard responds, "I see you know *Macbeth*."

35. All sound was recorded in postproduction. Some sounds are obviously extradiegetic and others obviously diegetic, but Rivette plays around with the difference between live and recorded music. A recording of seagulls is heard as Anne enters the Théâtre du Châtelet, for example. Juan's recording of his guitar music heard near the end of the film is also diegetic. But the guitar music first heard at a party is only belatedly identified as live, and the sitar music heard in French-American Terry Yordan's apartment is never identified as diegetic (if the sound is diegetic, its source is an LP record). Moreover, the music on Juan's tape is virtually identical to the music played at Gérard's party. LP records show up in the first scene of the film as Juan's sister lays her head down on her bed next to a record.

36. On Sergei Eisenstein's montage editing, see Eisenstein, "The Montage of Attractions," in *The Film Factory: Russian and Soviet Cinema in Documents, 1896–1939*, ed. Ian Christie and Richard Taylor (New York: Routledge, 1994),

87–89. The montage of Bridget, the Finnish model, introduces a disjunction between numerous photos versus the near invisibility of the photo of Juan, seen only very briefly in one shot, but a disjunction between sound and image: one can't pay full attention to Bridget's voice-over narrative about Philip and watch the briefly held shots of photos of her at the same time.

37. The Pont Neuf shot is not an interior memory of Anne's, in my view. However, along with the shortly earlier two shots of Anne and then of her brother being killed, the shot of the Pont Neuf may perhaps be read, especially in the wake of visions the main women characters have in two of Rivette's later films, *Celine and Julie Go Boating* and *Love on the Ground*, as Anne's vision. As such it would still not be a memory, but an experience that takes Anne outside herself.

38. *Celine and Julie Go Boating*'s happy ending is partly that the film doesn't end but instead loops back to its beginning, with the characters changing places.

39. All translation of the French titles and dialogue are mine.

40. Out of thirteen cast members, only three are men.

41. Morag and Erika perform the lines 3.5.98–107 and 3.5.133–410 of *The Revenger's Tragedy*.

42. As R.A. Foakes observes of *The Revenger's Tragedy*'s Gratiana and Castiza subplot, "Gratiana and Castiza temporarily change roles, and both play the parts of the temptress and virtuous woman scorning temptation before they are reconciled in honour," ed. R.A. Foakes, Revels Plays edition of Cyril Tourneur, *The Revenger's Tragedy* (Manchester: Manchester UP, 1966), xliii. Rivette mixes plot and subplot of *The Revenger's Tragedy*, repeats the inversion of roles, and does not provide closure in the form of reconciliation.

43. All citations are to the Revels Plays edition (see note 42).

CHAPTER 11

Alex Cox's *Revenger's Tragedy* and the Foreclosure of Apocalyptic Teleology

James R. Keller

The seventeenth-century drama *The Revenger's Tragedy*, believed to have been written by Thomas Middleton,[1] constitutes a parody of the theatrical revenge genre represented by plays such as Shakespeare's *Hamlet* and Thomas Kyd's *The Spanish Tragedy*. Much of the scholarship produced on *The Revenger's Tragedy* focuses on its reliance on the morality traditions of late medieval drama.[2] The play was adapted for the screen in 2002 by Alex Cox, who reshaped the content to offer commentary on contemporary politics, namely, the protracted hostility between Britain's lords/commons, Protestants/Catholics, and rich/poor, issues shared by both the early modern and the postmodern eras and latent in the play itself. This chapter examines Cox's revision of Middleton's tragedy via postmodern theories, postulating the failure of the grand meta-narratives of the twentieth century to bring about a long expected millennial destruction and renewal. The discontented seek revenge against the bloated class system of postapocalyptic England, but find themselves trapped within a self-sustaining monolithic structure that cannot envision or countenance change even in the face of cataclysmic destruction.

The social impetus for the simultaneously celebrated and reviled decadence of Middleton's play may constitute a creative release of the apocalyptic anxieties of the populace following the long and reasonably stable reign of

Elizabeth I, a sentiment exacerbated by the perceived excess and debauchery of the recently installed Scottish court in England, which began with the ascension of James I to the throne in1603. Uncertainty over the monarchical succession and the subsequent consolidation of what was considered a foreign power in England combined to generate a powerful sense of impending cataclysm, followed by an unsatisfactory yet uneventful resolution. However, the anticipated destruction and cleansing that would confer meaning on the preceding monarchy—as well as the social and religious power struggles of the sixteenth century—did not transpire. The overdetermined and self-promoting mythology of the Tudor dynasty was deflated with all the dire events attending the "cess of majesty" exposed as political fictions, including the converse belief that the death of Elizabeth would bring about a providential liberation of English Catholics who had long suffered under the protestant queen. James I, despite several conciliatory gestures to the Catholic populace, revealed that he would rule as a Protestant and continue many of his predecessor's discriminatory policies, such as fines for recusancy. To many, the new administration was not only a continuation of the problems associated with the final Tudor monarchy, but an intensification of the same because it could not muster sufficient dignity to inspire monarchical awe; the king was perceived as decadent, and, to some, his installment resembled an invasion. English courtiers complained of the increasing predominance of Scottish accents in the royal court, suggesting that the throne had been quietly usurped by a foreign power. Moreover, the liberality of the Stuarts—represented by the elaborate and expensive court feasts and entertainments, not to mention the notorious bisexual proclivities of the newly crowned king—was abhorred by the English Puritans, who mistrusted the son of the former Catholic pretender to the English throne—Mary, Queen of Scots.

Indeed, *The Revenger's Tragedy* can be understood as a commentary on the degradation of the English monarchy following Elizabeth's death. Vindice swears revenge while sighing over the skull of his murdered fiancé, Gloriana, blaming the corrupted and lascivious Duke for her poisoning because "she would not consent unto his palsied lust" (1.1.33–33). "Gloriana" was, of course, a common poetic epithet for Elizabeth I,[3] and the ducal family embodies the sensual/sensory intemperance mistrusted in the Stuarts. The moral binary separating the Duke and the revenger can also be aligned with national or ethnic sentiments. The resentment for the ducal family becomes a smoldering xenophobia. The second and more recent motivation for Vindice's revenge is the discontentment of his father who failed to gain preferment within the Duke's court, an advancement that Vindice regards as his father's due. This complaint may allude to the awarding of court offices to Scotsmen following the new King's coronation.[4] The play captures the sentiments and expectations of a group longing for the demise of an effete, decadent, violent, and wicked prince, yet the catastrophe of the ducal family fails to bring about the desired purgation of corruption and renewal of monarchical dignity, fails to deliver an apocalyptic conflagration and millennial promise.

A similar nationalistic antagonism can be read into Alex Cox's contemporary cinematic adaptation of the Jacobean drama. The director encodes one of the keys to his political allegory within the accents of his cast. All of the members of Vindice's family—Carlo, Castiza, and Hannah—speak with thick, Liverpudlian, working-class accents while the ducal family speaks with the more refined upper-class vocal intonations associated with London and the aristocratic and/or educated classes. Thus Britain's regional and linguistic hierarchy is progressively inverted, the revenger spending himself upon the once distant but now intruding and exploitative power structure. Vindice's kin are reluctant participants, perhaps even captives, to the debauchery and crass materialism of the British establishment, suggesting that England's provinces, its field full of folk, have been forcibly adjunct to material and territorial interests of the nobility, or more broadly the British class system.

The post-cataclysmic Liverpool setting of Cox's film is consistent with Middleton's satiric disputations on the decline of the realm, including the corruptive power of gold and women in human relations and the progressive decline of the old social hierarchy. Middleton's Vindice complains that "Were it not for gold and women / There would be no damnation" (2.1.25), and he laments that "farmer's sons agreed, and met again / To wash their hands and come up gentlemen" (2.1.16–17). His prophetic protests yearn for a dissolution in which divinity will summarily destroy all those players motivated by lust and greed within the depraved spectacle of the Duke's court. Although now somewhat dated in its theoretical approach, Una Ellis-Fermor's structuralist categorization of early modern drama into three phases—the optimistic Elizabethan, the apprehensive and millenarian late Elizabethan and early Jacobean, and the "satanic" late Jacobean[5]—is useful to this discussion. Middleton's tragedy belongs to the middle group, which registers its apprehension at an unspecified impending horror, first inspired, according to Fermor, by the anticipated transition of power that would follow the aging queen's death, and later by the inherent instability of the new dynasty, attempting to establish itself without provoking civil war.[6] Cox's film, on the other hand, seems consistent with the third phase of Fermor's schematic in which the impending horror has been either averted or endured, and the subjects are able to revel in the chaotic aftermath;[7] they can toy with the conventions of wickedness and doom without any real anxiety.

The world of the film is one in which the characters have faced apocalyptic destruction and suffering, finding them void of revelatory potential. They are the walking dead, a *danse macabre*, one skeleton leading a host of others to the grave.[8]

The promise of apocalyptic renewal has been thwarted or undermined within Cox's narrative, the culmination of the long awaited class struggle has been suspended, and hostilities over the inequities in material wealth and justice have survived the catastrophe and have even intensified. The social dissolution, resulting from the catastrophe, has not succeeded in wiping away the residual culture. Vindice's family represents a still point within this Babylon of desperate social climbers and lewd loves in the Duke's court. The flashbacks to Vindice's wedding party, just prior to the poisoning of Gloriana and most of the guests, reflect a period of stability in which social rituals and familial relations still seemed predictable and meaningful. Vindice's family is ostensibly a model of coherent relations, while the ducal family is a Freudian nightmare; none of the loyalties and prohibitions requisite to meaningful family bonds remain, their ambition and debauchery foiling the residual order and integrity of Vindice's kin. Indeed, the film is constructed largely upon the counterpoint of these antithetical groups, and such binary structures are common to apocalyptic narrative.[9] However, the resolution of *The Revenger's Tragedy* involves no triumph of good over evil, as there are no absolute standards of the same in the world of the play, which is too flawed to include pure virtue save in those already dead: Gloriana and Antonio's wife. The ducal family is incapable of fidelity, either social or sexual. The egotism, rapaciousness, and vaulting ambition of the Duke's kin differ from the virtuous, supportive, and forgiving behaviors practiced in Vindice's household. The individual members of the ducal family maintain no loyalties toward each other but are willing to annihilate their kin for advancement. In the lunge for power immediately following Lussurioso's death near the end of the film, Supervacuo kills Ambitioso, Spurio kills Supervacuo, and a security guard kills Spurio. They all die in an instant, falling successively in the upshot of Vindice's revenge.

Despite the numerous invocations to narratives of social cleansing and apocalyptic renewal, the expectations of a final destruction that sweeps away the old order, reestablishing justice and social harmony, remain unfulfilled. The narrative of Cox's film is not so much apocalyptic as anti-apocalyptic, a distinction that evokes the more traditional sense of the term, one that acknowledges the root word "apokalupsis," meaning "to uncover or unveil."[10] The term suggests a structure rather than a culmination. "Apokalupsis," and, by extension, "apocalypse," evoke a process that only implies a conclusion. "Apocalypse" is always in the process of becoming, thus the idea of destruction and renewal that shapes Judeo-Christian teleology must by definition always be looming and arriving, but never arrived. "Apocalypse" implies "to come" as well as "to reveal."[11] The narrative of human life is organized by knowledge of an impending end whether it is the individual life or the life of a civilization or our species; "each passing moment stands in some significant relation to a beginning and an end."[12] Frank Kermode concurs: "human meaning depends…upon his understanding of both a beginning and an end to things."[13]

However, much postmodern philosophy contends that humanity has been robbed of its end, that the apocalypse so important to the understanding of the twentieth century has been evaded or has been endured without creating substantive social change. In *The Illusion of an End*, Baudrillard argues that the idea of apocalypse can no longer signify because it can no longer be envisaged as a triumph of good over evil, legitimizing previous history as an incremental and meaningful movement toward revelation and apotheosis—toward destruction, cleansing, and renewal: "History, meaning, and progress are no longer able to reach their escape velocity.…Evil has become immanent and interstitial…there is no longer any abominable other."[14] Baudrillard cites "terrorism" as the new enemy,[15] one that has become invisible because it has infiltrated its institutional adversaries, thereby erasing the boundaries that delineated the antithetical camps of apocalyptic teleology and essentially eliminating the epic conflict that achieves apocalyptic proportions. The terrorist is limited in his/her reach, he/she can create havoc but cannot instigate doomsday, he/she cannot be completely eradicated, but he/she can be managed and even appropriated into the consolidation of power.

Cox's *Revengers Tragedy* illustrates the late twentieth- and early twenty-first-century perception, attributed to Lyotard, that our age has become suspicious of all "meta-narratives,"[16] overarching theories that form and predict a meaningful trajectory for human civilization. The familiar meta-narratives of Christianity or Marxism, for example, which lend coherence and purpose to the random events of human interaction and conceive a historical process culminating in a restoration of peace and social harmony—a vision of egalitarian justice that separates the damned from the saved (literally or figuratively), leaving the latter in possession of a newly rejuvenated earth—have lost their ability to signify.[17]

The narrative structure of Cox's *Revengers Tragedy* consistently undermines this process of destruction and renewal, this vision of a millennial tranquility, ecstasy, and stasis—this death impulse. The film debunks the myth of regeneration demonstrating through various micro-narratives that apocalypse is mythical, not inevitable or immanent. The world of Cox's film is both pre- and postapocalyptic. The catastrophe that preceded the opening of the film—the destruction of the Southern UK by an asteroid or meteor that conveniently wiped out the London-centered establishment has failed to erase the residual cultures that contributed to the abuse of the commons. Both the monarchy (the ducal family) and the government of peers (Lord Antonio) have survived the destruction and have become even more corrupt and comprehensive in their influence and in their exploitation of the working classes. The economic hegemony of the ducal family is apparently ubiquitous, the Duke's name or image attached to virtually every commercial and public enterprise. Thus the traditional symbol of divine judgment, the proverbial "bolt out of the blue," has not wiped away political and economic inequalities, but has exacerbated them, creating a dystopia in which the laboring classes still await justice.

The opening scene of the film depicts Vindice arising from the dead like the specter of revenge come to accept the trophies of his conspiratorial labors. As a public bus filled with corpses rolls to a stop, Vindice emerges as the only surviving creature. But the revenge he pursues—one that legitimizes a metaphysical system assuring that goodness, justice, and mercy will prevail—is not a foregone conclusion, and even after the success of his several machinations the new order that he has helped to establish turns out to be just as self-serving as the old and is indeed complicit with the same that is, presumably, overthrown. The pursuit of revenge reveals a faith in an idealized justice, the same that has been appropriated to legitimize and uphold the social structure condemned for its exploitation of and insensitivity toward the laboring class. Thus Vindice's plans reinforce a part of the same metaphysical structure that he needs to overturn in order to gain the justice he desires; the apocalyptic mythology is appropriated to both the maintenance and the subversion of power. One does not produce a revolutionary or reform structure without acknowledging, positing, and legitimizing that which it seeks to overthrow. So Vindice must wrest the signifiers of justice and legitimacy from those who abuse them for their own interests—the ducal family or the aristocratic class—but this same process ensures that the social struggle will have made no progress in the transformation of society. It will have only replaced one tyrant with another, and at the end of Cox's film Vindice and his coconspirators are surprised to find that they have come full circle; they have helped to install a man in power who is as unprincipled and selfish in his political objects as were the Duke and his heirs. Lord Antonio is chiefly interested in his own survival and is willing to circumvent justice in the maintenance of power. Thus apocalyptic or fundamental change fails to materialize. There is no rejuvenated earth to inherit but only a continuation of the same injustice that "breeds all black malcontents."

While the structure of castigation and reward operates productively within the context of Vindice's family, such as when the disguised avenger tempts his mother to operate as a bawd to his sister, then upbraids, threatens, and reforms her, similar patterns seem to miscarry everywhere else in the film. Justice is constantly foreclosed within the narrative, signaling the failure of the post-cataclysmic society to affect revolution or revelation. No one has learned from the event that destroyed the center of power before the film opened, the old order having survived to redouble its self-serving power and influence. Perhaps this points up the emptiness of harbingers and portents and the presumed manifestations of divine judgment and displeasure. When all is done, a rock fell out of the sky; it signaled no millennial or intelligent design; the benighted souls of postapocalyptic UK continue as they are without illumination. The condition of the legal institutions of the surviving state is captured in the image of the judge who presides over the Youngest Son's rape trial. The judge wheezes and rasps his way through his oratory, struggling for each breath even as he sucks oxygen from a tank. The image, of course, suggests that justice is on life support. The Duke's interruption and postponement of the impending guilty verdict is heralded as the death of justice: "Delayed, deferred, and if judgment have cold blood, flattery and bribes will kill it" (1.2.89–90). The law is unable to punish those who victimized Lord Antonio's wife; the rapaciousness of the ducal clan ranges unchecked.

While justice scarcely clings to life, the ducal family enjoys a world without impediment to the fulfillment of their most base desires, one in which there is no sublimation of the pleasure principle. Vindice's efforts to destroy them with their own villainies are repeatedly foiled by the counter machinations of the same Machiavellian group. When he alerts Lussurioso to the Duchess's sexual indiscretions with the bastard son Spurio, the ducal heir bursts in upon what he believes is an incestuous coupling, only to find the Duke and Duchess together. Vindice expects Lussurioso's imprisonment and execution, but the suspicious Duke overturns his rash judgment against his son when he sees the vigor with which his other children counsel their brother's death. The miscarriage of Lussurioso and his brothers' malignant designs would seem to be sufficient impetus to abandon treachery, ambition, and dissimulation, yet members of the ducal family are not reformed by their experiences; indeed they are so unregenerate that the same ambition destroys each in his turn in the denouement of the film/play. Yet being "hoist upon their own petard" does not constitute divine judgment or legitimize a narrative structure that assures the eventual triumph over villainy, lust, hypocrisy, murder, and avarice—the antimasque of moralities that is the ducal clan.

The agents of social change, Vindice's family, are not capable of seeing their own complicity in the corruption. The unrepentant dukes drop one after the other, but the expected triumph of the avenging family is undercut by their own misjudgment of Lord Antonio's gratitude. The apocalyptic narrative structure that should conclude with the doling out of punishment and reward to the wicked and virtuous respectively, instead sees the chastising revenger and his family facing the same punishment they dispensed—even those members most guiltless of intrigue—and all of this from a rising politician whose fortunes have been lifted by Vindice's seemingly just labors. Lord Antonio's claim that the revengers are capable of murdering him as well as the aged duke neglects to articulate the motivation for revenge that drove Vindice. In the context of the seventeenth century, the deposition and murder of the nobility, at least within the political mythology and rhetoric of the age, was never acceptable, and even in contemporary society vigilantism is not condoned, but both audiences probably would relish the sight of justice exercised upon unrepentant villainy, and the modern audience would even be content to see the revenger live.

Antonio's execution of Vindice's family exposes and condemns him as an ingrate and a Machiavellian villain. He is not a vulnerable old man who is frightened by the idea of Vindice's untamed violence, but rather a scheming politician who feigned grief over his wife's suicide and exploited the national outpouring of sympathy for his own cynical ambitions before viciously turning against those who brought him the retribution that law could not provide. His sentence against Vindice is not the production of a desire to see order restored, but a ploy to eliminate those to whom he is indebted for his power, those who may claim special privilege. In the final scene of Cox's film, Vindice becomes Antonio's unwitting accomplice. Thus the narrative expectation that villainy and virtue will be extricated from each other with order, harmony, and openness restored is subverted. There is no renewal or regeneration of government; the courts are still populated by a collection of fraudulent and self-serving politicians who place personal power before the collective good. The class and social hierarchies that Vindice has labored to dismantle by removing the executive privilege of the duke and his family is restored, and the laboring class punished for its presumption in overstepping its degree. Of course, the final event of Cox's film includes what may be the death of Lord Antonio, but the result of such an eventuality does not create a sense of hopefulness but rather a power vacuum that will no doubt be filled by more dissembling, strong-arm politicians. Indeed there seems to be no one of note left to assume the mantle of power.

The overall structure of Cox's narrative also undermines the expectations of apocalyptic cleansing. The world grows older and more degenerate, and yet it cannot bring its downward slide to its nadir from which to mount a virtuous ascent. The long predicted conflagration from which a millennial society will emerge seems just as remote as ever. The movement of the narrative toward its denouement suggests that meaning and purpose will be revealed; divine plan will be manifest, but there is an absence of providential intervention at the conclusion. As the protagonist and his family hurry toward their destruction, they witness a celestial portent (a comet or asteroid streaming across the sky) not unlike that which must have preceded the prior cataclysm, which left a water-filled crater where once southern England sat. Yet the players do not pause to question or reflect upon the anomaly, nor does it signal the advent of millennial events; the beginning and ending that would lend the celestial event coherence have been stripped of their ability to confer meaning. The former meteor strike did not signal the death knell of the establishment, and there is no reason to believe a second will. Indeed the first strike has demythologized the sky bourn portent. The revengers' failure to acknowledge the traditional harbinger may suggest that they have already lost hope in providential change even before the betrayal of Lord Antonio. Either way, the anticipations of cast and audience are countermanded by a cynical loss of faith in the traditional teleologies. The apocalypse can never arrive, or perhaps it already did but failed to manifest the recognizable signs.

Released within the first two years of the twenty-first century, Cox's film coincides with the dismantling of one false teleology and the construction of another; the first, a collapse of apocalyptic expectations surrounding the end of the second millennium, and the second, a violent genesis of a global and open-ended campaign against terrorism. The 9/11 attacks and the subsequent Barcelona train bombings and London Tube bombings function as the beginning of a new and dangerous historical epoch in which Western democracy and capitalism are under a threat from Islamic terrorism so pervasive that it compels fundamental and aggressive change in the operations of defense. The dualistic structure of the apocalyptic narrative reemerges, including a world populated by moral antitheses—innocents and monsters. The result is a defense that operates via naked aggression. The attacks of 9/11 serve as a reference point, the beginning of an ideological and military trajectory that has no definable object and no identifiable conclusion. It is war against a frame of mind—not a nation or alliance or even an identifiable social subgroup. The terrorist is a phantom enemy who does not exist in any one place or even one ideology, but can be anywhere at any time. The proliferation of referents for the appellations "terrorist" and "terrorism" and their usage as nationalist rallying cries within a variety of only marginally related circumstances exposes the fluidity of the new power base that can demonize or legitimize social processes based upon their relative relationship to the ongoing struggle against the hidden and ill-defined enemy, one whose shape changes as it suits our governing institutions. Cox's sensitivity to these ideas may be manifest in the original opening of the film, which included images of the 9/11 catastrophe that were later edited out.

Unlike the apocalyptic teleology that developed over the course of the twentieth century with the proliferation of nuclear weapons, the war on terrorism can offer no mutually assured destruction to stay the hand of violence. It can offer no final resolution since its object has no national boundaries, no population, no government, and no army, but only an attitude and resolution toward the Western World, one that can fall and rise as the vicissitudes of international politics dictate. The enemy can emerge even within our own national boundaries and among our own citizenry. The resulting actions involve a self-annihilating chaos in which state institutions make war upon themselves and their own populations. The culmination of this struggle exists as an ideal, a final eradication of an amorphous extremism that will result in a millennial dawn of universal peace. But an enemy, like Vindice (the representation of social and political dissent), who changes shape to suit the political milieu, cannot be eliminated but must be constantly reproduced to justify still further performances of hegemonic invulnerability. Thus the expected conclusion and resolution shapes the content of the events that produce it, but since the end can never be realized and operates only so long as it is able to hide its own mechanisms, the seemingly measured and incremental movements toward a denouement, a manifestation of a final and enduring justice are rendered random and incoherent, constantly overturned, reinvented, reinterpreted, and reproduced.

The inability of the protagonists in Cox's film to realize their revenge—a sociopolitical and juridical revolution—reflects the conditions of the post-9/11 mind-set and is indicative of the foreclosure of meaning for such narrative structures as well as the inveterate dreams of destruction and renewal. Revenge cannot bring about fundamental change, but only perpetuate a cycle of violence that reinforces those institutions that produce class or regional inequities. In Cox's film, the establishment is not overthrown or even reformed; it is simply repopulated and reinvigorated by a new enemy who signifies its radical alterity, its threat from within and without against which it must be constantly vigilant and of which it must be constantly sanitizing itself. Lord Antonio's ruthless suppression of Vindice's vigilantism signifies the rapid transition to a national security state in which conflict is met with exaggerated resolutions justified by the heightened vigilance in a self-created and even cynical paranoia. Lord Antonio's own rapid demise suggests the same insofar as the state cannot seem to operate with any punitive and judicial discretion or subtlety, but immediately adopts repressive violence at the first sign of disorder; it loses its ability to discern justifiable from antisocial violence. Lord Antonio's government, in an effort to restore order and security, perpetuates the injustice that wrought Vindice's crimes and produces its own form of state terrorism.

Notes

1. For the purposes of consistency and clarity, I have chosen to ascribe authorship to Middleton and not Cyril Tourneur, since Cox does so in the opening credits of his film. All citations are from *The Revenger's Tragedy*, ed. Brian Gibbons (New York: Norton, 1967) and are quoted parenthetically in the text.
2. L.G. Salinger offers a comprehensive articulation of the Morality Tradition in the *Revenger's Tragedy*. "The Revenger's Tragedy and the Morality Tradition," *Scrutiny* 6 (1938): 402–24.
3. Karen Robertson maintains that the naming of Vindice's dead beloved Gloriana "evokes a golden age of regal virtue" (226). Michael Neill warns us against drawing a close connection between the skull of Gloriana and an "Elizabethan nostalgia," since such a correlation could too easily be construed as an unkind parody of the "cosmetic grotesqueries of the old queen's last years" (413).
4. Christopher Lee discusses Robert Cecil's ability to maintain power and influence in the transition between Elizabeth I and James I in spite of the king's frequent awarding of court offices to Scotsmen. see *1603: The Death of Elizabeth I and the Birth of the Stuart Era* (London: Review, 2003), 202–203.
5. Una Ellis-Fermor, *The Jacobean Drama: An Interpretation* (New York: Vintage, 1964), 1–27.
6. Ibid., 2.
7. Ibid., 25.
8. See Salinger, "The Revenger's Tragedy," 415.
9. David Ketterer, "New Worlds for Old: The Apocalyptic Imagination, Science Fiction, and American Literature," *Mosaic* 5 (1971): 37–57, 41.
10. Ibid., 39.
11. Ibid.
12. Malcolm Bull, *Seeing Things Hidden: Apocalypse, Vision, and Totality* (London: Verso, 1999), 47.
13. Qtd. in Ketterer, "New Worlds," 43.
14. Jean Baudrillard, *The Illusion of an End*, trans. Chris Turner (Stanford: Stanford UP, 1994), 119, 40–41.
15. Ibid., 40.
16. Jean-Francois Lyotard, *The Postmodern Condition: A Report on Knowledge*, trans. Jeff Bennington and Brian Massumi (Minneapolis: U of Minnesota P, 1984), xxiv.
17. See Klaus R. Scherpe and Brent O. Peterson, "Dramatization and De-Dramatization of 'The End': The Apocalypic Consciousness of Modernity and Post-Modernity," *Cultural Critique* 5 (1986–1987): 95–129, 95–97.

CHAPTER 12

Forget Film: Speculations on Shakespearean Entertainment Value

Donald Hedrick

> ...written on purpose, with much study to no end.
>
> —John Taylor, the Water-Poet

If Shakespeare studies have at times had an imperialistic habit of mind threatening to conquer the space of English studies, just as English studies have a way of being perceived to dominate other literatures, so has film in its global domination had a way of becoming an ally of Shakespeare, albeit a provisional one. Theater, however, has experienced a trajectory of prestige-decline and subsequent legitimation crisis, as theater departments and the recent job market can testify, carrying with it the decline of nineteenth-century Shakespearean theater as an elite cultural form. Except for the musical, theater generally receives a smaller and smaller demographic, and a more elderly one. The decline itself has been appropriated as theatrical entertainment in Mike Daisey's current, one-man performance, *How Theater Failed America*.

Film's cultural transcendence was monumentalized by one film moment of its provisional alliance with Shakespeare, that moment when we took consummate pleasure in the spectacular and creative opening of Kenneth Branagh's *Henry V* (1989). In this much noted scene, Derek Jacobi wanders as Chorus through the darkened room of an isolated and abandoned film studio, suddenly lit with floodlights to replay the festive reveal of the Elizabethan theater of Olivier's *Henry V* (1944). The film's moment speaks to us profoundly: we not only identify the parallel between Elizabethan theater and contemporary film as popular arts, but also triumphantly acknowledge the reigning glory of cinema itself, thus given a cameo role in Branagh's version in keeping with film's contemporary celebrity status.

The linkages of Shakespeare to theater generally vary with their cultural capital, as Shakespeare audiences are to film audiences as opera audiences are to rock concert audiences. In combination with film, resulting Shakespearean cinematic productions are often imbued with a barely submerged sense of their competition with other film and television popular culture—horror film *Macbeth*; noir film *Richard III*; teen exploitation films of *Othello*, *The Taming of the Shrew*, *Twelfth Night*, and so on. In piggybacking on the popular, Shakespearean performance is clearly in an era of what I have elsewhere termed "late Shakespeareanism."[1] Yet a common observation about news journalism's response to its popularized commodification (news anchor stars, jazzy visual layouts) might well give Shakespeareans serious pause: that in attempting to compete with popular entertainment, an institution such as journalism must, even before it starts, *inevitably lose*, registering an implicit desperation.[2]

This is not to disparage the strong and fascinating work of the society of Shakespeare on Film. Yet here I want to exercise a tactical resistance to the hegemonic paradigm of the film machine over interpretation, a machine to whose operations I have myself contributed. The hegemony is apparent. Laurie Osborne, for instance, describes the way that the field of film has come to stand in for all mass culture.[3] Even early on in the field of Shakespeare on Film, Roger Manvell proposed what was at the time more counterintuitive, that the "situation of Elizabethan theatre" was in many respects "remarkably parallel to that of contemporary film and television."[4] Now, more popularly, Ron Rosenbaum claims that film techniques may give us access to "a vision of Shakespeare that *is closer to the original* [my italics] than most stage productions."[5] Speaking for the most sophisticated Shakespearean research and theory, Richard Burt suggests that "dominant" Shakespearean scholarship "has begun self-consciously recasting early modern media in terms of new media."[6] In attending to this prominence, I do not, however, mean to achieve a kind of residual allegiance to everything earlier or to an imaginary past of interpretation. Nor do I participate in the familiar resistance to popular culture that so frequently inhabits Shakespearean criticism and, as Katharine Rowe has argued, often underlies attempts to define and privilege media specificity.[7] I want, however, as part of my larger project of theorizing "entertainment value," to suggest a possibility that, in our submission to the film machine, we have elected the *wrong* popular culture, and that we might consider serving a different master for awhile. To Douglas Brode's boosterish remark that "apparently, William Shakespeare, once hailed by Orson Welles as the original screenwriter, is alive and well in Hollywood,"[8] I want to counter that Shakespeare is alive, yes, but in a witness protection program, hiding out in a location to be revealed in this chapter.

The competition with popular culture noted in contemporary Shakespearean theatrical production is in fact historical and even constitutive of Shakespearean theater. What Fredric Jameson regards as the "rivalry" of media characteristic of postmodernism is easy enough to project backward onto the pre-postmodern of early modern England.[9] Even prior to the period the notion of a competition among the arts and their artists was a traditional aesthetic formation of the Renaissance known as the *paragone*, particularly in the visual arts. Leonardo da Vinci, for instance, boasted that he was able to execute "sculpture" in any medium of marble, bronze, terracotta, or even painting in *paragone* with his rival artists.[10] What we observe in Elizabethan-Jacobean culture, however, is the transformation of the *paragoni* into commercial terms, or into what I term "relative entertainment value." The rivalry of Shakespeare's theater with other London entertainments has often been noted in passing in scholarship, especially traditional scholarship—"in passing" because of the typical dismissal of what is "just entertainment."[11] Two tendencies, however, reduce our consciousness of this rivalry. The first is the tendency of theater history to defuse in some way the growing competitiveness, endemic to an era of growing capitalization, within the profession and the institution. Thus, Andrew Gurr idealizes Shakespeare's company as the most democratic of the theater duopoly of the time, with Henslowe as the model of the predatory businessman and capitalist.[12] Capital becomes therefore more a matter of personality. Or, Roslyn Knutson stresses the cooperativeness of the traditional guild system of artisanship, as it was transferred to the new institutions of the purpose-built, admission-charging theaters.[13]

New historicism, as it happens, also deemphasizes the competitiveness among entertainment venues, by creating an ideological overview and master narrative of "subversion" (although I take its general thrust as important and convincing in capturing resistances to different kinds of domination). Thus, we find Steven Mullaney arguing that the theaters and brothels were ideologically "synonymous" in resistance to power.[14] Similarly, David Wiles describes bear-baiting and theater not in opposition but "homologous activities."[15] And yet, if we were to consider Shakespeare's inclusion of what must have been rather contemporaneous brothel scenes from London into the historical Greek setting of *Cymbeline*, we would hardly be able to see the satiric portrait as the equivalent of contemporary "product placement" or covert advertising for products that appear offhandedly in movie scenes.

Competitiveness, rather than the ideological synonymity, would be what is forcefully brought out as the virtuous young woman Marina manages to take down the brothel by her virtuous persuasions directed at its customers: the brothel owners end up looking silly and even old-fashioned.[16] While Marina's reasons for putting the brothel out of business are moral ones, the *entertainment unconscious* of the scene registers what is instead a *business* competitiveness. That the competition is of rival entertainment industries is registered by her fantasy of how she will employ all the whores put out of work by her convictions and their reforms, as she promises to "make gain," hence profit, by so doing:

> MARINA If that thy master would make gain by me,
> Proclaim that I can sing, weave, sew, and dance,
> With other virtues which I'll keep from boast,
> And I will undertake all these to teach,
> I doubt not but this populous city will
> Yield man scholars.
>
> (*Pericles,* Scene 19, 194–99)[17]

Moreover, in keeping with the entertainment logic of miscellany or variety in her hostile takeover, Marina promises to teach a variety of the entertainments for which she possesses skills, again alerting us to the entertainment unconscious of the "populous city" of London.

The competitiveness of entertainments, and the effects therefore of what I will term "relative entertainment value," is a reflection of the explosion of entertainment opportunities available in London early in the seventeenth century. In early modern scholarship, London has been called somewhat offhandedly an "entertainment culture" or an "entertainment industry," but the full implications and consequences of this have yet to be explored more thoroughly, particularly as they impact Shakespeare's plays themselves. The impact is reflected in the gallants' conversation that Thomas Nashe imagines in *Pierce Penniless*, when their wealth combines with their boredom to produce the following portrait of the choice—and therefore the commercial rivalry—of entertainment options.

> …saith one, "Let us go to the Steelyard and drink Rhenish wine."
>
> "Nay, if a man knew where a good whorehouse were," saith another, "it were somewhat like."
>
> "Nay," saith the third, "let us go to a dicing house or a bowling alley and there we shall have some sport for our money."[18]

The trajectory of their boredom points in the direction of what Theodor Adorno would describe as a certain logic of mass culture, which he termed "sportification."[19] This tendency of all entertainments to approach the condition of sport, I would argue, is a feature of the effect of capital and profit maximization. While capital is sometimes thought to promote competition, its "sportification," however, might be considered just the opposite, as a promotion of anticompetition, in that the choice of one opportunity might exclude or defeat another, pitting the choices against one another. As Jeremy Lopez has observed about developing theatrical convention, the love of variety and the excess of stimulus became prevalent.[20] We may thus expect them to have become integral features of everything from audience reception to aesthetic design insofar as the number of entertainment opportunities expands, like capital, theoretically without limit. Variety would take on the competitive nature of one-upsmanship, in a "maximization of affect" and style that conforms to Adorno's paradigm of "sportification."[21] Shakespeare will thus frequently incorporate the element of *choice of representations or entertainments*, often of alternative shows or characters, as he does explicitly in *A Midsummer Night's Dream* when Philostrate offers a menu of entertainments to Theseus for his wedding night, thus spending considerable stage time before "The Tragedy of Pyramus and Thisbe" is inevitably selected, and the process of choice and taste by Theseus (and Hippolyta in her resistance to his choice) comically anatomized, rejecting several of the proferred entertainments as shopworn or inappropriate to the occasion. The logic of the miscellany, variety, or entertainment alternatives informs representations of entertainment in Shakespeare from the early example of the "competition" of actor "Worthies" in *Love's Labour's Lost* to Mamillius' offering to his mother of a choice to hear a sad or a merry tale in *The Winter's Tale*, a play in which the audience is offered up two distinct genres. The flip side of the boredom exhibited above is clearly novelty, although it should be emphasized that both sides are constitutive of the reification of entertainment choice.

Combinatorial or cross-fertilizing entertainment moves are, of course, familiar in the period, as the theaters borrow from the court masque, and as the court masque, especially its anti-masque, borrows from the popular elements of the public theaters. The institutionalization of such combinatorial logic reaches an extreme in Henslowe's plan to make the Hope Theater a combination theater and bear-baiting arena on alternative days, with the theater—in an eerie premonition of theater's often dependent status in contemporary culture—perhaps to be carried along financially by the more profitable entertainment of animal-baiting. Perhaps the most prominent of the paratheatrical activities, however, would have been the stage *jig*, often attached to the end of even tragic plays as a kind of supplement.[22] How to think of the jig is problematic, as it is so often disregarded in scholarship because of a dearth of information in the archive, as well as its unprivileged role as mere entertainment. From its contemporary reception, however, it is clear that it could be regarded as an almost integral part of an entire "entertainment package," whether or not the theaters charged additional admission, as is currently unknown, for jigs at the end of the plays. But dancing itself would be subject to "sportification," as rival theatrical venues developed their own identifiable dancing styles associated with celebrity dancers of jigs; we read notes from the era about the competing "fat fool" of the Curtain Theatre and the "lean fool" of the Bull.[23]

The jig's disreputable history suggests that it was even more than the plays a *participatory* mode of entertainment, if the riots that eventually surrounded it may be taken as evidence. Such a participatory mode marking entertainment logic was known, of course, beyond the commercial theater, as a characteristic of public spectacle. Thus, Foucault has instructed us of the sheer theatricality and performative nature of public punishment and incarceration, which would transform the power of theater into the social and political realm. The reverse of this, however, has been seldom noted by Shakespeareans, namely, the use of the theaters themselves as sites of punishment and incarceration. From a pamphlet of Will Kempe's we learn that it was not uncommon to capture pickpockets in the theater and tie them to a post of the stage during the performance—an additional or supplementary show like that of the jig, and another instance of entertainment turning "real."[24] Elsewhere I have speculated on unpacking the implications of the practice, particularly in the circumstance of a relation created between onstage criminals of a play and the offstage "real" criminals in their proximity.[25] For the present purposes, however, what is significant is the "liveness" of what otherwise would be merely an *image* of criminality, or the fiduciary or substitution relationship between offstage and onstage criminal.

The extreme popularity of the jig suggests that it was not only especially participatory, but that it involved the audience to the extent that it ratcheted up anarchic energies, producing the out-of-control behavior that eventually brought on the authorities and the rulings. While clearly separate from the plays themselves as a theatrical event, the logic of the jig could show up in the relative entertainment value of the plays. Following Nashe's description of some London entertainments as "extreme pleasures," it is no stretch to think of the post-play jigs as pushing the envelopes of decorous taste and verse. Having acknowledged its force, we may glance at the relative entertainment value provided by the promotion of excessive dance within the play narratives. Sir Toby Belch in the festivity-rich *Twelfth Night*, for example, watches

Sir Andrew dance offstage while he competitively shouts, "Higher, higher!" in an instantaneous command for entertainment value. This mode of reception reflects as well what might be a typical audience's vocal involvement in the show, for which the term "reception" is a theoretical understatement for what may have been rather a request, demand, or even command for *more*. To watch the excess grow more excessive structures the key scene as drunken Toby and his company build to a "caterwauling" that interrupts Malvolio's sleep and initiates the "revenge," which then structures the play's dark turn into excess through the humiliation of Malvolio.

The Value of Little, Less, Nothing

Paul Yachnin, in arguing for what he terms a "populuxe" theater of Shakespeare's in the process of manufacturing ersatz cultural products of prestige value, suggests that in the marketing of plays the players had an interest to "maintain the worth of what they were selling to the public."[26] While his interpretation of the situation of the theater admirably attends to its market matters and would seem a rather unexceptional claim, I want to challenge its apparent universality as a comprehensive description of the mechanism of the marketplace and its evolution. That is, I want to replace Yachnin's logic of *raising* value with the more technically capitalist logic of achieving the most value for the least input, that is, the maximization of return on investment. Entertainment logic, I believe, takes this more economic principle of *return*, as opposed to strict *value*, to its extreme or limiting case: the ability to make a profit off of *nothing*.

I might be permitted an economic example, itself trivial, involving a souvenir I almost bought at the museum shop of the Victoria and Albert recently. The novelty was a clear plastic bubble-shaped container, which held, as its packaging promoted, absolutely *nothing*. It was as light as air because it was in fact only air. Its buyer was to become the proud owner of something deliberately, even spectacularly, overpriced, presumably to be bought (if my shopping style may be generalized) *because* it was so overpriced. The economy here was an overpricing that was *itself* the producer of exchange value, as the uniqueness of the novelty allowed the toy to be audaciously priced at two pounds, as I recall. Its pricing was thus totally fictional or imaginative, since the use-value of nothing is presumably nothing, produced with no labor except its packaging, and whose price determination was wholly arbitrary (though perhaps not, in a sense, since the manufacturers of this nothing could not arbitrarily place any price on it; had they priced it too high no one would want to buy nothing). And yet, like any art object bid up by being bid upon, this nothing carried an economic lesson in itself. In a sense, the little plastic bubble furnishes a model of the financial dealings and financial bubbles that were growing up during the nineteen-eighties and nineteen-nineties around the lax economic regulation and the inventiveness of financial novelties or "derivatives," directly leading to financial crisis and worldwide collapse sometime later. As if to prove the agenda of "presentists," the crucial factor among these derivatives was the device of "short-selling," which, perhaps not coincidentally, dates from European practices of the beginning of the seventeenth century, and was as controversial then as it became in the Great Depression and now. Whether or not the sale of "nothing" was intended to have an ironic meta-significance about late capitalist economics is doubtful, but it was nonetheless prophetic for past and present. Aside from that speculation, however, the point to be made here is that the souvenir marks the peculiar, problematic, and recursive economic nature of entertainment value.

Shakespeare notes the "nothing value" phenomenon in many places in his plays, although it is not usually interpreted by Shakespeareans in this more economic sense. The token of "nothing" is usually present in hyperbolic or rhetorical gambits, such as when Theseus in *A Midsummer Night's Dream* describes the poet as "giving to airy nothing a local habitation and a name," or Iago's commentary on the power of the jealous imagination to transform "trifles light as air" into "proofs of holy writ" (3.3.26–28). The play *King Lear* proves to its willful protagonist monarch that he is in error in telling his daughter, "Nothing will come of nothing" (1.1.89), echoing a principle of classical Aristotelian natural science. As explicitly entertainment value this nothing is directly represented, however, when the pickpocket Autolycus boasts about distracting the sheep-shearing festival audience with his song, by describing their "admiring the nothing of it." The "trinkets" he offers for sale he explains receive such a hypnotic response from the crowd "as if my trinkets had been hallow'd and brought a benediction to the buyer," thus conjoining the religious sense of fetishism with the economic, as Marx was to do in describing the founding nature of capital (*The Winter's Tale* 4.4.601, 613).

The elevation of what is acknowledged to be worthless or trivial begins, I believe, to mark the habitus of the entertainment market in rather remarkable ways. We know, of course, this logic in our own entertainment epoch, particularly in the universally decried and profitable "reality shows" of television, where anything at all can be filmed and observed, even in its quotidian banality, and even become a profitable series. Such shows, cheaply or relatively cheaply produced, not only generate an inevitable, public outcry that they are worthless trash, but it may also be that their very economic success and popularity depends on this common disparagement, rendering them productively worth nothing if the contempt becomes nearly universal. The aesthetic sensibility of this would seem to conform to usual concepts of the postmodern or modern. To complain that such "reality" is either trash or not *really* reality is evidence that its strategy is successful and works exactly as entertainment value logic demands.

This phenomenon is not unfamiliar to the present age. One candidate for its contemporary origins in the artistic field would be pop art, with its deliberate banality, as Andy Warhol silk-screened images of ordinary soup cans for his art. Yet, as we seek to historicize the aesthetics of this, or rather to seek its origins, we are driven back further historically. Certainly, we could include along with Warhol's "trifles" Marcel Duchamp's noted found object, "Fountain," the commercial urinal put on display as a cheeky entry into a Paris art exhibition in 1917. This artwork has not only been valued in histories of art for its shock value, but now, some hundred years later, it has been judged by an extensive survey of art historians to be the most important and influential work of the twentieth century. Like Autolycus, the modern artist becomes a pedlar of whatever he finds lying around, virtually *inviting* the charge against its worthlessness.

We may go further back for the phenomenon, however, at least until the growth of the entertainment industry in the purpose-built Elizabethan theaters, which arguably were as revolutionary as these noted works of art. The possibility of much further retracing back of this elevation of the trivial and the everyday constitutes the chief agenda of the present examination of the early modern paradigm of entertainment. Some of the best examples of this phenomenon can be culled from the work of a single entrepreneur/ entertainment promoter, John Taylor, who theatricalized ordinary everyday experience in an explosion of pamphlet writing, in the process of which his inventiveness ranged from everything from the first work of nonsense to some of the very first experiments in journalism and news.[27] Although a frequent customer of the theater and of Shakespeare's plays, as we know from his citations, Taylor's tactic of relative entertainment value would be to compete in an alternative media: the pamphlet, competitively sold at one or twopence, in natural equivalence to the theater's admission prices. His pamphlets were often linked to a wealth of other promotional activities and stunts devised by Taylor, thus marking the explosion of entertainment options in the early seventeenth century. Not the least of these projects/ stunts was the production of the very next folio edition after Shakespeare's of 1623, Taylor's "All the Works," following in 1630 and capitalizing on his ephemera. That rivals for Londoners' pennies were in a kind of collaborative competition, as opposed to a fully cutthroat one, is evidenced as well by the fact that such pamphlets, like food and drink for sale, were hawked in the theater itself at performances, and could thus bear some relation to the plays being performed. Thus entertainment values would be in play with each other, particularly, for example, if the anti-theatrical complaints were true that prostitutes would locate customers among theater audiences.

It may be even more striking, but understandable, that the early modern logic of entertainment also produced virtually the exact equivalent of the contemporary reality show, in one of Taylor's many "projects" or schemes, described in his pamphlet, *The Great Eater of Kent*.[28] In it, Taylor wittily describes his plan to stage the gargantuan Nicholas Wood (using some evident spirit of Rabelaisian excess of descriptions of food for Gargantua), of extensive local fame in his hometown of Kent, in a public London theater rented for the occasion. Wood's fame was his ability to eat enormous amounts of food, reputedly a quarter of a sheep at a single setting, and a good deal of the pamphlet is a more or less tongue-in-cheek praise of Wood's unique talent. What the reader gets, however, is much less than less: the described scheme was not carried out, since Wood got cold feet, perhaps fearing to become a laughingstock. With even less to work with than before, Taylor recounts in this same pamphlet his *lack of success* in the scheme, betting that the failure itself—a kind of nothing—would be worth a curious customer's pence. Exactly like the marketing coup of getting someone to pay something for nothings, Taylor's pamphlets, schemes, and rhetorical ploys continually play on the idea of his getting something for nothing, or the idea of his readers paying something for his self-confessed worthless work—the writer going beyond the traditional "humility" *topos* in audacious extremity.

Taylor was not, however, the only such entertainment value maximizer. In terms of "something for nothing," perhaps the most famous of entertainment fiascoes in Shakespeare's time, certainly competing for the honor with the described "non-stunt" of Taylor, was that of the advertised entertainment in 1602 of "England's Joy"—the phrase itself become synonymous with either the maximum audacity of a "projector," or the maximum gullibility of audiences. This infamous scheme by Richard Vennar, whose posted bill survives, was a promise of the stage performance spectacle that would involve actual nobility, acting as amateurs to perform historical characters and dancing. The shilling-paying audience arrived to find the event a sham, its schemer having escaped and being pursued by officers. Years later, however, Vennar would outdo this very audacity by writing an ostensible "apology." Yet, introducing the forgotten entertainment stunt for new entertainment value as a pamphlet about the stunt, he manages yet another insulting move: he complains that the gullible public should actually realize that it got its money's worth after all, since the value of such a show is in the *anticipation* of it, not in its necessarily disappointing fulfillment.[29]

The "reality show" characteristic of the London entertainment industry, and its newly found skill in profiting off of nothing, produced other phenomena affecting the theater and involving the economy of the para-theatrical. Our sense of the early modern theater business naturally tends to be involved in "box office" issues of profit from the audience paying for admission, presumably a chief novelty of the permanent theaters built in London. Our mental model of the historical event of the admission price tends to be governed by our habits, particularly our habits of attending cinema, where, unless one also attends its concession stand for refreshments, the ticket price involves the rather simple economics of supply and demand. In such a case the event produces, in a sense, a loss for the audience in return for the pleasure of the performance. We assume, further, that the wealth of theater owners and the personal financial gains of a writer-shareholder such as Shakespeare were proportional to or commensurate with the quality or value of the performance—not as we would judge it but as the paying audi-ence would judge it. Yet what if the overall theater business had a somewhat different determination, affected by the relative entertainment value of a rival, alternative choice for customers?

What throws off the simpler economics thus described is a factor underestimated in analyses of the early modern theater industry, namely, its apparent reliance upon a different "extreme pleasure" allowed within its walls. Here I speak not of prostitution, even though we recall the Puritan diatribes describing the theaters as meeting places for sexual assignations to be performed, like the jigs, afterward, and thus also a part of a broader consideration of theater economics and profitability. Instead, I want to consider gambling, not in the prevalent dicing houses of London, but as it immigrated into or was informally appropriated by its rival, the theater. We know, as it happens, that informal gambling occurred with respect to acting, with betting on actor success or ability, a clear example of the logic of sportification increasingly driving the overall economics of the entire industry.

Like the jig or the onstage incarceration of criminals, this additional aspect of the "real entertainment" offered by the public theaters as part of relative entertainment value and entertainment choice has been underes-timated in importance. The logic of sportification of entertainment tied theater to the promotion of gambling in any number of ways. We learn, for instance, just before the closing of the theaters, that the acquaintance of young, rich gallants with actors was a sure way of losing their wealth, and the most expeditious way of accomplishing great wealth loss would likely have been to gamble it away.[30] In Shakespeare, for instance, we see a reflection of this when Beatrice in *Much Ado About Nothing* declares that if Claudio attaches himself to Benedick as this month's "sworn brother," the unworthy friendship will "cost him a thousand pound" (1.1.71).

To have been lured into gambling and into dicing houses by the semi-reputable or disreputable pretenders (as Subtle and Face do to Surly in Jonson's *The Alchemist*), however, was not the only way in which gambling and the theater could be linked as economic competitors and collaborators. Gambling could occur as part of the theatrical experience, as we know from instances of "wagers" on actors described as having been typical.[31] While we don't know the extent or exact nature of such betting, the fact of a gambling *mindset* when entering the theater seems additionally confirmed by the audience portrayal of the comic spectators of *The Knight of the Burning Pestle*, the middle-class grocer and his wife who interrupt and intervene in the performance of a city comedy, paying the actors to rewrite the script as a chivalric romance starring their apprentice Rafe. Throughout the performance and their interruptions of it, we hear again and again about wagering on some aspect of the performance. Many times the examples, while not referring to an actual wager, indicate the mind-set of gambling, as when Nell asks George if he thinks Rafe will beat the Giant Barbaroso, and George responds, "I hold my cap to a farthing he does" (3.2.134).[32] But the gambling referred to could be literal as well, as when George, responding to Nell's observation that Rafe performed a tragedy at a guild performance, adds his commendation that Rafe "should have played Jeronimo with a shoemaker for a wager" (Induction, 85–88).

Even in its spoofing of middle-class aesthetic taste, the prevalence of their mind-set establishes that gambling could be a central paradigm for the "sportification" of theatrical experience and its participatory logic. While I know of no evidence of the amounts of such wagers, it might seem more plausible that they were not as extravagant as the gambling at competitor venues, but the fact of the entertainment combination itself could have a profound effect on our usual literary sense of the evaluation and especially developing expectations of audiences regarding plot, characters, and performances. What does it mean that one might come back from a performance with more than one's admission fee? The question can only be asked from a perspective of entertainment value.

The central entertainment value premise of the most return from the least investment, thus applies to the logic of London's early modern entertainment alternatives, whose proliferation would favor sportification, applying it to everything from the jig to onstage incarceration to in-theater wagering. These are features, of course, that tend to move us away from the film paradigm challenged here, toward something similar but distinctly different.

I noted earlier my intention to reveal the location of the living Shakespeare. What I intend by this, however, is linked to the way that Walter Benjamin regarded his Arcades project, as he examined Paris' earliest shopping centers. As Benjamin describes his project, the object of historical analysis of the nineteenth-century shopping venues is to discover where "capital is hiding."[33] The answer I propose here is that it hides in *entertainment value.* For our modern era, the capitol of capital, as it were, is not Hollywood but Las Vegas, whose casinoism replicates what I suggested is a broader framework for considering the early modern entertainment culture of London, one in which theater, while an important part, was necessarily only a structural part. For the immediate present, moreover, Las Vegas provides an archetype for the same casino capitalism and destructive bubble-building we now experience all too well, with massive, international consequences.

We may now retell the story of the closing of the theaters, a story told in Shakespearean scholarship with lamentations for the depredations and antitheatricality of the Puritan revolution. In most accounts, the termination figures as tragic, recalling the ending of Chekov's *Cherry Orchard,* whose mournful sound of felling trees offstage signals a world-shaking historical transformation. We may retell it instead as the similar story of an economic bubble that, as it expanded and proliferated, would inevitably burst. Las Vegas' presence has always seemed both more "real" and more fantastical than that of film, for the reasons I have begun to suggest here.

As Benjamin regarded Paris as the capital of the nineteenth century, so we might regard Las Vegas as the capital of the twenty-first century, with strong parallels to the past for reasons of an anticipatory economic formation and its subjective corollary. The casino sensibility ushered in the exploding of monumental financial firms, taken down with the same perverse spectatorial frenzy as the public celebrations held to demolish famous Las Vegas casino-hotels such as the Sands. Spectacular, gargantuan devastation is transformed into civic spectacle. The incorporation of this site of economic value into what Paul Smith examines as the "subject of value"[34] is a consequence of the revolution in Shakespeare's time. Furthered by Shakespeare as an epigone of Marlowe, under the conditions of the profit-driven, purpose-built theaters, the revolution of entertainment value might even be called, were the term not so overused, its *invention.* Its nature has been ingeniously captured in the recent marketing campaign of the MGM Casino and Hotel, urging all of us to release our "inner Las Vegas." Here, I translate the slogan into a methodological call to excavate within Shakespeare's plays, however trivial the evidence might seem, an entertainment unconscious corresponding to the Las Vegasization of London. We might then revise Smith's concept to speak not of the "subject of value," but more profitably of the "subject of entertainment value"—to describe a special subjectivity, familiar under the current economic regime, common to the condition of the Elizabethan entertainment industry.

Learning from Las Vegas as opposed to learning from Hollywood requires some adjustments to differences between the two research-generating paradigms, differences that themselves may provide additional illumination. The most general difference is that of Las Vegas embodying the participatory, as the location to which one physically relocates for the experience. Las Vegas cannot be brought to you, and certainly not into your home, except when represented in film. Its much touted "unreality" is therefore problematic, since with its simulations of monuments and of locations from France to New York to Egypt, the simulations themselves are more "real" than images, as in Baudrillard's "hyperreal," even if the reality is sometimes that of a stage prop. The "unreality" claim is similarly disturbed by peculiar scale: the city's version of the Eiffel Tower in the Paris Casino and Hotel, for instance, is *just above* one-half scale—neither a screen miniaturization nor a true replica, and it must be experienced in its own bodily and fantastical terms. More Bakhtinian than Lacanian, Las Vegas requires no screen for its bodies, which become productively profitable more through locomotion than through sitting in place, with the exception of a few diehard zombies fastened to their favorite slots. The narrative of film is replaced by the narrative of wandering, with distinct locales designed for distinct niche markets and classes.[35]

With the introduction of two reputable art museums and some traveling exhibitions in Las Vegas there has been some distinct movement toward the "educational," but the tenor there is largely more antieducational than one finds in the educational impulses of film, particularly Shakespearean film as collaborator with academia. What passes for educational in any case becomes just another niche market, much like the "populuxe" of ersatz upscale goods posited by Yachnin. Unlike the signs of titles and credits in film—signs that have even become objects of interpretation themselves—the signs of Las Vegas, so crucial for Venturi's architectural analysis,[36] are more permeable, even serving as support systems for roller coasters that ride through them. They are, literally, experienced in embodiment. While the film apparatus, even in more avante-garde versions, relies upon the directing of the gaze, the Las Vegas scene scatters the gaze in distraction, providing no preselected, framed choice of viewpoints, along with its offering up of a variety of experience choices.

In the context of its participatory character, Las Vegas' realm of choice is expansive rather than limited, say, to the choice-events offered when in a movie theater: either by viewing the sequence of film trailers for future consumption, or by standing in line at the concession stand. In terms of the visual, the difference roughly follows what Barthes distinguishes as the *studium* of a photograph, the organizational character of its viewing, with the *punctum,* or non-interpretable point of fascination or distraction, the inexplicable or intriguing detail noticed somewhere in the picture.[37] The "winnings" of film are controlled by the Academy and other awards, in cultural capital, whereas the winnings of Las Vegas from gambling are real, if temporary, like the comparable money of the financial world. Or, like the simulacral locations themselves, the winnings are not so much hyperreal, as constituted by shuttling back and forth from "real" to "fictional."

The following provisional chart may serve in summary and speculative conclusion:

HOLLYWOOD	LAS VEGAS
films on "location"	real locations and *simulacra*
"image"	"real"
focus	distraction
platea, screen between audience and players	*locus,* audience in place
titles and credits	signs, permeability and inhabitability
passive	participatory
screen limits	no limits
Lacanian, body as seen	Bakhtinian, body as experienced
hidden prostitution	open prostitution
choice of images, limited	choice of experiences, expanded
"screenplay" = text	lose the text
film narrative	wandering in the city
unproductive sitting	productive sitting, moving
scopic control	distraction
risking a ticket (money, time)	unlimited risk
no money back	potential money back
democratized audience	niche audience
choices for agency (trailers, concessions)	any or all entertainments
educational or noneducational	noneducational or antieducational
studium	*punctum*
taste and judgment, awards	"sportification," winnings

The present speculative analysis is not intended to discount the *enterprise* of interpreting Shakespeare and the perennial primacy of the text, traditions nevertheless maintained in the shift to a dominant and progressive use of film for interpretation. Yet a profitable, collective project of identifying the "inner Las Vegas" of Renaissance drama, in a mode entirely alternative to the supposedly "popular" provided by film, has only just begun.

Notes

1. Donald Hedrick, "Bardguides of the New Universe: The Cultural Logic of Late Shakespeareanism," in *Shakespeare After Mass Media*, ed. Richard Burt (New York and London: Palgrave, 2001), 35–57.
2. This situation of nostalgia for Shakespeare's seemingly unopposed cultural capital may in part account for Richard Burt's illuminating focus on the Shakespearean as "loser critic" within popular culture representations.
3. Laurie Osborne, "Introduction," *Colby Quarterly* 37.1 (March 2001): 10.
4. Roger Manvell, *Shakespeare and the Film* (New York: Praeger, 1971), 5.
5. Ron Rosenbaum, *The Shakespeare Wars: Clashing Scholars, Public Fiascos, Palace Coups* (New York: Random House, 2006), 320.
6. Richard Burt, "Introduction: Shakespeare, More or Less? From Shakespeareccentricity to Shakespearecentricity," in *Shakespeare after Shakespeare: An Encyclopedia of the Bard in Mass Media and Popular Culture*, ed. Richard Burt (Westport, CT; and London: Greenwood Press, 2007), 6–7.
7. Rowe, "Medium-Specificity and Other Critical Scripts for Screen Shakespeare," in *Alternative Shakespeares 3*, ed. Diana E. Henderson (London and New York: Routledge, 2008), 35–53.
8. Douglas Brode, *Shakespeare in the Movies: From the Silent Era to "Shakespeare in Love"* (Oxford: Oxford UP, 2000), 242.
9. Fredric Jameson, *Postmodernism, or, the Cultural Logic of Late Capitalism* (Durham: Duke UP, 1991), 62.
10. Rona Goffen, *Renaissance Rivals: Michelangelo, Leonardo, Raphael, Titian* (New Haven and London: Yale UP, 2002), 31.
11. For this observation in a contemporary theorization of entertainment, particularly in terms of the musical comedy, see Richard Dyer, *Only Entertainment* (London and New York: Routledge, 1992).
12. Andrew Gurr, *The Shakespeare Company, 1594–1642* (Cambridge: Cambridge UP, 2004), 88.
13. Roslyn Lander Knutson, *Playing Companies and Commerce in Shakespeare's Time* (Cambridge: Cambridge UP, 2001).
14. Steven Mullaney, *The Place of the Stage: License, Play, and Power in Renaissance England* (Chicago: U of Chicago P, 1988), 144.
15. David Wiles, *Shakespeare's Clown: Actor and Text in the Elizabethan Playhouse* (Cambridge: Cambridge UP, 1987), 167.
16. For a further social-economic explanation of the scene, see Hedrick, "Bardguides of the New Universe."

17. References to Shakespeare are to *The Norton Shakespeare*, ed. Stephen Greenblatt, 2nd ed. (New York and London: Norton, 2008).

18. Thomas Nashe, *Pierce Pennilesse*, in *Thomas Nashe*, ed. Stanley Wells (London: Edward Arnold, 1964), 64.

19. Theodor W. Adorno, "The Schema of Mass Culture," in *The Culture Industry* (New York and London: Routledge, 1991), 89.

20. Jeremy Lopez, *Theatrical Convention and Audience Response in Early Modern Drama* (Cambridge: Cambridge UP, 2003), 33, 81.

21. For these and the initial theorizations of early modern "entertainment value," see Donald Hedrick, "Advantage, Affect, History, *Henry V*," *PMLA* 118, 3 (2003): 470–87, and "Male Surplus Value," *Renaissance Drama* n.s. 31 (2002): 85–124.

22. For a thorough account of the jig, see Charles Read Baskervill, *The Elizabethan Jig, and Related Song Drama* (Chicago: U of Chicago P, 1929).

23. Ibid., 119.

24. William Kempe, *Nine Daies Wonder* (London, 1600), B1r.

25. For an account of the theater experiment with onstage incarceration, see Donald Hedrick, "Real Entertainment: Sportification, Coercion, and Carceral Theater," in *Thunder at a Playhouse: Essaying Shakespeare and the Early Modern Stage*, ed. Matt Kozusko and Peter Kanelos (Selinsgrove, PA: Susequehanna UP, forthcoming).

26. Paul Yachnin, in Anthony B. Dawson and Paul Yachnin, *The Culture of Playgoing in Shakespeare's England: A Collaborative Debate* (Cambridge, UK: Cambridge UP, 2007), 41.

27. For selected information on Taylor, see Bernard Capp, *The World of John Taylor the Water-Poet, 1578–1653* (New York and Oxford: Oxford UP, 1994).

28. John Taylor, *The Acts and Exployts of Wood the Great Eater, in Kent, in All the Workes of John Taylor the Water Poet* (London, 1630), n.p.

29. Richard Vennar, *An Apology* (London, 1614).

30. Anon. *The Actors Remonstrance* (London, 1643).

31. For the references to actor-wagers, see B.L. Joseph, *Elizabethan Acting* (London: Oxford UP 1964), 93–94. For further consideration of the implications of actor wagers for "entertainment value" and "real" entertainment linked to the theater, see Donald Hedrick, "Real Entertainment."

32. Citations are to Francis Beaumont, "The Knight of the Burning Pestle," in *English Renaissance Drama*, ed. David Bevington, Lars Engle, Katharine Eisaman Maus, and Eric Rasmussen (W. W. Norton: New York, 2002).

33. Walter Benjamin, *The Arcades Project* (Cambridge, MA: Harvard UP, 1999), 804.

34. Paul Smith, *Millennial Dreams: Contemporary Culture and Capital in the North* (London: Verso, 1997).

35. Naturally, "participatory" offers no hard-and-fast distinction, since media do not have essences and since the history of entertainment alternatives develops unevenly and disjunctively. Earlier cinema reminds us of a venue notorious for giveaways, gimmicky audience and promotional schemes, make-out balconies,

and the like; moreover, residual participation survives in cult film ritual (*The Rocky Horror Picture Show*, *The Sound of Music*).

36. Robert Venturi, Denise Scott Brown, and Steven Izenour, *Learning from Las Vegas* (Cambridge, MA: MIT Press, 1972).

37. Roland Barthes, *Camera Lucida: Reflections on Photography* (New York: Farrar, Straus, and Giroux, 1981).

Contributors

Richard Burt is Professor of English and Film and Media Studies at the University of Florida and the author of *Medieval and Early Modern Film and Media* (2008); *Unspeakable ShaXXXspeares: Queer Theory and American Kiddie Culture* (1998); and *Licensed by Authority: Ben Jonson and the Discourses of Censorship* (1993). He is the editor of *Shakespeares After Shakespeare: An Encyclopedia of the Bard in Mass Media and Popular Culture* (2006); *Shakespeare After Mass Media* (2002); and *The Administration of Aesthetics: Censorship, Political Criticism, and the Public Sphere* (1994). Burt is the coeditor of a special issue of *Exemplaria* on "Movie Medievalism" (2007); *Enclosure Acts: Sexuality, Property, and Culture in Early Modern England* (1994); *Shakespeare the Movie: Popularizing the Plays on Film, TV, and Video* (1997); and *Shakespeare the Movie, II: Popularizing the Plays on Film, TV, Video, and DVD* (2003).

Deborah Cartmell is Reader in English in the Faculty of Humanities, and Director of the Centre for Adaptations, at De Montfort University. She edits the journals *Shakespeare* (Routledge) and *Adaptation* (Oxford University Press), is general editor of the Screen Adaptations Series (Methuen), and has written on Shakespeare and adaptations of canonical and popular literature. She is currently writing *"Pride and Prejudice" on Screen* (Methuen) and cowriting *Impure Cinema* (Palgrave).

Melissa Croteau is Associate Professor of Literature and Film Studies at California Baptist University. She has presented papers on Shakespeare and film at numerous international conferences, and her recent publications include an edited volume for Press Americana entitled *Reel Histories: Studies in American Film* (2008) and the coedited volume *Apocalyptic Shakespeare: Essays on Visions of Chaos and Revelation in Recent Film Adaptations* (2009).

Adrienne L. Eastwood is Assistant Professor of English and Comparative Literature at San Jose State University. She earned her doctorate in 2004 from UCSD, specializing in early modern literature and culture. Dr. Eastwood is currently investigating early English wedding poetry and the uses of epithalamic conventions in Shakespearean comedy. Her other current research interests include early modern women authors and gender and queer studies.

Donald Hedrick is Professor of English at Kansas State University. He has published widely on Shakespeare and Renaissance studies, including *Shakespeare Without Class: Misappropriations of Cultural Capital* with Bryan Reynolds (2000). He has been a visiting professor at Cornell University, Colgate University, and Amherst College; was a recent Fulbright Scholar at Charles University in Prague; and has directed student tours to London and Prague.

James R. Keller is Professor of English and Chair of English and Theatre at Eastern Kentucky University. His research includes five monographs, the most recent of which is *"V for Vendetta" as Cultural Pastiche* (2008), and four collections coedited with Leslie Stratyner, the most recent of which is *The Deep End of South Park* (2009). Keller has published over fifty articles, notes, and chapters on a variety of subjects, including early modern literature, gay and lesbian studies, film, and popular culture.

Courtney Lehmann, Professor of English and Film Studies at the University of the Pacific, is the author of numerous articles on Shakespeare and film and such books as *Shakespeare Remains: Theater to Film, Early Modern to Postmodern* (2002), with Lisa S. Starks, *Spectacular Shakespeare: Critical Theory and Popular Cinema* (2002), and *The Reel Shakespeare* (2002).

Amy Rodgers is currently a fellow at the University of Michigan's Institute for the Humanities, where she is finishing her dissertation "The Sense of An Audience: Spectators and Spectatorship in Early Modern England." Her fields of interest include early modern drama, visual and mass culture, audience studies, film theory, and the historiography of early American cinema.

Greg Colón Semenza is Associate Professor of English at the University of Connecticut. In 2003–2004, Semenza published his first book: *Sport, Politics, and Literature in the English Renaissance*. His other books include *Graduate Study for the 21st Century: How to Build an Academic Career in the Humanities* (2005; 2nd ed. 2010) and, with Laura L. Knoppers, *Milton in Popular Culture* (2006). He is currently at work on a monograph entitled *Fictional Milton*. He has published numerous essays on such pop culture topics as Tim Blake Nelson's *"O,"* children's versions of Milton's *Comus*, and *Shakespeare: The Animated Tales*.

Kevin J. Wetmore, Jr. is Associate Professor of Theater at Loyola Marymount University, author of multiple books on theater and popular culture including *Empire Triumphant: Race, Religion And Rebellion in the Star Wars Films* (2005), coauthor of *Shakespeare and Youth Culture* (2006), a professional stage combat choreographer, and the founding artistic director of the Unseam'd Shakespeare Company.

Deborah Willis is Associate Professor of English at UC Riverside. Her book *Malevolent Nurture: Witch-hunting and Maternal Power in Early Modern England* (1995) explores the dynamics of witchcraft accusation through legal documents, pamphlet literature, religious tracts, and the plays of Shakespeare. Other published work include "Marlowe Our Contemporary: *Edward II* on Stage and Screen," in *Criticism: A Quarterly Journal for Literature and the Arts* (1998); and "The Gnawing Vulture: Trauma Theory, Revenge, and *Titus Andronicus*," in *Shakespeare Quarterly* (2002). Current projects focus on representations of witch-families in early modern England and on early modern languages of trauma and addiction.

Ramona Wray teaches in the School of English at Queen's University of Belfast. She is the author of *Women Writers in the Seventeenth Century* (2004) and coeditor of *Screening Shakespeare in the Twenty-First Century* (2006), *Reconceiving the Renaissance: A Critical Reader* (2004), *Shakespeare, Film, Fin de Siècle* (2000), and *Shakespeare and Ireland: History, Politics, Culture* (1997).

Index